By
God's
Grace

"WE MUST LEARN to give, give,
and give like the sun, and like Mother Ganga,
with no hesitation, no expectation,
no vacation, and no discrimination."

By GOD'S GRACE

THE LIFE AND TEACHINGS OF
PUJYA SWAMI CHIDANAND SARASWATI

Sadhvi Bhagawati Saraswati

Foreword by
HIS HOLINESS
THE DALAI LAMA

Preface by
RABBI DAVID ROSEN

MANDALA
PUBLISHING
San Rafael, California

"THE BEST WAY to honor God in our lives is through serving humanity."

MANDALA
PUBLISHING

PO Box 3088
San Rafael, CA 94912
www.mandalapublishing.org

ART CREDITS

Page 14: *Krishna and Radha*, by B. G. Sharma. © B. G. Sharma/Mandala
Publishing. Page 18: *Dhruva Narayana*; lithograph; ca. 1910s; Ravi Varma
Press, Karla-Lonavla; collection of Mark Baron and Elise Boisante.
Page 22: *Rama in Palace*, by Indra Sharma, © Indra Sharma/Mandala
Publishing. Page 30: *Ganga on Crocodile*. © Mandala Publishing. Page 46:
Saraswati, Goddess of Learning, by B. G. Sharma, © B. G. Sharma/Mandala
Publishing. Page 51: *Mahadev Shiva Holding Trident*, by Indra Sharma,
© Indra Sharma/Mandala Publishing. Page 54: *Goddess Lakshmi Holding the
Pot of Nectar*, by Indra Sharma, © Indra Sharma/Mandala Publishing.
Page 76: *Gayatri Ma* © Rahul Goswani. Page 113: *At Badrinath in Himalayas*,
by Indra Sharma, © Indra Sharma/Mandala Publishing. Page 125: *The Ganges
Descending to Earth*, by Indra Sharma, © Indra Sharma/Mandala Publishing.

Design by Dagmar Trojanek

ROOTS of PEACE   🌲 REPLANTED PAPER

Insight Editions, in association with Roots of Peace, will plant two trees
for each tree used in the manufacturing of this book. Roots of Peace
is an internationally renowned humanitarian organization dedicated
to eradicating land mines worldwide and converting war-torn lands
into productive farms and wildlife habitats. Together, we will plant two
million fruit and nut trees in Afghanistan and provide farmers there with
the skills and support necessary for sustainable land use.

Manufactured in China by Insight Editions

10 9 8 7 6 5 4 3 2 1

Contents

Foreword

BY HIS HOLINESS THE DALAI LAMA

All the world's major religious traditions are similar in having the potential to help human beings live at peace with each other and with themselves, while taking care of our natural environment. Therefore, harmony among our different religions is essential for world peace. In order to develop genuine harmony, it is extremely important that we cultivate genuine respect for one another and come to appreciate the value of others' faith traditions.

Since I was a boy in Tibet, I have regarded India with great respect and admiration. Its civilization has given rise to a long series of great teachers endowed with both human intelligence and a sense of responsibility towards the community. Consequently, a rich and sophisticated philosophy of non-violence, tolerance, and pluralism has flourished here. To me, the greatest lesson of India's example is that genuine religious pluralism and toleration are achievable and, indeed, have been a historical fact. I often refer to *ahimsa* and religious harmony as India's treasures, and they have great potential to build a happy, compassionate, and non-violent society.

Swami Chidanand Saraswatiji is someone who seeks to put these ancient Indian traditions into practice today. We have met during interfaith meetings such as the Parliament of World Religions in Capetown in 1999 and in Melbourne in 2009. Subsequently, I made an enjoyable visit along with other spiritual teachers and leaders including Mr. L. K. Advani, the former Deputy Prime Minister of India, to Haridwar and Rishikesh in April 2010, attending the launch of the admirable *Encyclopedia of Hinduism* project that Swamiji has initiated and the Sparsh Ganga campaign to clean and preserve the Ganges, to which he is particularly dedicated.

This book tells Swamiji's story, from his childhood eagerness to follow a spiritual way of life through his years of training to the present time, when as a spiritual leader, his responsibilities take him to many countries. In the twenty-first century, if spirituality is to contribute to positive change in the world, I believe well-intentioned words are not enough; the meaning of such words needs to be put into effect by taking practical action. There are many instances in the book of Swamiji doing this.

I feel sure that readers will find much in this book to interest and inspire them. I hope they may be encouraged by what they read to take practical steps according to their own circumstances to contribute to making the world in which we live a happier, more peaceful place.

Preface

BY RABBI DAVID ROSEN

It would be a very great privilege for anyone to be asked to write a preface to a biography of one of the most remarkable spiritual teachers and exemplars of our times. However, when the person asked to do this is from a different religious tradition and cultural background, the privilege is even greater—and, indeed, I am deeply appreciative of the honor.

I would, however, presume to state that for those of us who have been blessed to know and learn from Swami Chidanandji, it is not especially surprising that a rabbi would be asked to pay tribute to him, for Pujya Swami's spirit and vision transcend all boundaries—cultural, ideological, and geographical.

Indeed, it seems to me that he embodies the critical challenge for religions in our times, and that is to be true to their respective heritages while moving beyond their past limits. In other words, to be authentically rooted in their particularity while expressing a universal morality.

In our times, it is more evident than ever before that a spiritually healthy person is one who has a strong particular identity. Indeed, social scientists have pointed to the drug culture and violent abuse found in even the most affluent societies as the search for stimulation on the part of the bored, as the search for identity on the part of the deracinated and alienated. Our particular religious and cultural heritages embody so much wisdom and beauty they guide our lives accordingly. Too strong an identity, however, can lead to insularity; a deep religious immersion can often be so self-preoccupying one can become almost oblivious and even insensitive toward others. This becomes particularly evident in contexts of conflict.

Pujya Swamiji is not just a noble son of a noble tradition and not only a great teacher of that tradition. His life is devoted to making it known in an authentic manner, both within and beyond its historical boundaries, as evidenced in the magnum opus that he has taken on,

the *Encyclopedia of Hinduism*. He presents a spiritual consciousness, an awareness, and a message that is relevant for people everywhere and in every tradition. Above all, he demonstrates how we should relate to each and every person, as created in "the Divine image." This is particularly evident in his extensive and impwressive social and philanthropic projects.

Among the sayings of the Jewish sages from some two thousand years ago is the well-known passage in the name of Ben Zoma (Ethics of the Fathers, 4:1), who rhetorically asks, Who is wise? Who is mighty? Who is rich? Who is honorable? He declares, A wise person is one who learns from all people; a mighty person is one who controls his passions; a rich person is one who is happy with his portion; an honorable man is one who honors others (or dignifies others).

In modern society, one would not normally receive such responses. For most people today, a wise person is one who has accumulated much information and/or has many degrees; a mighty person is one with muscular strength, or a general of an army; a rich person is one who has accumulated money or property; and a honorable person is one who has titles and awards. But these answers reflect the fact that we all too often see people in terms of what they have accumulated. The sage Ben Zoma is not talking about having, but about being—about what one is. His observations could not be more appropriate than for the person and life of Swami Chidanandji.

Pujya Swamiji not only is a man of knowledge but also a truly wise man whose wisdom has come through his encounter with humanity. He is a mighty man, in that he became and is a true master of his will and passions. He is a rich man as a paradigm of gratitude and appreciation for whatever he is able to enjoy and provide. And as much as he is a revered man, his greatest dignity is the product of his dignified treatment of all, from the most humble to the most exalted.

It has been my great privilege and joy to have been with him in many different interfaith contexts and international fora. Perhaps most notable of these have been the Hindu-Jewish leadership summits in New Delhi and Jerusalem. My wife, Sharon, and I (and our daughter, Amirit) have had the great pleasure and honor to have been his guests at Parmarth Niketan. Each encounter with him is indeed an encounter with the beauty of true wisdom, power, richness of spirit, and genuine honor.

On the occasion of his sixtieth birthday, I know that I speak on behalf of his myriad admirers when I pray that One Source of All will grant him the health and energy to continue to be the remarkable blessing and guide that he has been and is for many more decades to come.

Introduction

When I first met Pujya Swamiji, I did everything I possibly could to get him to accept a compliment. "You are the most wonderful person I've ever met!" I'd exclaim with exuberance singular to twenty-something females. "You are the most divine, most amazing, most incredible being I've ever encountered," or something more specific: "You have the most heavenly singing voice."

His answer never varied. "It's all God's grace."

To a twenty-five-year-old American Jew this concept was unfathomable. Sweet. Beautiful. Endearing. But unfathomable and occasionally exasperating. "Yes, yes, I know," I would say, trying to mask my exasperation and sound as if I, too, was living in constant awareness and appreciation of God's gifts. "But it's *you* I'm talking about," I would contend. "It's *you* who is so incredibly amazing and divine."

"It's all God's grace," he would reply.

In more than fifteen years of living in his *seva*, being with him in vastly differing environments across the globe, watching him interact with people ranging from the Dalai Lama to Bill Clinton to Uma Thurman to homeless children on the streets of both Delhi and Durban, I have never heard him respond to a compliment in any other way. He knows that the common response to a compliment is "Thank you." He hears everyone else say it all the time. However, to him, any praise, any appreciation, any acknowledgement of a project he's completed, a mission he's accomplished, a blessing he's bestowed, or even speech he's given is praise for God. He is an inconsequential medium, a vessel who happened to be in the right place at the right time. "A microphone would never take credit for a speech, would it?" he asks if one should ever be foolhardy or adamant enough to insist he, not God, is the one you're praising. "Wouldn't it be ridiculous for a microphone to say 'Wow! I got a standing ovation tonight. The audience loved me. I gave a wonderfully inspiring talk.'" He truly views himself as that microphone: a vehicle, not the power or the source.

Pujya Swamiji is as awed by God's grace as others are of him. "Look, look how Ma (Mother Goddess) takes care of everything," He exclaims frequently when a project to which he's given hundreds of hours of time and attention bears fruit. "God is really great," he whispers, eyes wet with tears, as he watches schools, orphanages, women's vocational training centers, medical clinics, disaster relief programs, and rural development projects take shape. That he has planned, guided, overseen, and inspired every aspect of the project from beginning to end is of no consequence. Yes, of course, he is fully aware that he spends more than fifteen hours a day planning, guiding, and overseeing dozens of humanitarian projects. But him as doer? No. To him, the Doer is God. He has merely been blessed with an opportunity to serve as a vessel, to use his time, energy, abilities, and innumerable pads of paper in the service of humanity.

How does he choose the charitable projects? How does he decide the next location for a free computer center or an orphanage or a medical health camp? He doesn't. God does. He believes that whatever appears in front of him comes from God and that he is supposed to accept it. So we never wonder what our next project will be. We are sure that long before we have completed one, another will fall into his lap. "No more new projects," Pujya Swamiji has been known to say when the list of current *seva* activities is longer than anyone can remember. However, we all know that what that really means is no new projects until a new project falls in his lap. A mother can only stand so many minutes of her child's wailing before, despite her resolve to let him cry himself to sleep, despite the advice of child-rearing experts, she is pulled by a force beyond herself to his bedside and rocks him back to sleep. Pujya Swamiji lives like the mother of the world, and he too can tolerate a bare minimum of pain in his children before—despite any prior decisions to the contrary—he rushes to their aid.

WRITING THIS BIOGRAPHY

Writing this biography has felt like trying to describe the warmth of the rays of the sun. For one who has felt his body relax, release, and melt into a delicious patch of sunshine, no explanation is required. No words can even approximate the feeling. The mention of sunshine causes a cascade of neuronal reactions reminding him—intellectually, emotionally, and somatically—what the sun feels like. Yet, for one who has never felt the heat of a summer's day, for one who has lived his life indoors or in a part of the world covered twelve months a year by frost, no words are sufficient to give even a hint of the experience.

Similarly, this *is* Pujya Swamiji's biography and this is also *not* Pujya Swamiji's biography. It is the factual account, as accurate as I could piece it together, more than half a century later, of the sixty years his body has been in existence. Even this part is incomplete. In traditional India, particularly until recent decades, no one paid very much attention to what were seen as inconsequential details. Few people bothered with exact dates or time frames. "It was summertime," you'll hear people say. Or, "it was during the dark half of the month of Phalguna." In Hindi, there are fifty-two letters in the alphabet, permitting innumerably more combinations of words than in English. There are dozens of words for "water," depending on whether that water is running or still, pure or impure, from a river or from the toilet. However, the same word with the same spelling and the same pronunciation means both "yesterday" and "tomorrow." I mention this trivial yet fascinating fact simply because it explains the lack of specificity in people's recollections of dates and time frames. In Hindi, there really are only two types of time—the present moment and everything else. This is a phenomenal way to live, but is the subject for another book. Its only relevance here is that while I have attempted to verify the details wherever possible, most people's memories of time other than the present moment tended to be less than sharp.

However, a simple, chronological biography, merely telling you about Pujya Swamiji, would have been incomplete in another, much more profound way. It would tell you what he did, what he said, where he went, whom he met. But it would not give you the experience, the knowing, the awareness of Pujya Swamiji, just as reading about the sun can not warm you on a snowy day. For this reason, I have tried to create more than simply a chronological biography. I have tried not only to tell you about Pujya Swamiji but also to give you the experience of Pujya Swamiji. I have tried to give you, as he would say, "not only the teaching but also the touch." It is my prayer that this book will be both interesting and inspiring and also that it will touch a deep part of you, a part upon which the sun may not have shown in many years.

HOW THE BOOK CAME TO BE

I have wanted to write Pujya Swamiji's biography since the first week I knew him. I felt that the nature of who he is, how he lives, and what he teaches is so universally meaningful that it should be shared with the world. Having been born in the West and having received all of my education in elite schools and universities of the West, I knew how desperately these teachings were needed. My intentions were pure but I made the mistake of mentioning them to Pujya Swamiji. "Oh, sure," he responded. "Just as soon as you've finished this little bit of work I have for you." As that little bit of work grew, expanded, and multiplied, I realized that I would have to make specific time to write, rather than waiting for a time when I wasn't otherwise occupied. Every few years I would remind him, "I really would like some time to write your biography."

"Oh, yes, of course," he would reply lovingly. "Just as soon as this project is done." Sometimes that project was a particular school or vocational training program that required planning or expansion. Sometimes it was a medical camp at Parmarth in Rishikesh. Sometimes it was a *yatra* to Mansarovar and Mount Kailash where he built three ashrams (rest houses) on sacred, holy land in Tibet. Finally, it was the *Encyclopedia of Hinduism*. "Just as soon as you finish reading every single word in eleven volumes of seven thousand entries and copyediting them, then, sure, of course you can write the biography."

By the time the first volumes of the *Encyclopedia* had been launched by His Holiness the Dalai Lama, and my *seva* for the entire *Encyclopedia* was complete, it was April of 2011. Now, I felt, sure, I could finally start working on the biography. However, Pujya Swamiji had launched, by His Holiness's hands, not only the *Encyclopedia of Hinduism* but also a huge new initiative to save Mother Ganga. Named Ganga Action Parivar, it has become a global family dedicated to protecting and preserving the river that is both the Mother Goddess to more than 1 billion Hindus and the source of water for drinking, bathing, cooking, and irrigation for more than 450 million Indians. The first major conference of Ganga Action Parivar took place on April 21 and 22, 2011, at Parmarth, and was attended by Nobel Laureate Dr. R.K. Pachauri and dozens of other eminent scientists, engineers, and activists. There was, of course, much work to be done.

I wrote and deleted two drafts of the manuscript over that summer, while traveling in America and Europe, overwhelmed by the task of turning the life of the man who brought light to darkness around the world, whose presence was itself a miracle in the lives of countless people, into ink on a page. Nothing I wrote felt right. I wrote and rewrote, deleting words, sentences, pages, and even, finally, discarding two nearly complete manuscripts. What I wrote may have described Pujya Swamiji, I felt, but my prose did not convey him; it did not give the experience of him. I was desperate to begin anew, and to finally get it right.

Back in Rishikesh, I couldn't write in ten-minute bursts between other *seva*, phone calls, visitors, programs, events, and travel. Finally, bereft and with deadlines looming if the biography was to be ready for his sixtieth birthday, I decided the only solution was to observe silence and a special "writing meditation" for the nine days of Navratri

that fall in late September/early October. They are the most sacred days of the Hindu year for those who, like Pujya Swamiji, worship God in the form of the Mother. As I sat down at my desk, phones transferred to the reception office, automatic reply on my email account, earplugs in to block out distractions, basking in the freedom to finally write, I understood. Ah, of course. The Mother. Her Grace. Pujya Swamiji had orchestrated it all so that this book would be written during Navratri, that it would come to me only by God's grace.

LAYOUT OF THE BOOK

There are three parts to this book. There are eleven chapters of biography, running mostly chronologically, capturing a wide variety of events and experiences from Pujya Swamiji's early childhood to today. There are also sidebars. These deep-orange pages provide additional information about a concept raised in the text. Lastly, there are the teachings. These are in Pujya Swamiji's own voice and encompass some of his most specific tenets and philosophies. "What are Pujya Swamiji's teachings?" is a common question for newcomers to the ashram or friends brought by friends to one of his lectures, *satsangs*, or retreats abroad. The question is simple but the answer is quite profound. For the teaching depends on the person to whom he is speaking. I have heard him give seemingly contradictory answers to the same question on innumerable occasions. "But Pujya Swamiji, last week someone else asked you the same question and you gave a completely different answer," I've observed. "Yes," he says. "Because I am not answering the question. I am answering the questioner." Different questioners need different teachings even if they seem to have asked the same question. For this reason, the teachings I've chosen for this book are the ones that I felt are applicable, touching, and meaningful to everyone and from which, I hope, everyone will be both taught and touched.

CHAPTER ONE

A Saint Is Born

"I ALWAYS KNEW I WOULD GIVE ONE OF MY CHILDREN TO GOD," SWAMIJI'S MOTHER, MATASHRI, SAYS. "AS I SAT IN THE *YAGNA* FIRE CEREMONY, WHEN SANTJI WAS STILL BREAST-FEEDING, I PRAYED TO GOD TO ACCEPT ONE OF THE FLOWERS OF MY WOMB

as His own." Eight years later, the child they had always called Santji for his serene, saint-like qualities came home and announced, "I want to be a Swamiji. Matashri, please make me a Swamiji."

Swamiji's father, Pitashri, was renowned throughout the village for his devotion to saints. No rupee of income from the prosperous family shop was saved in a mattress or deposited in the bank. Not a single rupee was put away for a rainy day. It all was given freely, with open hand, to saints, sadhus, and spiritual institutions. He had four sons and a daughter, all under the age of ten, and some may have thought it was frivolous and irresponsible to donate such a large percentage of one's inc e without saving for

the possible needs of his own family. However, Pitashri's choice was purposeful, deliberate, and made after great contemplation. "The saints are my insurance," he replied when anyone questioned his ways. "What can be greater insurance for my family than the blessings of spiritual masters?" Every time a sadhu came come to town, it was Pitashri who would rush to the saint's feet and plead for the opportunity to do some *seva*. At a young age, he earned the nickname Bhagatji ("the devoted one").

One morning, a revered wandering saint, clad only in a scrap of jute tied around his waist, came to their town. As soon as word reached Pitashri that a saint was in their local temple, he rushed with Santji and prostrated at the

opposite Santji (as Pujya Swamiji was known as a child) holds an image of Pujya Swami Brahmaswarupji, his guru.

guru's feet. "Swamiji, please come and have lunch at our home after your *satsang* in the temple," Pitashri begged the saint.

Pujya Swami Brahmaswarupji was a fakir, one who needed nothing, depended on no one except God, and was unattached to any needs or desires of the flesh. He replied, "If I am still sitting here at noon, I will come home for lunch. If I have left before then, God will provide my lunch somewhere else on the path."

Therefore, Pitashri instructed young Santji to sit there, in the temple, at the guru's feet, and should the Swamiji try to leave, Santji should immediately run home and call his parents, who would come quickly and bring Swamiji to their house. Santji sat, quietly transfixed, at the feet of the guru, surrounded by a small group of devotees, as Pujya Swami Brahmaswarupji began, silently, to transform him.

Santji's mind was clear and calm and seemed to be held by the gaze of the holy man. "Neither of us spoke. He was sitting on a cot in the room of the temple, and I was sitting on the floor at his feet. I remember the incredible sensation of peace and love which filled the room," Pujya Swamiji recalls.

Suddenly, Pujya Swami Brahmaswarupji motioned to Santji to approach him. As Santji stood in front of him, the saint placed his thumb firmly on Santji's "third eye," the place just between the two eyebrows, known as the *ajya* chakra, or seat of divine knowledge and wisdom. Pujya Swamiji explains,

I lost all consciousness of the outside world. It was as though the vessel of my individual consciousness was shattered and—just like the air in a pot merges with the air outside as soon as the pot is broken—my personal consciousness suddenly became one with the universal consciousness. I was simultaneously aware of nothing and aware of everything. Behind my closed eyelids, with the inner, divine eye, I beheld a bright white light into which everything dissolved. Out of the white light emerged a vision, a premonition prophesying more aspects of my future life than I realized. I

was standing on one foot in vrekshasana *(tree pose) somewhere deep in the forest, surrounded by trees whose leaves and branches refracted the early light of daybreak. My eyes were half shut, yet I was distinctly aware of being able to behold all of that around me as well as all of that within me. It seemed that the position of my eyelids was due merely to the comfort of the lids themselves rather than bearing any relation to my field of vision. My hair hung down nearly to my ankles, cascading off my head in long, flowing locks. Slithering around on the ground beneath me were cobras, pythons, and other poisonous snakes. I could feel them as they swirled around my one foot planted on the ground, and yet there wasn't a trace of fear or apprehension. I knew, beyond a doubt, that they would not hurt me.*

The vision was prophetic—both literally and metaphorically. Undergoing intense *sadhana* in the forest, spending hours each day on one foot in meditation, and having vision that sees beyond the realm of the physical eye were all literal events that would soon come to pass in his life. Similarly, on a literal level, being surrounded by snakes and scorpions would be an inextricable part of his childhood, to be spent in realms inhabited more frequently by serpents than by people. There was an even deeper aspect to the clairvoyance, an awareness that throughout his life he would forever seem to be balancing on one foot—firm and steady as a yogi—and yet always with one leg up, raised high to take the next step forward, never ceasing, never needing to regain a state of balance or to plant both feet on the floor. People who know Pujya Swamiji well today confirm that he is always in more than one place at a time, one foot in each of the realms he occupies. Additionally, he knew that throughout his life there would be snakes, serpentlike people, and deadly situations that would be more than enough to take the life (or at least the resolve) of an ordinary man. And yet, they would neither harm him nor even upset his balance and inward focus. They would exist, but low on the ground, an inherent part of his existence, yet never able to touch him.

After some time, the vision merged back into pure white light, which gave way to a vision of Lord Krishna, hand raised in blessing. These visions kept the young saint captivated and mesmerized for hours.

The next thing I remember, he was touching my third eye again, and my consciousness returned to normal. However, although my vision and consciousness came back to the world I inhabited, my relationship with that world had forever changed. I had seen the truth. I had been plugged into the divine powerhouse and knew that I was meant to remain connected only to Him.

The guru agreed to come for lunch. Upon entering the house, just behind Pujya Swami Brahmaswarupji, young Santji exuberantly called out to his mother, "Matashri, I want to be a Swamiji. Please make me a Swamiji."

Matashri, engrossed in preparing lunch for the beloved guru, assured her son lovingly, "Sure. Of course. But now go wash up and get ready for lunch." Little did she realize in that moment of half awareness that her dream of giving one of her children to God had just been fulfilled. The divine hand had reached out and chosen His gift from among her children, a gift that was, of course, already His, but which, through his maya, he enabled Matashri to feel she had spontaneously offered.

When lunch had finished and Pujya Swami Brahmaswarupji was preparing to depart, Santji clung to his cloth dhoti. "Take me with you," he pleaded with the saint. "Wherever you are going, please take me. I need to be with you."

Swamiji was not a saint used to being encumbered by even a cloth bag. He carried nothing. Traveling barefoot, refusing to touch money, permitting the divine plan to make his bed each evening, he was not enthusiastic about having an eight-year-old along with him. Nor was he sure the child was ready. He told Santji, "Not yet. I will return soon, and then we will see."

Bhagawan Sri Krishna.

AWAITING THE RETURN OF THE GURU

The following months dragged endlessly for Santji as he awaited the arrival of his guru, believing each morning that today would be the day. Even prior to meeting his guru, Santji's choice of pastime was never sports or frivolous play. Rather, he would gather together the neighborhood youngsters and enact dramas of "Satsang" or "Buddha" in which he donned the role of the Swami or the Buddha, giving lectures, advice, and blessings to his gathered friends.

These months passed in the same way. After school and on weekends, Santji would play the role of Swami or Buddha for the neighborhood children and then return quietly to his room for meditation. "Whenever I closed my eyes, I would feel my guru's finger

Pujya Swami Brahmaswarupji.

on my third eye. The bounded container of self would expand and expand until it disappeared completely. I spent hours a day in that divine state of complete oneness with the universe."

SILENCE

As suddenly as he had appeared the first time, Pujya Swami Brahmaswarupji reappeared many months later. Elated, Santji exclaimed, "Now, please, take me with you."

"Not yet," his guru replied. A life of *sanyas* is not granted easily or recklessly. The *sanyasi* stands as a symbol, an embodiment of strength, courage, self-resilience, autonomy, and complete detachment from anyone or anything other than God. To grant it or take it in haste undermines its very nature. *Sanyas* is a shedding of a life past and an embracing of life anew—in a different form, with different values, goals, and meaning. It is not the decision a guru can permit an eight-year-old to make. "Before you can come with me, you need to ready yourself. You need to detach fully from the world around you and reattach only to the inner world, the world of the Divine. The antennae of your life and your perception must be aligned not externally, picking up sights and sounds and smells of the outside world, but rather internally, picking up the nuances of the internal world."

Perhaps he wanted to test the tenacity and sincerity of young Santji. He instructed the child that for the next year he was to remain in silence and seclusion, physically in the house of his family but otherwise removed from it. He was to live in one room, seeing no one, speaking to no one, engaged fully, all hours of the day, in silent meditation, sometimes seated, and—for eleven hours a day—standing on one foot in *vrekshasana*. Once a day, Santji was permitted to have a bowl of dal (lentils) boiled in water, plain, simple, saltless, and with neither ghee nor spices, and two dry wheat chapatis. Upon Matashri's entreaties that her beloved son would perish from malnutrition, the guru added permission for a glass of hot milk each evening.

Thus, the next year of Santji's life was spent moving deeper and deeper, further and further, into the unknown reaches of the inner world, into the depths of the divine realm. "But how did you stand on one leg eleven hours a day?" people ask him today. Typical hatha yoga classes demand that students hold various asanas, including *vrekshasana*, for anywhere between thirty to sixty or perhaps ninety seconds, by which time one's hips, knees, and thighs burn from muscle fatigue and twitch with the buildup of lactic acid. Advanced practitioners might be able to maintain the posture for five to seven minutes. Eleven hours is inconceivable. "How did you do it? Didn't you get tired?" everyone who has ever attempted the difficult balancing posture asks him.

The answer is simple, seemingly simplistic, and yet fraught with lessons about life and its challenges. He replies, "If I got tired, I just switched my legs." The challenge is nonnegotiable. One cannot bargain with life if one wants to move forward on any path. However, deep within ourselves, deep within the bones and muscles and blood-filled passageways that run as veins and arteries along the vascular network of our body, is an infinite amount of inner resource, an infinite number of possibilities, infinite adaptations, treatments, and cures. Doing fewer than eleven hours was not an option. It was the guru's instruction. Going back to regular life was not an option. He had stepped, seamlessly and perfectly, as the Alakananda and Mandakini merge into Mother Ganga—separate streams only momentarily until their destined union is complete—into the life that he was to lead. To turn back was to go against the flow of nature, much like trying to distill Alakananda and Mandakini streams out of Ganga when She has already reached the sacred ghats of Hari ki Pauri in Haridwar. There are no separate streams anymore. There is no Alakananada; there is no Mandakini. There is only Ganga, and there was no other life for Santji. He had merged completely into the stream of Swami, a stream that flows in only one direction.

Being beaten by the challenges of the task was not a possibility. Nor was fatigue or pain or discomfort. He had to draw on the possibilities within himself to overcome any obstacles on the path. The river Ganga, as She flows downstream, does not stop and freeze, thwarted or petrified, at sharp turns in the river or at oversize boulders. She flows around and around them, increasing and decreasing Her depth and breadth as needed. When Santji got tired of standing on the left foot, he simply changed to the right foot. When the right foot tired, he switched to the left.

Months passed. As the world outside contracted, with no sight of his friends, family or anything beyond the four walls of his bedroom, the world inside expanded. Each day took him deeper into the realm of consciousness in which there are no boundaries between self and other, in which the cells of the self merge with the cells of not-self until one is palpably aware, experientially aware, of the complete, unbroken unity of all of existence, a place in which the true yoga (union) of self with the Divine is complete.

MILK OR MEDITATION?

Mothers are always mothers. The mother of a saint and the mother of a sinner may be oceans apart in their values, ethics, and the lessons they instill in their children. Yet, in their basic maternal instinct, they are identical. Thus, as Santji traveled further and further away from identification with the body, Matashri worried about the health, strength, and sustenance of that very body. Boiled lentils and dry chapatis are the type of food that cause prison riots. They are not sufficient for a growing boy, the beloved Santji of a well-to-do family. However, stronger even than her maternal instincts was Matashri's faith in her guru, Pujya Swami Brahmaswarupji. She never would have dared or even dreamed of violating his instructions. Yet, there are times in which instructions leave room for interpretation or honest, well-meaning misinterpretation.

Such was the case with Santji's evening milk. As his mother explains, "He had never said what size the glass of milk should be." The instruction had simply been for one glass of milk. What size and what thickness weren't mentioned, let alone explicitly dictated. In India, even today, more than fifty years later, milk comes not from cartons, pasteurized and homogenized, but straight from the cow. It is delivered to the door or picked up at the local Mother Dairy, packaged in disposable thin plastic pouches, meant to last

merely for short transportation, or in individual, reusable steel containers. The milk is neither pasteurized nor homogenized and therefore is boiled promptly upon arrival at home. Other than in the heat of summer when people indulge in "cold coffee" made with boiled milk kept in the refrigerator, milk is always served hot. As the milk has not been treated in any way, it still contains all the fat meant for young, growing calves. In a country where the expression for "losing weight" literally means "becoming weak," fat is seen as a positive attribute. Those who can afford the extra milk will frequently boil it and boil it until a pint of fresh milk becomes condensed into a cup of thick, rich dairy delight, or even half a cup of nearly solid milky dessert, to which the addition of sugar is a common but unnecessary redundancy.

Matashri spent hours each afternoon and evening boiling pints of fresh milk into a thick, fat-filled, milky substance that she poured into a glass and served to Santji each evening at his appointed "milk time." She added nothing other than time and love, thereby violating none of the guru's specific instructions. Her heart was at ease, knowing that her son was getting each evening the nourishment he missed during the day. Santji, too, enjoyed his evening treat. "I would look forward to it so much each evening that my mind became more and more focused on milk rather than meditation! My meditations late in the day could be described as 'milk meditations,' as I waited, with an empty rumbling belly, for my nightly delicacy."

The system established with his mother during these months of *sadhana* was that his meals (the daytime lentils and chapatis and the evening milk) would be left on a small table just outside his room, and a light knock would be the signal that he should come out and take the food. By the time he opened the door, his mother was gone, so as not to violate the rule that he must not see any family members during this time of austerity.

One evening, just after his mother had left his milk on the small table outside his room and—as customary—knocked gently on his door before retreating into the kitchen, Santji heard another knock on his door. This night, the second knock had a different tone. It was beckoning, rather than simply informative. Santji quickly went to his door and opened it. Towering at the threshold of his room was his guru, Pujya Swami Brahmaswarupji. "I immediately fell at his feet in *pranam*, and—as I was in silence—I motioned for him to have a seat on the chair while I sat at his feet."

Matashri immediately appeared, the first time child and mother had beheld each other in several months. She bowed at the guru's feet and said she was bringing his dinner right away.

"I will not take dinner," he replied simply. "I have come just to see my Santji."

In Indian tradition, it is inconceivable that one would not feed a guest, particularly a holy man. *Athiti devo bhava*, one of the most fundamental tenets of the tradition, says, "Adore the guest as God." Meals, rooms, clothes, and even savings are handed over to guests without a second thought by all Indian families. And that is true whether the guest is a mere acquaintance, a stranger, or even a beggar. When the guest is the guru, the incarnation of God Himself, the injunction takes on even greater importance. There is no such thing as "no" when a host offers food to a guest. One simply cannot refuse. Having already eaten, not being hungry, being on a diet—these are inconsequential, insignificant details, of no value as negotiating tools. One might as well not even bother to refuse.

Therefore, when Pujya Swami Brahmaswarupji refused supper from Matashri's hands, she was tenacious. "You must have something. If you won't have supper, what will you have? At least a cup of hot milk, you must have," she entreated.

"I will have milk, like Santji," the guru replied. Santji's covered industrial-size steel glass of milk was still sitting on the table where his mother had left it before Swamiji's arrival. He would, however, wait until his guru's milk arrived before touching his own. Thoughtfully, Matashri brought her guru's milk in the same-size glass as Santji's, to diffuse any possibility of suspicion on his part.

As she set it down on the table before him, he reached over and took Santji's glass instead. "I will drink his milk and he will drink my milk," stated the guru flatly.

She panicked. Santji's milk was the product of hours of careful boiling and condensing, a veritable hot milkshake, while Swamiji's milk was fresh, just boiled once, as thin as when it came from the cow. Should he see the consistency of his disciple's evening milk, he would immediately understand, and her loving subterfuge would be exposed. "Oh, no, Guruji," she pleaded. "Your milk is fresh. It just came from the dairy. Santji's milk is from the morning. It's not fresh at all."

Pujya Swami Brahmaswarupji replied, "Santji is the one doing the intense *sadhana*. He should have the fresh milk. I will drink the morning milk." With that, he took the cover off Santji's glass of sweet, thick, condensed milk and began to pour it from the glass into a small bowl. Santji's "milk" fell from the glass in thick, sweet clumps and globs, the product of hours of careful tend-

"Meditation is the best medication for all agitations."

ing over a low flame. Swamiji looked from mother to son, then back to mother and back to son. "Is this the way you drink your milk every night?" he asked.

Santji nodded, eyes lowered and brimming with tears of shame.

"Do you want to be a yogi or a *bhogi*?"

Santji was silent, still in the imposed twelve months of silence. He didn't want to break another rule. As he raised his eyes up to look at his divine guru, it was clear that his was the path of a yogi, not a *bhogi,* or sensual enjoyer.

His guru lay a hand on his head and said, "Do you think I came here tonight just to see you and drink milk? Do you think that I don't know what has been going on? Do you really think it is the thick, condensed milk that has been sustaining you all these months? I have come here to tell you that it is not the milk but the meditation that will sustain you (*dhood nahiy, balki dhyan*). Do you not realize that He who created the cow, He who put the nourishment in her milk, He who gave you a mouth with which to drink and a stomach with which to digest is He who ustaining you? From this day forward, there will be no more milk in the evenings." He stood and left as quickly and unceremoniously as he had come, his milk untouched on the table.

Now was the time of the true test for Matashri. Inside, perhaps, she was devastated. Her maneuverings—as benign as the intention had been—were exposed before her guru, and now her son had lost the very thing on which she had placed her confidence, and which had enabled her to sleep at night and had eased her maternal concerns. However, she was not an ordinary mother. She had come onto Earth with a special purpose: to bear and raise someone who would lead people from all over the world on a path toward divinity, on a path of surrender to the divine will, a path in which the whirling, tempestuous currents of their own egos, desires, pain, and obstacles would get swept up into the flowing river of divine consciousness. She was sent with special and unique gifts to prepare her for this.

MOTHER OF A SAINT

Several years earlier, when Santji was four or five, a relative had come to visit, and following Indian custom, the entire family had gone to the railway station to see him off. Matashri had lingered a moment too long in her good-byes on the train, and by the time she turned to exit, the train had started. It is common to jump off slowly moving trains onto the long concrete platforms at stations. However, it is not simple. One must angle oneself properly with the platform and jump, counterintuitively, in the exact direction the train is going. Matashri jumped, not exactly perfectly, and slipped off the platform into the narrow space between the platform and the moving train. Her family's screams could barely be heard over the roar of the train; the pull of the red emergency cord served only to bring the train to a halt one hundred yards away, after it had traveled through the entire station and over what they were sure was her mangled body.

As the last carriage rolled, now at great speed, over the place where she had fallen onto the tracks, Matashri's family rushed to what they knew would be a scene of graphic and bloody tragedy. Yet, there she was, kneeling ever so still, ever so erect, hand held on her heart, lips chanting, "Satguru, Satguru, Satguru," without a scratch, completely untouched by the train, which had just passed closer than a hair from the space in which she fell. "Satguru saved me," she says simply, as though it were an everyday occurrence, like the rising of the sun.

From that day onward, still in the peak of youth, she vowed to devote the rest of her life only to God. "I knew—even more than before—that now every breath, every moment, every word, and every action should be only for Him. I had borne five children, four boys and a girl, and my duties in that realm were complete." She remained at home, as a loving, doting, devoted wife and mother, but her life became that of a renunciant. She gave away all her clothes and wore only white. She forsook the comforts of a bed for the hard floor and spent long hours early each morning motionless in the family temple, engaged deeply in prayer and meditation.

Marital relations with Pitashri ceased as well. As she explained, her childbearing duties were

OPPOSITE *Young Santji during his year of silence and sadhana at home.*

Bhagawan Sri Krishna and Radha, the epitome of divine, non-physical love.

over, and anything else would be mere indulgence of the flesh, a path she had renounced. Fortunately, Pitashri was also a deeply religious man, who roused his sleeping children each morning at 4:00 a.m. to take them on a walk before showering and settling down for morning prayers. "There was no breakfast without prayers. If you didn't pray, you didn't eat," Pujya Swamiji explains now, encouraging families to be as committed to rearing spiritual children as his own parents were.

Being deeply religious, being deeply connected to God, and being human can all go seamlessly together. Pitashri was pious and devout, simple, humble, and selfless. But he was also human, and his young wife's abrupt termination of marital relations was not easy. Pujya Swamiji recalls one summer evening:

We were all sleeping on the rooftop because of the heat. It is very common in India to sleep on the roof in the summertime, under the stars and in the fresh breeze. Late in the night, I awoke thirsty and headed downstairs for a glass of water. As I reached the bottom of the staircase, I could hear my father knocking on my mother's door. It was dark, so my father could not see me. From inside the room my mother asked calmly and tenderly, "Yes, what is it?" My father explained, "Look, this is too much. You are my wife. There is nothing wrong with honest, loving relations between and husband and wife. Open the door." However, my mother remained firm and reminded him of her vow to a life of renunciation and full dedication to spirituality. Finally, my father, exasperated, pleaded, "Even Krishna had loving relations with the gopis." I will never forget the sound of my mother's voice or the words she said. Without a trace of annoyance or condescension, but with great resolve and in the tone that made you know the conversation was over, she replied, "Perhaps He did. First go and become Krishna. Then come back and we can talk."

Thus was the spiritual strength of Pitashri further heightened and his path defined. In having to overcome physical longing for his wife, while maintaining the deep connection and love between them, he had only one route—to sublimate all desire, channeling that energy into spiritual practice. The only way was to connect beyond the body rather than with the body. "My father had always been spiritual," Pujya Swamiji describes. "But after my mother's imposed abstinence, he delved much deeper, and a new light began to shine through his eyes."

So Matashri was a woman who had, by the time God selected Santji as the flower from her altar, great reserves of spiritual strength and resilience. On the night that her guru rescinded the one way she felt that she was able to provide nourishment to her beloved son, she was able to draw on those reserves, and she consoled her son, "Don't worry, child. Look at how blessed you are. Your guru came from so far away just to teach you such an important lesson. No matter where he is, he is always with you. And he is right; it is not the milk that gives you strength. It is his grace and his blessings."

Despite the pangs of guilt, sadness, regret, and concern for the future she must have felt, she displayed none of it in front of Santji. For him, she maintained a face and demeanor of perfect, gracious, and grateful acceptance. And she never again brought him a glass of milk.

INTO THE FOREST

Finally, the year came to a close, and Pujya Swami Brahmaswarupji returned. Santji was ecstatic that now he would be taken by his beloved guru; that now, having passed the test, having undergone the year-long austerities, his guru would keep him near forever. His heart full of joy, his mind stilled and withdrawn from the year of intense *sadhana*, he rushed to the feet of the guru, ready to be swept up eternally into the guru's loving embrace. "Not yet," was Pujya Swami Brahmaswarupji's terse reply when Santji reiterated his insatiable desire to never leave his side.

"I couldn't believe it," Pujya Swamiji recalls. "He had promised that after a year of *sadhana*, he would take me with him."

The tests and trials of a *sanyasi* are never ending. Pujya Swami Brahmaswarupji explained, "A *sanyasi* must be like a military man: completely self-sufficient, scared of nothing, brave, courageous, and a master of his own body and mind. For this you must go into the jungle."

"Don't worry if you don't believe in God. He believes in you. Faith is important for ourselves, for our own peace and spiritual growth. But, God is there with you all the time, whether you believe or not."

For a young boy who had never been beyond city limits, the jungle was the place of nightmares. The mystery, romance, and adventure associated with jungles and forests in other parts of the world don't pertain to India's elite. The jungle is where, at best, *dacoits* hide out under the cover of trees, avoiding capture and arrest. At worst, it is the abode of man-eating lions and tigers and huge wild elephants that crush villagers' bones like dry leaves underfoot. For young Santji, it was the place of ghosts. "All I could think about was the ghosts," Pujya Swamiji says. "My guru was taking me there to become one with God, but my mind was not filled with God. It was filled with ghosts. I was sure that I would not survive."

However, Pujya Swami Brahmaswarupji was a guru of extraordinary power—spiritual, mystical power and the power to breathe courage, strength, and serenity into a heart bursting with anticipation and fright. "Ghosts?" he said to Santji. "Ghosts are nothing compared to the power you will have. I will give you a mantra with which even Brahma cannot stop you!"

On a summer day, young Santji was officially initiated into *brahmacharya* and given the name Sant Narayan Muni. As he bent down to touch the feet of his father, then

FOLLOWING PAGES *Young Muniji in his years of meditation and* sadhana.

his mother, upon departure from the home, Matashri quickly wiped the streams of tears from her eyes. Yes, she had prayed to God to accept a flower of her womb. But the roots of the flower grew more deeply into her heart than she had realized. As God plucked the flower of Santji out of the garden of her house to make His own, she felt the tendrils, which she had always taken to be part of her own heart, ripped out violently, and her heart resembled the broken, trampled earth from which a deeply rooted plant has been pulled.

Young Santji, now young Muniji, was off on a journey that would take him from the home of his parents and blood relations. His possessions consisted of a long, thin cotton robe, pale yellow in color (the color worn by young spiritual seekers); one thin mat, a

Dhruv is blessed by the appearance of Lord Vishnu to whom he had prayed in the forest.

small Bhagavad Gita in original Sanskrit; and a framed picture of Dhruv, the prince who— through an unfulfilled wish to sit on the knee of his father the king—became an enlightened sage and *rishi*.

The story of Dhruv is one of the most famous stories in the Indian scriptures, an allegory of finding true wealth by leaving behind riches, of becoming a true king by leaving behind a kingdom, of finding the true Father, by leaving the home of the father. Dhruv spent years in the forest, doing *tapasya*, awaiting—on one foot in *vrekshasana*—the vision of Lord Vishnu. Therefore, it was this picture of God in the form of Bhagawan Vishnu appearing before young Dhruv in the jungle that was given to Muniji to meditate on during his days and nights alone.

Throughout India, in villages and even in the jungles, there are thousands of tiny shrines, seemingly abandoned and yet home to the faith of any poor, wandering villager, shepherd, or sadhu. Pujya Swami Brahmaswarupji chose one of these small dome-shaped shrines, housing a Shiva Linga, built along a dirt path in the mountainous jungle, hundreds of miles from his parents' house, as Muniji's new home. Attached to the shrine was a tiny hut, measuring approximately four feet by four feet, in which Muniji was to sleep. For how long? Pujya Swami Brahmaswarupji didn't say. He merely left his disciple with strict instructions to maintain complete silence, to beg for food once a day in the nearest villages, and to spend all of his time in meditation. A young child, armed with nothing more than a small Bhagavad Gita, an image of Dhruv, and a mantra that his guru assured him would stop even Brahma in his tracks, clad in a thin cotton robe, alone in the farthest reaches of the jungles, miles from the nearest small village. This is how Pujya Swamiji spent his youth.

The first few nights were really difficult. My guru had said I would be protected, but I was a child. I was afraid, particularly of ghosts. Every sound I heard, I thought it was a ghost. I remember the first night I had to go out to the bathroom. The jungle is frightening in the daytime. In the nighttime it is much worse. I barely made it a few feet away from the hut and I heard the snapping of twigs. Convinced it was a ghost coming to get me, I ran—duty unaccomplished— back into the hut. Regardless of what I did, I could not muster enough courage to venture back out into the dark of night. Pained by a full bladder, yet unable to empty it, I spent the night awake, in tears of discomfort and fright.

The next day I decided I would avoid the problem by not drinking any water in the afternoon or evening. However, the mechanisms of the body are not always predictable, and tragically, the urge came upon me. I had to go. Again the drama of the previous night unfolded, and again, bladder painful but less compelling than fear of the ghosts, I kept awake all night—shifting positions to ease the strain on my bladder—waiting for sunlight.

On the third day I had an idea. I held the picture of Dhruv being showered with blessings from Lord Vishnu. I looked deeply into Bhagawan Vishnu's eyes and said, 'Okay. We will go outside together. If anyone tries to hurt you, I will save you, and if anyone tries to hurt me, you will save me.'

A DEAL WITH GOD

The faithful logic of a child cannot be shattered, and Muniji confidently embarked on an evening journey into the trees to answer the call of nature. He gripped the framed image tightly, on the lookout for anyone who might try to harm the Divine that he carried so gingerly in his small arms. The presence of God—even in the form of the two-dimensional image—filled him with such confidence that he easily succeeded in his mission, without a trace of anxiety. After all, he had a deal with the Divine. He was prepared to fulfill his part, so he was sure, beyond any doubt, that God would similarly fulfill His. After going to the bathroom, he pumped the iron hand-pump to wash his hands and feet.

In India, the villages and even jungles have ubiquitous hand-pumps, bringing the gift of water to hundreds of millions of villagers who would otherwise be without. It is still rare today, and even rarer half a century ago, to find running water outside major cities. The vast majority of villagers use a hand-pump for their daily drinking, bathing, and cooking needs. As the tradition of saints, sages, *rishis*, and renunciants wandering through the jungle is so com-

"The GPS in our cars stands for 'global positioning system,' but our lives also have GPS: God's perfect system. That quiet, still, divine voice within us is our lifelong GPS. If we follow our divine GPS, we will never get lost or go astray."

mon, and as so much of India is populated by shepherds who wander over vast areas each day with their flocks, these pumps are common even far off the main roads or paths. Pujya Swami Brahmaswarupji had been sure to leave his disciple near a pump so that, despite the rigorous austerities he dictated, young Muniji would not be without access to water.

On this night, the third night of what was to become many years of jungle existence, Muniji had lovingly placed the divine image on a tree stump while he went to the bathroom in the trees and washed up. As he pumped water in the dark of night, a nail came loose from the rusty pump and fell onto the iron base, startling him.

I couldn't imagine what it was. It is only in retrospect now that I realize it must have been a nail from the old, unmaintained pump. At the time, I was sure the ghost was upon me and ready to snatch me up in his hands within a moment. I rushed, full of fright, as fast as I possibly could, back into the safety of my hut. Only upon catching my breath inside did I notice the missing picture and I remembered my arrangement with God. I was bereft to realize that, despite all my best intentions, I had abandoned Him when it mattered most. I had sworn to protect Him, but when the ghost came I had completely forgotten and selfishly cared only about my own safety. I was overcome with a guilt and remorse I had never known previously and have never known since. I felt as though I had truly let down God. He had depended on me. We had made a promise to each other, and I had broken my promise.

All night, an ocean of tears poured down his cheeks. Wave after wave of guilt, anguish, shame, and unbearable regret filled his head. Sleep did not visit him for even a minute. Yet stronger than the guilt and remorse was the ever-present fear of the ghost. "Even knowing that God was out there alone, that I had abandoned Him and broken my promise, even worrying that the ghost was probably devouring Him at that very moment, I still could not muster enough courage to return to the dark night in the trees, the playground of the ghosts."

Only when the first light began to creep through the branches and onto the leaves did he venture outside. With the curtain of the night raised and the light of day on the stage of his life, he rushed out to see what had become of his beloved God. "Miraculously, there He was, untouched, unharmed, exactly where I had left Him on the tree stump." With tears of joy flowing over the path the rivers of sorrow had laid on his cheeks during the night, he grabbed the picture and held it tightly to his chest, his heart opening into the divine eyes of Vishnu. "Suddenly, as I held the picture up to gaze into the eyes of my Beloved, as I poured out my apologies and regret, a voice came from the portrait. 'Do you think I am only in this picture? Do you not realize that I am everywhere, always with you, always taking care of you? I will never leave your side. If I am here, what is there to fear?'"

From that moment on, his life changed. "God became my best friend. He became my mother, my father, my closest confidante. I would talk to Him the way people talk to their closest, trusted friends. My thoughts, my fears, my ideas, my experiences—I would sit down and share with Him in the way that children run home and tell their mothers about everything that happened that day. And He would speak back to me. I heard His voice clearly—in my ears and in my heart—sometimes guiding me, sometimes consoling me, sometimes just letting me know that He was listening."

NARAYAN HARI

The first year passed easily for Muniji. Days were spent standing on one foot, gazing into the inner world with open eyes. Each day, as the sun rose high in the sky, he would walk several miles to one of the nearby villages, careful to alternate so that no one would tire of feeding him. "Narayana Hari," he chanted, the well-known expression of sadhus asking for alms. "Narayana Hari," the only words he was permitted in his strictly imposed vow of silence. Sometimes the villagers fed him, touched perhaps by compassion for the slender child undertaking the austerities of ancient *rishis*. Others fed him due to deep-seated belief in Hindu culture that one obtains good karma and divine blessings for feeding brahmins, particularly those engaged in *sadhana*.

However, many did not feed him. The Himalayan jungles are filled with people who are barely eking out a living themselves, farmers who work, dawn until dark, to provide for their families. Thus, Muniji's sweet chanting of "Narayana Hari," the request for a meal, was sometimes belligerently refused: "Kamake khao (Work and earn a living to eat)," they shouted as they chased him away, sometimes with sticks and rocks, sometimes with their dogs.

The rule was three houses. He was permitted to beg at three houses each day. If, within those houses, he managed to receive food, it meant that he was destined to eat that day, and he would return to his hut with a full belly. If, from those houses, he received nothing but admonition, insults, and threats, it meant that God wanted him to fast. On those days, he would return with empty hands and an empty stomach.

Young Muniji in his years of meditation and sadhana.

Summer turned to the rainy season, which turned to autumn and then winter, with no sign of the master. Having been instructed that he was to beg only for food and nothing else, Muniji withstood the temptation to beg for a blanket or a shawl to protect his thin frame against the whipping Himalayan winds. All shrines in India, except for the big, public temples, have no doors. Roadside shrines and the small *mandirs* in villages and jungles have no opening or closing hours. The dome-shaped entrance facing the deity is always open. Thus, in the wintertime, when Muniji lay down and curled his small body up next to the Shiva Linga, there was nothing to shelter him from the wind and snow outside. If it was windy outside, it was windy inside. If it snowed outside, it snowed inside. Neither socks nor a sweater nor any form of covering was available to him. However, slowly, from within, the body's inner resources began

to mobilize. "I just stopped feeling cold," he explains. "Yes, I was aware it was freezing, but the inner experience of discomfort, of shivering, was no longer there. It was freezing outside, but I was warm on the inside."

This mobilization of inner energy stayed with Pujya Swamiji long after his childhood years. Nearly fifteen years later, when he moved to Pittsburgh, Pennsylvania, to found the Hindu-Jain Temple, he was seen shoveling snow wearing nothing but a thin dhoti. "I only learned of thermals very recently. They just didn't exist in my experience."

Finally, green sprouts began to peak out from beneath the blanket of snow, and the ground again became soft and fertile. A few months later, as the summer heat began to rise early in the morning, the master reappeared. Wordlessly, in a language heard and understood only by guru and disciple, he asked Muniji how he was faring. Was he okay? Were there any

insurmountable difficulties? The light shining forth from Muniji's young, dark eyes and the gentle smile as he bowed at his guru's feet were the only indication necessary that he was doing well. "One more year," his master said casually, as though he were telling a tired sprinter to take just one more lap around the track, rather than requiring a child to live for twelve months more in jungle seclusion.

BACK TO SCHOOL

After another year, his master returned and announced that it was time for Muniji to complete his academic education. "He told me that I must get my degree first and then I could become a *sanyasi*. In fact, he had tried to convince me in the beginning not to give up my studies, but I was firm in my decision. After that moment of enlightenment, there is no going back."

Although his spiritual master had acquiesced at the beginning and had allowed Muniji to stop his studies in order to undergo the *sadhana* at home and in the forests, he now changed his mind. Or, perhaps, like many masters, he wanted to give his disciple one last taste of the world he was renouncing. So, he sent Muniji back to school. Despite being out of school for so long, he did not need to begin where he had left off or learn what he had missed. Through his *sadhana*, he entered right back into the stream of studies with the rest of his classmates.

"I would go to see my spiritual master in the morning before school, do his *seva*, do *seva* at the temple like cleaning the floors, and do my meditation and *japa*. Then, I would attend school, but I would leave early in order to be back with my master in the afternoon, sitting at his holy feet. Yet, I somehow absorbed everything and I got the top marks on all my exams."

The only activity at school that interested Muniji was drama. "I would play the role of Lord Buddha or of Shravan Kumar, or of Lord Krishna or Lord Rama, in the dramas.

I felt not that I was *playing* them, but that I *was* them. The role of Lord Buddha especially captured my entire being and consciousness. I lived the role, and everyone at the time used to call me 'Buddha.'"

His spiritual master was a wandering saint; thus frequently Muniji—unable to be separate from his master—would disappear from school and home to join his guru in the forests. Weeks later he'd return at his master's orders, attend school, and then rush off again for his guru's *darshan* and divine company in the secluded jungles and rural villages.

Even living at home, even attending school, Muniji was already well onto the spiritual path and his destiny was laid out clearly before him.

One day after school, Muniji was sitting in meditation below a tree. When he first sat down, he was protected by the cool shade of the tree, for the sun was directly overhead and the sun's leaves and branches cast a shadow over him. However, after a few hours the sun had shifted across the sky, and the shadow no longer fell onto Muniji but rather onto the far side of the tree. Muniji opened his eyes from meditation to see that he was in the direct sunlight. The intense heat of the sun bore down upon him, causing drops of perspiration to fall from his forehead. His *sadhana* was strong, and he did not move to the cooler, shady part of the tree. Rather, he closed his eyes again and continued his meditation, witnessing the way the hot sun felt on his head and face.

Within a moment, his body became cool and he could see, through his closed eyelids, a dark shadow move across his field of vision. Opening his eyes, he expected to see a large animal standing in the path of the sunlight, perhaps preparing to have Muniji as its lunch. What he saw was the large hood of the divine cobra, Naag (the cobra who is always with Lord Shiva, hovering over his head), moving directly above his head. He could see the shadow of the serpent on the ground by

OPPOSITE *Bhagawan Sri Rama, an incarnation of Lord Vishnu and the divine hero of the epic Ramayana. This is the role that young Muniji played in the school and neighborhood dramas.*

his feet and the neck stretched up from the ground to the height of Muniji's head. Then, towering above his small body, the cobra opened up its hood, blocking out every ray of the sun. Muniji noticed that the cobra itself was not there; rather, only its shadow had come to protect him from the afternoon heat.

"I knew this was a sign that God is always there, always protecting you, always just above you, giving you shelter and shade."

The time back in school passed quickly for Muniji, as he says, "I was not really there. My mind and my heart were still in the forest. Even sitting in school or sitting at home I would be doing my mantra. Whenever I had the chance, I would go to see my master."

FROM THE SCHOOL OF BOOKS TO THE SCHOOL OF LIFE

Barefoot, silent, owning nothing other than the clothes they wore, a Bhagavad Gita, Muniji's image of Dhruv with Lord Vishnu, and Swamiji's *kamandal* (begging bowl, typically made of either wood or brass), they traveled for much of the next several years throughout the forests and jungles of Punjab, Himachal Pradesh, Haryana, and what would later become Uttarakhand.

Periodically, with neither warning nor anticipation nor recognizable pattern, Pujya Swami Brahmaswarupji would leave Muniji somewhere along the way. Sometimes it was a cave, sometimes it was a small abandoned hut, sometimes it was a small shrine like the one in which he spent his first few years. The rules were always the same—no money, no possessions other than the Gita, the picture, and the thin mat on which to lie, and the vow of silence other than for his daily noontime chant of "Narayana Hari." Sometimes Swamiji would return after a few months, sometimes after more than a year.

The instructions were no less severe when they traveled together; in fact, it was even more difficult. "He was really strict," Pujya

Swamiji remembers. "Anything I did wrong, he'd slap me. One day I received twenty-one slaps." The slaps were not the result of a guru without control over his anger. Rather, they were the careful slaps that a potter makes as his piece of art spins on the wheel. With one hand, the potter holds the bowl. With the other, he slaps and hits it into shape. There is a practice in Zen Buddhism in which the Zen master walks, silently, up and down the rows of meditating students, whacking each of them periodically on the back with a long bamboo rod. Should one's mind have wandered, the stinging welt from the bamboo rod is sure to bring it back. Upper backs and shoulders are red and bruised, but minds are focused, sharp, and ever aware.

One of the instructions Muniji was given was that he should chant his mantra continuously and that his lips should move silently, without a break, every minute of the day.

I remember one time Guruji was resting on his back in the afternoon under a tree. He had covered himself with his chaddar *(thin cotton shawl) from head to toe. The* chaddar *was tucked in under the back of his head and again under his heels to keep any mosquitoes or flies off his sleeping body. I was fanning him. However, I was also tired. We had been walking continuously since 4:00 a.m., and the soporific afternoon heat began to overcome me. My fanning never ceased, but as sleep crept up upon my consciousness, my lips stopping moving with my mantra. Although his eyes were closed, although he was sleeping, and although he could not even see me because his eyes were covered by the* chaddar, *still he knew somehow that my mantra had stopped. From under the* chaddar, *instantly came his open palm, landing in a sharp slap upon my cheek.*

Another time, as they were wandering—barefoot and possessionless—through deserted meadows, sparsely populated farming communities, and rustic villages, they came to a crowded city. Having had nothing to distract him other than the trees and birds, Muniji became engrossed by the billboards in the city. One after another, they just kept coming, advertising an infinite array of products and services, each with a carefully scripted slogan. He began reading them, one by one.

An inherent limitation of the mind is that it can't actually pay attention to more than one thing at a time. We say, "Oh, I have one hundred things on my mind," but actually at any given moment, the brain can only think of one thing. We may have a hundred thoughts in such rapid succession that they seem simultaneous, but they are not. They are sequential. Therefore, as he began to silently read the signs, his attention, focus, and concentration were lost. His lips stopped chanting *japa* as his mind started chanting slogans for soda pop. Enthralled by the catchy sayings, the rhymes, and the clever advertising, and with his head facing upward rather than downward, he didn't notice that his guru had stopped. He kept walking, right into the back of his guru. His master turned around, immediately understood what had happened, and addressed the lack of attention with a hard slap on Muniji's cheek. "Suddenly I was right back with my mantra. Suddenly there were no more billboards, no more wandering mind, no more slogans. Only my mantra remained."

Another important instruction, common for young *brahmacharis* in spiritual training, was to have no interactions of any kind with the opposite sex. Ultimately, as *sadhana* deepens, from the rich soil of *tapasya*—watered with sacrifice, upon which the rays of God's grace have fallen—blossoms the flower of divinity, and one loses all temptation toward calls of the flesh. Desires drop off like the outer, dry, wilted petals of a rosebud, leaving behind only the deep, fragrant petals of balance and inner ecstasy. However, in the early days, gurus are very careful to ensure that young *brahmacharis* are not ensnared by the sticky ropes of maya or any of her allies—lust, greed, jealousy, and anger.

Thus, young Muniji was strictly forbidden from any direct contact with girls or young women. Traveling barefoot through the jungles with his guru and living in seclusion made

Young Muniji during his late adolescent years when he was mostly traveling with Pujya Swami Brahmaswarupji.

this mandate an easy one to follow. However, one day their travels brought them through a more populated area. Muniji had been taught to always keep his head pointed down, to stare at the path in front of him, so that his mind could be free to continue the *japa* rather than getting distracted by the sights and happenings around him. Although he kept his eyes focused only on the path in front of him, as they passed a relatively busy area in the town, he accidentally brushed against the arm of a young woman coming in the other direction.

As he hadn't been able to see her approaching, due to his downward gaze, he was unable to anticipate or avoid the encounter until it was too late. Fortunately, it was a minor enough brush that the woman seemed not to notice and continued on her way. No words were spoken and she didn't even turn her head to look at the boy whose arm had brushed her own.

Swami Brahmaswarupji, walking a few paces ahead of Muniji, had eyes not only in the front of his head, but also in the back and

"God and the Guru are not vending machines where you put in the money and push the button and your choice of snack comes out. God gives us what we need, not always what we desire."

on the sides. He spun around and slapped Muniji. "Did you like that? Did you like the way you managed to touch a woman thinking I wouldn't notice?"

Muniji simply looked down at his feet, crusted with the dry earth of Indian villages. Even if he hadn't been in silence, he knew there was nothing he could say. Another slap, now on the other cheek, nearly knocked him over, and he caught himself just before falling to the ground.

One time, I almost threw myself under an oncoming train. I had had enough of his slaps. I told him, breaking my silence as I thought they would be my last words, "Forget it. I have had enough. It is better to die than to endure this day after day." Although his slaps were part of my daily life, and were dished out for the slightest infractions, they never extended beyond an open-palm smack on the cheek. This time, however, as I readied myself to jump in front of the approaching steam engine, he deemed a stronger hand was necessary.

"What? What did you say?" he shouted as he looped his kamandal high in the air and then down quickly toward my head. He must have thought that if I didn't have any sense, he would beat it into me. Perhaps he thought that when I regained consciousness I would have clearer vision. However, I was young and agile and filled at that brief moment with a spirit of rebellion and discontent. Thus, as the kamandal was about to come crashing down onto my face, I threw up my arms and caught it, thwarting it in its path.

Our hands touched as—for a brief moment—we were each holding the kamandal, him bringing it forcibly down and me averting the blow. As our hands touched, our eyes locked. Mine filled with tears. The veil of ignorance was torn off my eyes.

He turned and began to walk away. I followed him, silently and meekly, for quite some time until he decided I had repented enough and his arms were again open to me.

I realized, in that moment as our fingertips touched around the hardness of the kamandal, that he was not beating me due to his own anger. He was molding me, shaping me, beating out any vestiges of attachment and ignorance, beating down my ego. He knew, every step of the way, exactly what he was doing, and he was in full control. He did not slap me because he lost his temper. He slapped me because it was the quickest, clearest, and most direct way to literally knock an idea or a concept into me or out of me.

FEEDING THE SOUL BUT NOT THE BODY

As they traveled together, nights were spent sleeping under trees, in crevasses dug into fields for drainage in the rainy season, and occasionally in the home of a devotee. As they carried no money and vowed not to touch it, meals were dependent on the compassion and generosity of villagers. Usually they received food at least once a day. Sometimes, they did not. "One time, I remember we had gone three days without any food and I was famished. One afternoon, after being turned away for the third straight day by every home we approached, we came upon an ashram. Weariness turned to relief as we knew that, according to inviolable ashram tradition, all guests are fed. We entered the ashram and were ushered into the room of the main Swamiji. Right before our eyes he proceeded to eat his lunch from a silver plate without once asking us if we would like to eat."

Ashram tradition dictates that all guests and pilgrims, especially sadhus, must be fed without their asking. Some of the bigger ashrams in populated areas have *bhandaras* (free feasts) running twenty-four hours a day. Even those that don't run continuously are obligated by spiritual law to feed those who appear at mealtime. As fundamental as the rule of feeding wandering sadhus, the converse custom is equally binding: sadhus should never have to resort to begging. They may and sometimes must beg in the cities, towns, and villages, where it is understood that people are focused only on themselves and without coaxing would be loathe to part with wealth in any form. In ashrams, where the purpose is to serve and provide a place for sincere spiritual seekers, a sadhu must never lower himself to begging. It is understood that his needs will be met.

"So, we sat there, stomachs rumbling from hunger, bodies weary with fatigue, watching this swami eat chapati after chapati. We were confident that, once he had had his own meal, he would offer to feed us. But, amazingly, he never did." As the swami rose from his meal, he sent a helper to take the two sadhus to a room where they could rest. Pujya Swami Brahmaswarupji politely refused the offer and led his disciple out of the ashram. As they exited, he explained, "If they cannot even feed two sadhus, it is not a place in which I want to spend even another moment."

They continued to walk throughout the afternoon and into early evening. Muniji was beginning to feel overcome with hunger. "As it was, I didn't have an extra ounce of body fat on which my body could draw. Swamiji was huge and never seemed to lose a pound. I was always quite small and thin, though, and as the third day neared a close I wasn't sure how much longer my body could continue to walk eighteen hours a day without any fuel." Just as those thoughts began to take precedence in his mind over the ceaseless chanting of his mantra, a farmer approached them. He touched the saint's feet and then requested, "Please, Swamiji, come into my home and allow us to feed you supper."

Swamiji blessed the farmer but refused. According to a tradition that he faithfully observed, he did not eat after sunset.

However, the man was persistent. "You must let me feed you something. If you won't take a full meal at least let me give you some mangoes from my tree and a glass of fresh milk. Please. I will throw myself in front of a truck if you do not accept my gift."

The guru looked back and forth between the farmer, who had appeared inexplicably out of the depths of his fields in the dark of dusk, and his famished young disciple. Finally he acquiesced. The man carefully peeled three mangoes, which he insisted on feeding to Muniji with his own hands, and he wouldn't let them leave until they each drank a full glass of milk.

"So, God was always with us," Pujya Swamiji explains. "Whenever things became really difficult, He would appear in one form or another in order to take care of us. That stubborn farmer was not a coincidence. He did not just suddenly decide that feeding mangoes to sadhus after sundown was more important than his own life. Rather, God put him there."

Faith in God's Perfect System

ONCE THERE WERE THREE MEN SITTING UNDER A TREE IN THE GARDEN AND THEY STARTED talking about God. One man said, "I don't believe that God is perfect. In fact, there are so many things that even an ordinary, reasonable man would be able to plan better than God. For example, look over

there." The man drew his friends' attention to the pumpkin patch where hundreds of pumpkins were growing, large and round. "God has put these huge, heavy pumpkins on the end of tiny, thin vines that always collapse under the weight of their enormous fruit."

One of the other men joined in. "Yes, you're right," he said. "Look at the mango trees. Huge, strong, sturdy trees. And their fruit? A tiny four-ounce mango! What kind of backward planning is this? Put the heavy fruit on the thin, weak vine and put the light fruit on the tall, strong tree? I agree that God definitely is far from perfect."

However, the third man was not persuaded. "What both of you are saying certainly is compelling. You are right that it might have made more sense to put the heavy fruit on the strong tree and the light fruit on the thin vine, but I believe that there must be a bigger, better, Divine plan. I believe that God knows exactly what He's doing and that His planning is perfect, even if we don't understand it."

The two friends chided the third for his simplicity and blind faith. "Can't you see with your own eyes how stupid it is? Even an idiot would know better!"

Wounded by the other men's criticism, yet secure in his faith, the third man stood up and went to rest under

a nearby tree, separate from his two friends. All three drifted off into a deep, afternoon slumber in the shade of the mango trees.

A strong wind rose and whipped through the trees. Branches swayed in the heavy wind, causing the ripe mangoes to fall. The sleeping skeptics woke, startled by mangoes falling on them and all around them.

One of them exclaimed, "Our friend the believer was right! It is certainly a good thing that only mangoes hang from these branches. The weight of a falling mango was enough to startle me from sleep and bruise my cheek. Had it been heavy pumpkins falling on us, we would have become pumpkin pie! It is very good those heavy pumpkins grow so close to the ground!"

Frequently in life, we doubt God's path. We wonder, "Is this really the way?" We become skeptical of the divine plan; we lose heart; our faith falters. God's ways are frequently mysterious; we fail to see the full picture until it is unveiled for us.

These days in the West all the cars have GPS navigation systems that give directions on how to reach your destination. As you sit in the car, you enter your destination, and throughout the journey a pleasant voice guides you. However, after you've entered the destination but

before the guided instructions begin, you must press the "accept" button on the screen. If the button is not pushed, the guided route will not begin, and you will be left on your own to reach the destination.

GPS stands for "global positioning system," but it also stands for "God's Perfect System." He knows the way to the destination of our life, to the fulfillment of our unique, special, and divine mission. He has designed the map, laid the roads, created the mountains, rivers, highways, and train crossings. He knows every turn, every corner, every one-way street. God never loses His way.

If we don't push "accept" on the GPS system in the car, our journey will be filled with tension and worry. At each intersection we will have to gauge whether it is best to continue straight ahead or to turn left or right. We will have to stop and ask directions from passersby who may not be any more acquainted with the roads than we are. We may eventually reach the destination, if we are focused, efficient, and lucky, but we will likely be late and the journey will have been tense.

Alternatively, if we press "accept," we will be guided gently and correctly at every step. We will know where to turn, where to continue straight, and where to stop. Our minds will be free to contemplate God, to think pleasant and peaceful thoughts, to converse with others in the car. The journey will be peaceful, smooth, and enjoyable.

We must continue to "accept" the guidance given by God's Perfect System whether we are familiar with the route He is taking us or not. He is the creator, the planner, the driver, and the guide.

Chapter Two

The Call of Ganga

THE CRYSTAL CLEAR, BLUE, RUSHING WATERS OF MOTHER GANGA CUT THROUGH THE FOOTHILLS OF THE HIMALAYAS, CARVING OUT THE MOST SACRED RIVERBED IN THE WORLD. OUT OF THE MOTHER GLACIER MORE THAN THIRTEEN THOUSAND feet above sea level, 150 miles north of Rishikesh, the Goddess Ganga—daughter of King Himavat, the king of the Himalayas, and Queen Meru, sister of Uma, Bhagawan Shiva's divine consort—is said to have descended upon Earth, an act of grace and compassion to bring liberation to the fallen sons of King Sagara. Lord Brahma, pleased by King Bhagirath's *tapasya*, directed him to undertake prayers to Lord Shiva, who would catch the powerful, intractable force of Ganga's waters in His infinite locks, releasing Her flow from heaven gently so that She would bring healing and liberation rather than decimation to Earth. Thus, Goddess Ganga gracefully departed from Her heavenly abode and took the form of a flowing river; Lord Shiva released Her from His tresses into seven streams or tributaries, the main one being the river Bhagirathi from the glacier known as Gaumukh ("cow face"), for it appeared to some to be shaped as a cow's mouth. Joining at Dev Prayag with Her sister rivers Alakananda, coming from Badrinath, and Mandakini from Kedarnath, Bhagirathi becomes known as Ganga—the confluence of these three sacred rivers from three of the holiest sites. Rushing rapidly through curves and bends in the mountains, flowing across the holy flora of the Himalayas, accumulating mineral-rich soil in Her waters, Ganga finally arrives in Rishikesh where Her breadth increases, Her speed decreases, and She seems to pause, permitting all to have *darshan* of Her majestic form.

OPPOSITE *Goddess Mother Ganga who descended to Earth to bring purity, life, and liberation to all of humanity.*

ABOVE (left) The founder of the ashram, Pujya Swami Shukdevanandji Maharaj. ❋ (middle and right) President of India, S. Radhakrishnan, visits Parmarth Niketan.

The riverbanks are lined with rocks, softened and smoothed by Her waters, large ones on which one can sit for hours, medium-size ones that fit perfectly in the palm of one's hand, for holding and meditating on, and small pebbles, one or two collected by the pious so that Mother Ganga may flow through their home as well.

Off in the distance *aarti* bells ring in one of the ashrams or temples, calling the devotees to prayer. "Om Jaya Jagadish Hare, Swami Jaya Jagadish Hare . . ." The sound of *aarti* in the temple rides the wind, up and down the river, mingling with the mooing of cows, the vendors' lyrical announcement of the types of vegetables on their carts, and the lull of Ganga's waters washing over the rocks.

This is Rishikesh, a land known as the "home of the *rishis*." The alternate spelling of Hrishikesh refers to Lord Vishnu as Lord of the Senses. It is, therefore, a land in which to conquer one's senses, to conquer the call of desire, to become master of oneself.

This is the land through which young Muniji, now seventeen, and Pujya Swami Brahmaswarupji passed as they walked from the mountains of Badrinath toward the plains of Haryana.

Nearly everyone has had a moment in life in which he or she feels "I have been here before. I have seen this, known this before. This place is not new. I am meant to be here." Some people refer to this as déjà vu, but merely "already seen" does not encompass the internal awareness of "meant to be." For it is not merely that

I have seen this place before, in a dream, in a vision, in a past life, but rather that this is exactly where I am meant to be. This place is the lock for which my key was made. Pujya Swamiji had this experience upon entering Parmarth Niketan ashram, a serene spiritual abode founded by Pujya Swami Shukdevanandji Maharaj in the 1940s.

Years prior, high in the mountainous paradise of Kashmir, the wandering sadhus had visited the ashram of the Shankaracharya math in Srinagar. When his Holiness Adi Shankaracharya traveled from the south to the north of India in the late eighth and early ninth centuries, spreading his great message of unity and the oneness of all creation, he stopped at four main places along the way. These places—Sringeri, Dwarka, and Jyotirmath, and Puri, plus Kanchi, where he lived in the south—are now revered as Shankaracharya's ashrams, and those who head the maths (monasteries) are seen as direct descendants of Adi Shankaracharya, and therefore revered as the highest post in all Hindu culture.

Pujya Swamiji remembers: "When I stayed in the ashram in Srinagar I felt so inspired, so touched by Shankaracharyaji's message and the meaning of his life. I vowed that I, too, would dedicate myself to uniting and inspiring people and to bringing harmony among them."

While there he had met many saints who encouraged him to complete his studies, who explained that in addition to divine inner wisdom and vision, if one truly wants to accomplish something in the world, if

OPPOSITE (top) *Rama Jhula area of Rishikesh in the 1960s and 1970s.* ❀ (bottom) *Parmarth Niketan as seen from across Ganga in the 1970s.*
THIS PAGE *Parmarth Niketan interior in the 1970s and early 1980s.*

one wants to guide, inspire, and lead people toward noble and worthy causes, one must also have an education. They dispelled the idea that inner wisdom was enough. "If you only want to stay in the jungles, then yes, it is enough. But you are destined to accomplish great things. Your arms are destined to reach far beyond the boundaries of North India. You will lead and touch people from every walk of life, every culture, and every country. You will be a leader of this nation and of the world," they foresaw. "Plus, you are very smart. You will have no difficulty in studies. You must get an education."

These words continued to ring in young Muniji's ears as he walked through the villages and jungles of Kashmir, Punjab, and then Uttarakhand with his guru. He was not pre-occupied with the idea, for his near decade of intense *sadhana* had gifted him a complete and unfailing faith in God's plan. He knew that he was being guided and protected.

However, when he entered Parmarth Niketan and saw the sea of young boys, clad in yellow dhotis and kurtas, engaged deeply in the study of Sanskrit and philosophy, the injunction of the saints came back to him. Coupled with his own inner calling to delve deeper into the Vedanta of Shankaracharya, he realized that—now fully established in his spiritual strength—he should return to the academic world and complete the studies he had left behind.

Thus, with the blessings of his spiritual master, who knew that his responsibility was fulfilled, he stayed back at Parmarth Niketan and enrolled in the Sanskrit Mahavidyalaya. Despite having never attended high school, with his mind fully aligned and free from the distractions, fluctuations, and temptations that affect most people, he thrived in the world of higher education. His scores consistently ranked among the highest in the country, earning him a variety of awards and accolades, including a gold medal in the All India Sanskrit Exam Board.

Young Muniji, upon emerging from the forests and arriving at Parmarth.

EARLY YEARS AT PARMARTH

Days were spent imbibing the ancient richness of the Sanskrit language, philosophy, and spiritual tradition. Evenings found Muniji reviewing the day's lessons or walking on the banks of Ganga, head tilted down as his years of wandering through the forests had trained him. At that time, there were no shops or carts or hotels encroaching on his path. One could walk for miles, on the pebbled pathways or dirt roads, lining the banks of the river, without ever encountering more than a lone villager, huddled over a single-burner flame, boiling cups of steaming tea for passersby, tempting them not with calls of "Chai" ("tea") but rather with calls of "Jai Gange" ("Glory to Mother Ganga").

As soon as classes let out for holidays, Muniji would return to the feet of his guru, wherever that might be. Sometimes, the master would be in a village or city, giving *satsang* and discourses in a local temple. Sometimes,

OPPOSITE *River Bhagirathi flows from Gaumukh, but the name "Ganga" is typically used to describe the sacred river after the confluence at Dev Prayag where the Bhagirathi meets the Alakananda and Mandakini.*

"MAKE EVERY DAY a holy day:
Start every day with prayer.
Fill every day with prayer. End
every day with prayer."

he would be wandering through the jungles. In either case, guru and disciple were reunited at every opportunity. "Spiritually we were never apart," Pujya Swamiji explains. "Yes, I was in Rishikesh studying and he was wandering through holy forests, but we were so connected on the spiritual level that we were always together. I could feel him, hear him, and even see him with me all the time, particularly as I watched the mist rise over Ganga. I would see his face in the mist or in the setting sun or in the shimmering ripples."

YOGA AS MEDICINE

Not long after Muniji had settled permanently into Parmarth, he was stricken with typhoid fever. Four weeks passed in feverish sweats, cold compresses, and a liquid diet. For Muniji, it was another opportunity to go inward, to sink even deeper into the divine realm within. "First God sent me to the jungle outside for *sadhana*; then with typhoid, he sent me to the inner jungle, to that silent, calm, secluded, and serene place untouched by the external world." Throughout Muniji's illness, Pujya Swami Vasudevanandji, the head of Parmarth Niketan, nursed him with the attention and love of a devoted mother. Gently and tenderly he wiped Muniji's feverish cheeks and

"Yoga is not a union of our hands to our feet or our head to our knees. It is a union of the self to the Divine."

brought him fresh juices. He sat on Muniji's bed and spoke of God, in all of His manifestations, chanting prayers, mantras, *shlokas*, and *stutis*, turning Muniji's bedroom into a temple.

With the grace of God and Pujya Swami Vasudevanandji's blessings and loving touch, Muniji soon began to recover. However, the progress was neither as quick nor as complete as Muniji felt it should be. The doctors urged him to take heavier and heavier doses of medicine. Since childhood he had an instinc-

Pujya Swami Vasudevanandji.

tive aversion to any form of chemicals, and his body—even now as he enters his seventh decade—can handle only the purest and most unadulterated food. His years in the jungle also habituated his body to being completely untouched by any synthetic material. Even natural additives such as chilis, spices, salt, and ghee don't suit him, and to this day he avoids them as much as possible. On Pujya Swamiji's fiftieth birthday, Pujya Sant Shri Rameshbhai Oza described his state of health perfectly: "Pujya Swamiji nirantar swasth rahate hain. Aur yadi cabhi bimaar hote hain, to Ganga jal se hi theek ho jate hain." ("Pujya Swamiji is always well, and if by chance he ever falls ill, it is by Ganga water alone that he cures himself.")

"I learned this in the jungle," Pujya Swamiji explains. "You never see any hospitals for animals or doctors for animals or drugstores for animals. Nor do you see them lying around moaning in pain and dying pathetic deaths due to lack of treatment. Rather, they are so in tune with nature, so in tune and in balance with themselves and with the universe, that they instinctively know how to cure themselves before they ever get sick. Eating less or fasting, taking rest, and lying in the sunshine are the miracle cures I learned in the jungle, and these are what I use to this day. The moment anything feels out of balance, whether a slight stomach upset or an imminent fever, an immediate reduction in food intake and rest are my medicine."

This pattern was already well established by the time he contracted typhoid in his student years at Parmarth. Hence when the doctors tried to give him heavier and heavier doses of the medicine in response to the stubbornness of his fever, he refused. "There has to be another way. Medicine is okay when you need it. I would not shun medicine on principle. But when you realize that it has done all it can do, that it has run its course and benefited you as much as it's going to and reached its capacity, then one has to search for alternative remedies."

In his case, after the typical course of the typhoid medicine, with the fever still lingering, he knew the answer was not simply to repeat the course that had been ineffective the first time. He intuitively knew that simply pumping his young, frail body with more chemicals was not going to restore its health. "I had developed a very basic yoga practice in the jungle. Eleven hours a day in *vrekshasana* formed the backbone, and of course, I sat for hours in *padmasana* while I practiced my *pranayama* and meditation. I felt the great pervasive benefits of these asanas and *pranayama*, and I knew that they held a key to complete health of the body and mind. Therefore when my fever would not subside despite the best attempts by the doctors, it was to yoga and *pranayama* that I turned."

Pujya Swami Bhajananandji, who had come to Parmarth in the 1940s with the founder, Pujya Swami Shukdevanandji, was a phenomenal yogi. Even at the age of eighty, Swamiji would spend more than thirty minutes each day in *shirshasana*, from 3:30 to 4:00 a.m. While the rest of the world slept, he was awake, upside down, head firmly on the ground and legs held high, strongly, in the air. Following *shirshasana*, he performed an intense sequence of other asanas before leaving for his ritual morning walk at 4:30 a.m. Muniji would frequently accompany Pujya Swami Bhajananandji on his walk, a practice that ceased when Muniji fell ill.

"I asked him to teach me more yoga so that I might heal and strengthen my body, so that the fever might leave me forever." So, along with the tender nurturing of Pujya Swami Vasudevanandji, Muniji began to receive *yogasana* lessons, which he practiced diligently and religiously. Soon, what chemicals could not do, yoga accomplished, and Muniji was well.

"It was from that time that I became a firm and ardent proponent of yoga and nature cure," Pujya Swamiji explains. His devotion to the natural way of health and healing has followed him throughout his life.

ABOVE *(left)* Pujya Swami Dharmanandji. ❋ *(right)* Pujya Swami Bhajananandji.

INTO THE LAP OF THE GURU

Parmarth Niketan, Rishikesh, is the headquarters of the Swami Shukdevanand Trust, a trust that also manages ashrams in Haridwar, Delhi, and other places. One day, Pujya Swami Vasudevanandji was going to the Haridwar ashram to meet with the head, Pujya Swami Dharmanandji, his guru-brother. Muniji had recovered from his bout with typhoid, but Pujya Swami Vasudevanandji's adoration of him had not faded. Hence, he took the young saint with him to see the Haridwar ashram and to have *darshan* of his guru-brother.

"Pujya Swami Dharmanandji and I immediately had a very special and very deep connection," Pujya Swamiji remembers. "I knew that he would play a very important, divine, guiding role in my life." After that, whenever he had the opportunity, Muniji would go to Haridwar to have his *darshan*, and Pujya Swami Dharmanandji came frequently to Rishikesh where young Muniji would sit for hours at his feet.

Remember Your Own Dharma—The Saint & Scorpion

ONCE THERE WAS A SADHU (MONK), LIVING ON THE BANKS OF A RIVER PERFORMING HIS SADHANA with great piety and determination. One day as the holy man went for his bath in the river, he noticed a scorpion struggling in the water. Scorpions, by nature, cannot swim, and the sadhu knew that if he did not save the scorpion, it would drown. Therefore,

carefully picking up the scorpion, the saint lifted it out of the waters and was just about to set it down gently on the shore when the scorpion stung his finger. In pain, the sadhu instinctively flung his hand, and the scorpion went flying back into the river. As soon as the sadhu regained his composure from the sting, he again lifted the scorpion out of the water. Again, before he could set the scorpion safely on the land, the creature stung him. Yet again, as the sadhu shook his hand in response to the pain, the scorpion fell back into the water. This drama went on for several minutes as the holy man continued to try to save the life of the drowning scorpion and the scorpion continued to sting his savior's hand before reaching the freedom of the river bank.

A man who had been out hunting in the forest noticed this drama between the holy man and the scorpion. He watched as the saint carefully and gingerly lifted the creature out of the water, only to fling it back in as his hand convulsed in pain from each fresh sting. Finally, the hunter said to the sadhu, "Revered Swamiji, forgive me for my frankness, but it is clear that the scorpion is simply going to continue to sting you each and every time you try to carry it to safety. Why don't you give up and just let it drown?"

The holy man replied, "My dear child, the scorpion is not stinging me out of malice or evil intent. It is simply his nature to sting. Just as it is the water's nature to make me wet, so it is the scorpion's nature to sting. He doesn't realize that I am carrying him to safety. That is a level of conscious comprehension greater than his brain can achieve. But, just as it is the scorpion's nature to sting, so it is my nature to save. Just as he is not leaving his nature, why should I leave my nature? My dharma is to help any creature of any kind—human or animal. Why should I let a small scorpion rob me of the divine nature that I have cultivated through years of sadhana?"

In our lives we encounter people who harm us, who insult us, who plot against us, whose actions seem calculated to thwart the successful achievement of our goals. Sometimes these are obvious acts, such as a co-worker who continually steals our ideas or speaks badly of us to our boss. Sometimes these acts are more subtle—a friend, relative, or colleague who unexpectedly betrays us or who we find has been secretly speaking negatively about us behind our back. We often wonder, "How could he hurt me like that? How could she do this to me?" Then, our hearts become filled with anger and pain, and our minds start plotting vengeance.

Slowly we find that our own actions, words, and thoughts become driven by anger and pain. We find ourselves engaged in cunning thoughts of revenge. Before we realize it, we are injuring ourselves more by allowing the negative emotions into our hearts than the other person injured us by their words or actions. They may have insulted us or plotted against us or sabotaged a well-deserved achievement at work, but we injure ourselves more deeply and more gravely by allowing our hearts and minds to turn dark.

Our dharma is to be kind, pure, honest, giving, sharing and caring. Due to ignorance, due to lack of understanding (much like the scorpion who doesn't understand the sadhu's gentle intention), or due to the way in which their own karmic drama is unfolding, others may act with malice, deceit, selfishness, or indifference. We, however, must not let their actions or their ignorance deprive us of

fulfilling our dharma. We must not allow ourselves to be lowered by their ignorance, their habits, or their greed. The darkness in their hearts should not be allowed to penetrate into the lightness of our hearts.

Sometimes people ask, "But Swamiji, how long should we continue to tolerate, continue to forgive, continue to love in the face of other people's aggression, jealousy, hatred, and malice?" The answer: *forever*. It is not our job to mete out punishment to others based on their actions. That is God's job and the job of the law of karma. They will get their punishment. Do not worry. They will face the same misery they are bringing to you. But it is not our job to hand that to them. It is God's job and—with the exacting law and science of karma—evildoers will receive punishment, but not by our hands. If we allow ourselves to injure, insult, plot against, or hurt them, then we are simply accruing more and more negative karma for ourselves.

If the sadhu had allowed the scorpion to suffer and drown in the river, he would have forsaken his own divine path in life. Sure, we can say that the scorpion deserved to die for what he had done to the sadhu. We can say that the sadhu had tried and tried to save the scorpion but the scorpion would not let him. We can give a list of explanations to excuse the sadhu for not rescuing the scorpion. But, to pardon bad behavior is not the goal. To excuse ourselves for failing to fulfill our duties is not the goal. The goal is to live up to our full, divine potential as conscious, holy beings.

So, let us remember that our dharma is to live lives of purity, piety, peace, selflessness, integrity, and love, and let us never allow anyone or anyone's actions—however malicious or crazy or poisonous they may be—to divert us from that goal.

CHAPTER THREE

The Rising of the Sun

SANYAS

SANYAS IS THE OFFICIAL RENUNCIATION OF WORLDLY ATTACHMENTS, TIES, EXPECTA-
TIONS, AND TEMPTATIONS AND AN OFFICIAL DECLARATION OF THE SURRENDERING
OF EVERY CELL OF ONE'S BEING, EVERY MINUTE OF ONE'S LIFE, EVERY OUNCE OF ONE'S

energy to the service of God and humanity. "Idam
Namamah," not for me, but for You. Not for me, but
for You. Nothing I have, nothing I know, nothing I can
do, nothing I achieve or attain or receive is for me. It is
all for You.

Although Muniji's path had been laid on the day that
Pujya Swami Brahmaswarupji touched him on the forehead (and, perhaps, had been laid the moment his soul
selected Matashri's womb in which to take birth), the official embarkation upon the life of *sanyas* is taken at the *diksha* (initiation) ceremony. Twelve years after taking vows
of *brahmacharya*, one is eligible for *sanyas*, in the Shankaracharya lineage.

Mahashivratri is a day on which Hindus across the
world abstain from food and stay awake all night in meditation on the element of the Divine that destroys what is
old and impure to make room for new birth. It is a day on
which, despite the infrequence of rain in the dry winter,
Ganga invariably falls from the sky. It was on this day in
1975 that Sant Narayan Muni received the saffron garb of
a *sanyasi*, the cloth dyed to resemble the color of the setting
and rising sun, to resemble the color of fire. Pujya Swamiji
explains.

*The sun gives and gives, with no hesitation, no discrimination, no
expectation, and no vacation. The sun never says, "I am too tired to
rise today. I think I'll take a day off." Nor does she say, "You haven't*

OPPOSITE *Pujya Swamiji in the mid-1970s, shortly after being officially initiated into sanyas by Pujya Swami Dharmanandji.*

Goddess Ma Saraswati, the bestower of true wisdom.

attachment, the identity, the personality and tendencies of the pre-*sanyas* life, and a new being rises from the flames. Hence, when a *sanyasi* dons the saffron cloth each day, he or she remembers that the old self has perished and been burned in the purifying fire.

On the holy day of Mahashivratri 1975, Pujya Swami Dharmanandji performed the ceremony of *sanyas* for Sant Narayan Muniji. As Muniji walked, naked and newly born, out of the rushing waters of Mother Ganga, his guru draped the saffron robes on his slender shoulders and anointed him as Swami Chidanand Saraswatiji.

"But what does your name mean?" so many people ask. Saraswati is the divine Goddess of wisdom, knowledge, and learning and also of music and fine arts. Seekers pray to her for everything from good marks on their exams to divine wisdom and enlightenment, and for blessings in their pursuit of the ancient, sacred arts of music and song. Ma Lakshmi is seen as the Goddess of Wealth, but the wealth bestowed by Ma Saraswati is no less valuable. One who has money without wisdom is impoverished indeed. One who has financial or professional success without the deep understanding of its place, its value, and its shortcomings will be thwarted rather than benefited by the prosperity. Thus, in many ways, true knowledge, true wisdom, is the greatest wealth and the greatest blessing. Ma Saraswati bestows this.

The Saraswati lineage is traced to Shankaracharya. It is a lineage where one seeks to attain the light of understanding and wisdom that burns through the darkness of ignorance and isolation. It is one of the main, traditional spiritual lineages of India.

Chid-anand literally means "bliss through wisdom." *Chid* does not merely refer to excellence in certain fields of study or mastery over particular subjects. Rather it is the true, divine, all-encompassing wisdom. It is the wisdom with which one discriminates between truth and falsehood, between reality

paid my bills. So I will not rise over your house today." *Nor does she shine more brightly on the homes of Hindus, or Muslims, or Christians, or Jews, or Indians, or Americans, or Africans. She shines equally for all—never sending a bill, never taking a vacation. When we say "the sun has set," she has actually risen somewhere else. It is her grace that she gives us half a day of darkness so we can take rest. But she is always on, just in a different part of the world. That is the meaning of* sanyas. *Give, give, and give, with no expectation—never demand or ask anything from anyone—no hesitation, no vacation, and no discrimination."*

The saffron color also symbolizes the flames of a fire. Part of the traditional *sanyas* ceremony is attending one's own cremation. All the items that connect one to the past and tie one down are burned, representing the final rites ceremony of the person who used to live. In those flames are burned the

"IF WE WANT to be torchbearers
of peace, we must first become rivers of love,
dousing all flames of discord in the waters
of our own compassion and serenity."

MAHASHIVRATRI

Shivratri is one of the holiest nights of the year. It is the night dedicated to the worship of Lord Shiva. The holiday of Shivratri is celebrated by performing special Shiva *puja* and *abhishek* and by remaining awake at night in meditation, *kirtan*, and *japa*.

Literally, "Shivratri" means "the great night of Shiva." It is celebrated on the thirteenth or fourteenth day of the dark half of the month of Phalguna (February–March).

In the trinity of gods, the divine trinity of Brahma, Vishnu, and Shiva, Bhagawan Shiva is the God who dissolves what is old and impure in order to make room for a new creation that is pure and divine. Lord Shiva annihilates our egos, our attachments, and our ignorance. Many fear Lord Shiva's destructive capacity, and yet it is destruction for the purpose of regeneration. Without death, life cannot begin anew. Without the annihilation of old habits, attachments, and ego, we cannot progress toward the goal of God realization and be filled with divine qualities. On this night of Shivratri, as we worship Bhagawan Shiva, let us pray that all within us that is old, holding us back, and keeping our lives in the shadows should be dissolved.

Bhagawan Shiva is portrayed with ash on His forehead, and devotees of Lord Shiva frequently apply sacred ash to various parts of their body. This symbolizes two things. Everything that today has a form on the Earth once was ash in the ground and again will be reduced to ash. Therefore, the ash serves to remind us that all that we are and do earn and acquire one day will be reduced to ash. Therefore we should live our lives dedicated to God and to serving humanity, rather than to the accumulation of fleeting possessions and comfort. When we apply the sacred ash or see it, we are reminded, "Ah yes, it is only by the grace of God that I am still here today, and that I have not yet been turned to ash. It is His grace that my home, my family, and my possessions are still with me and that they have not become ash. Therefore, I should remember Him, pray to Him, and devote myself to Him."

The stories and the messages of Bhagawan Shiva are innumerable. One of the most important is the story of how He, for the sake of humanity, swallowed the poison that emerged from the ocean.

The story says that the *devas* (divine ones) and their brothers, the demons, were churning the ocean in search of the pot of the nectar of immortality. After a great deal of effort, what emerged was not nectar, but poison! This happens in life, too. When we embark upon a divine plan or undertake a noble challenge, before our effort bears fruit, we frequently face failure, condemnation, or seemingly insurmountable hurdles.

The *devas* and demons knew that in order to continue churning, and ultimately to unearth the divine nectar, they could not simply toss the poison aside. Someone had to drink it. But no one was willing to drink the poison. Everyone had some excuse for being too valuable to be sacrificed. Finally, Bhagawan Shiva came forward. He said, "I will drink the poison if it will preserve peace in the family and enable my brothers and sisters to attain the nectar of immortality."

In our lives and in our families, we wait and wait for the divine nectar to emerge, but it seems that only poison comes. When we work for good causes, when we embark upon divine work, the poison often comes before the nectar. If the *devas* and demons had forfeited the churning at the appearance of poison, the nectar of immortality would never have emerged. We must have faith that the nectar will come. We must be willing to churn, be it poison or nectar.

On this night of Shivratri, as we worship Bhagawan Shiva, this is also the night that we pray for the strength to take His message to heart! Let us not only worship Him, but also emulate Him. Whoever is willing to swallow the poison and sacrifice for the family, for the community, and for humanity is the true Mahadeva (Great Divine One).

After drinking the poison to enable the churning to continue, Bhagawan Shiva held the poison in his throat—hence the name Neelkanth, which means "Blue Throat"—and went to the Himalayas where He sat peacefully in meditation.

You don't have to go to the Himalayas. Create your own Himalayas, wherever you are. First, be the one to accept the poison. Be the one to sacrifice, apologize, and concede humbly. Then go, sit, and meditate peacefully. This is not weakness, but divine strength.

On the night of Shivratri, as we remember the churning between the *devas* and demons for the nectar of immortality, we must take another lesson to heart. After the nectar emerged, the demons tried to abscond with it. If they had succeeded, they would have been ever more powerful and able to destroy their brothers, the *devas*. Through a series of divine interventions, the *devas* emerged the victors with the gift of immortality.

The night of Shivratri is especially auspicious for winning this same battle within ourselves—the battle between good and evil, between right and wrong, between poison and nectar, between death and immortality. Let us use our *puja*, our prayers, our meditations on this night to pray for divine intervention so that within ourselves the good might vanquish the evil, the nectar within us might emerge, so that we too may be carried from death to immortality.

Mahadev Shiva holding a trident.

Prime Minister Smt. Indira Gandhi visits the Parmarth camp in the Maha Kumbha Mela.

and illusion. It is the wisdom with which one realizes—deeply and experientially—that one is not the body, but rather the eternal Self that is simply inhabiting the body, and *chid* is the light of wisdom with which one can see the divine, externally as well as internally.

KUMBHA MELA

Kumbha Mela is the largest gathering of pilgrims in the world. Tens of millions of spiritual seekers flock to the site, yearning for inspiration and liberation. The land of Allahabad (or Prayag Raj) is seen as the holiest of the four Kumbha Mela locations, for it is here that the holy Ganga and Yamuna rivers meet the invisible Saraswati. To this sacred Triveni Sangam, people from across the world flock in the millions in order to submerge their bodies, their sins, their cares, and their worries in the convergence of rivers. For much of the year, the Kumbha Mela zone is covered by water. There are no permanent structures. It is only in the dry season of winter that the water levels drop, the land becomes parched and dusty, and camps are erected for the Mela. It is a feat of

unparalleled devotion to have the elaborate tent-camps, complete with electricity and running water, erected in a few weeks' time. The barren land becomes a land without one unoccupied inch. The eerie quiet melts into the booming sounds of competing *pravachans* blasting from loud speakers set up throughout the area.

The year 1977 marked Pujya Swamiji's first Kumbha Mela in Allahabad, particularly significant as a new *sanyasi*. He and Swami Shashwatanandji together traveled overnight by train from Haridwar to Prayag to erect a camp of epic proportion and unparalleled beauty on the cold, dry sand. To make water flow from a desiccated land and make electricity run where there is nothing but mosquitoes, to provide thousands of guests with accommodation that would block out the raging wind and the near-freezing cold—these are the tasks the two young sadhus undertook.

Parmarth and the Daivi Sampad Mandal were already established and respected names, particularly among the community of ashrams; with Pujya Swamiji's vision and energy, the Parmarth camp (established together with Bharat Sadhu Samaj) quickly

OPPOSITE *Scenes from the Maha Kumbha Mela, the largest spiritual festival on Earth, which takes place every twelve years in Haridwar, Allahabad, Nasik, and Ujjain. Tens of millions of people gather together. The Haridwar and Allahabad melas are traditionally the largest.*
FOLLOWING PAGE *Divine Mohini holds the pot of the nectar of immortality, the origin of the Kumbha Mela festival.*

"THE SHOP ADVERTISEMENT says,
'Buy one and get one free.'
God says, 'Buy me and be free.'"

Satsang on the train platforms for all passengers as well as local people.

became the hub of divine activity during the mela. Morning prayers, *satsangs*, yoga, meditation, and *pranayama* classes and divine *bhajans* kept the camp full of devotees and pilgrims from Magh Purnima in the frigid fog of early January to Maha Shivratri when the winter frost turns to spring sunshine in late February.

The camp received so much public acclaim that when Prime Minister Indira Gandhi came to have *darshan* of the Kumbha, it was Parmarth's camp she visited. Speaking to a huge crowd in a makeshift hall of unprecedented proportions and elegance, constructed on dry sand with neither machinery, nor running water, nor professional contractors or builders, Indira Gandhi spoke effusively about the Kumbha Mela, Parmarth's camp, and the ashram's dedication to humanity demonstrated by the charitable services and activities.

BHARAT DARSHAN

In 1979, Pujya Swamiji organized a train *yatra* (spiritual pilgrimage) of enormous proportion. The saints and nearly six hundred devotees of Parmarth Niketan rented an entire train and traversed the country, north to south, and west to east. The theme of the *yatra* was "Bharat Darshan," and it was organized so pilgrims would be able to have *darshan* of the diverse spiritual sites throughout the country. Further, for Pujya Swamiji, the deeper and more profound purpose of this train *yatra* was to bring the inspiration and message of Parmarth to people from every walk of life, every caste, and every creed. As Adi Shankaracharya had traveled from south to north spreading the message of oneness, similarly, Pujya Swamiji envisioned traveling north to south, carrying hundreds of people on a journey to discover not merely temples and sacred sites but also the inherent unity within all people, despite differences in language, region, culture, and caste.

As Mahatma Gandhi had emphasized the importance of the village people, the poor, and the tribal people, so Pujya Swamiji led the *yatra* through small villages, countrysides, and barren tribal areas, stopping to give the divine touch to local people. All *yatris* slept on the train in the nights and disembarked each morning for a quick *snan* (shower) on the platforms. At each station there was one platform that was the *snan* platform. The men filled buckets of water from the hand-pump and had their baths in the open. The ladies gathered into tight circles, forming a protective shield with their combined sarees, and each in turn went into the middle for her bath, the others shielding her from sight. Then, after bathing, everyone congregated on the station platform for morning prayers.

There, in the middle of bustling train stations, the saints, *yatris*, all the local devotees, and everyone who happened to be in the station at the time sat together and sang the glories of the Almighty, led by Pujya Swamiji's mellifluous voice. As he sang, thousands of miles from the Himalayas, on station floors that hadn't been cleaned in decades, as hot, stifling, diesel fumes filled the air, in any and all circumstances he carried the listeners effortlessly to the cool banks of Mother Ganga.

The days were filled with *satsang* at local temples, local halls, and—when there wasn't time to go into town—on the sanctified, concrete platforms of local train stations.

Sitting or standing, steel plates in hand, the 575 *yatris* plus all their family members ate *prasad* prepared by the ashram's own cooks. "Parmarth Niketan" means "an abode dedicated to the welfare of all," and it is a message and motto ardently upheld by all the saints who have headed the ashram. Thus, the idea of feeding only oneself is inconceivable. To eat means to feed those around. To this day, whenever Pujya Swamiji travels by plane or

train on a long journey, those who pack him *theplas* or *paranthas* (Indian flat bread) for the way always have to pack extra; inevitably he will feed all the flight attendants and nearby passengers before putting a bite in his mouth. In this way, as *bhandaras* sprung up on station platforms, the *yatris* ate and also fed everyone who had gathered to hear the spiritual discourses or to have *darshan* of the saints, as well as fellow travelers and those who had come to meet friends and family, and anyone who was just hungry. Pujya Swamiji remembers, "Sometimes by the time we were ready to sit down for our meals there was nothing left, or everything was cold. But, the joy was in serving, in feeding so many people. We were feeding not only their bodies but also their hearts and souls with divine connection."

Devotees in each town along the way would come and garland the saints.

THIS SPREAD *During the Bharat Darshan yatra, the saints and devotees visited local temples, gave satsang programs in halls and tents, had baths in holy rivers and lakes, and led processions throughout cities and towns across India.*

"DON'T ONLY light
the oil lamp in your temple, but light
the lamp in your own hearts."

Pujya Swamiji, already a visionary, realized that it was impossible for 575 people to crowd into one train compartment and listen to *pravachan* in the evenings as the train steamed past villages. So he made special arrangements for a public address system to broadcast the saints' voices throughout the train. In that manner, everyone could receive the divine message while sitting comfortably in their own compartments.

Everything went beautifully, with the inevitable hurdles that distinguish a *yatra* from a

"Life is about the journey, not the destination. Live in heaven now. Don't wait for it to come later. Live in *moksha* now. Don't wait for death."

holiday. However, one evening a small group was late in returning to the station for the train. Pujya Swamiji went back into town to look for them, as in those days there were no mobile phones or pagers or any immediate way of contacting someone. When he returned with the truant bunch, who had inadvertently lost track of time, Pujya Swami Dharmanandji mistakenly assumed that it was he who had been leading them and therefore he was to blame for their tardiness. He scolded his young disciple for being irresponsible and for delaying the entire train. Pujya Swamiji recalls the incident.

I felt the breath drain out of my body. Here was my beloved guru in whose seva *I was living, for whom I was doing everything, to whom I had surrendered my life. And he misunderstood? However, I never spoke back to him. I took everything he said and did as God's divine plan. Hence, this too, which was clearly a mistake and misunderstanding, I took as God's message. I had not been irresponsible this time, but surely sometime in the past I must've done something irresponsible. In the past, sometime, I was sure I had made mistakes. Therefore, I took his words not as a misunderstanding but rather as reproach for an earlier time, a time when I surely must've deserved it.*

When he finished his rebuke, I touched his feet and returned silently to my coupa *(compartment). Lying on my cot, I closed my eyes and allowed the soft, gentle melody of my mantra to soothe my heart.*

When time for dinner came, Pujya Swamiji refused. "I decided that I needed to fast to atone for whatever mistakes I had committed and to further greater introspection." A short while later, one of the *sevaks* knocked on his *coupa* door. "Maharajji is refusing his dinner unless you eat," the boy told him. He followed the boy to his guru's *coupa*. "Maharajji, please take your dinner. I am fine. I am fasting for my mistake," Pujya Swamiji pleaded tenderly with his guru.

In the hour between the censure and dinnertime, others had informed his guru what had happened that day. He realized he had unjustly scolded his dearest and closest disciple. "If you must fast for your mistake, then I shall fast for mine," Pujya Swami Dharmanandji replied. Realizing that his guru wouldn't take his meal unless he also ate, Pujya Swamiji told the *sevak*, "Okay. Bring us both our dinner."

In the more than twenty years of living in Pujya Swami Dharmanandji's *seva*, that was the only time he was ever scolded.

OPPOSITE *Bhagawan Shiva, the embodiment of the divine energy of dissolution.*

Endless Desires

ONCE, MANY YEARS AGO, BEFORE THE SEVERE VIOLENCE IN JAMMU-KASHMIR, WHEN I WAS YOUNG, we traveled to Kashmir to spend a few days meditating on the beautiful and heavenly Dal Lake. However, all the devotees enjoyed themselves so much that we delayed our departure date and remained there for one month instead of a few days.

Each week we would postpone our departure from that heavenly, pristine, glorious environment. "Just one more week," the devotees would cry, so we stayed.

Finally, after one month we knew we needed to leave, so we went to bid farewell and give payment to the kind boatman who had taken us out onto the lake each day. When one of the devotees offered payment, the simple boatman refused. He said, "I thank you for the money, but more than the money I want one special blessing from Swamiji. Could I please speak to Swamiji and ask his blessing?"

When the boatman came to see me, he fell in prostrations on the ground and finally looked up, tears in his eyes, and said words I will never forget. He said, "Swamiji, I don't know what horrible karma I must have performed to be stuck here in this lake for my whole life. I beg you to please give me the blessing that I may go one day and see Bombay."

I was amazed! We had come from all over India (and many devotees were from Bombay, Calcutta, Delhi, and other big cities) and we had fallen in love with the serene, divine atmosphere in Kashmir. The devotees from Bombay would have given anything to be able to stay forever on the lakeside. Tourists travel from every corner of the Earth to visit Kashmir. When there is not war going on in the area, it is known as the greatest natural paradise on Earth.

Yet, this man who had taken birth here, who lives every day in the midst of the most beautiful lake, dreams of nothing but Bombay! Those in Bombay are crying to take a holiday to Kashmir, and those in Kashmir are crying to go to Bombay.

One of the greatest plagues of human beings is our insatiable desires. We truly never feel satisfied. We never

feel that we have "enough." We are always looking for more and more and more. This pertains to almost every area of our lives. Obesity, diabetes, and heart disease are sky-rocketing because we always want "just one more" *ladoo, gulab jamun,* or piece of chocolate cake. Our bank accounts are getting fuller but our lives are getting emptier because we are always striving to close "just one more deal" or to take on "just one more project," thereby sacrificing the precious time that we could otherwise spend on spiritual pursuits or with our families or engaged in service for others.

It is through surrendering to God that we become desireless. Through being desireless we attain peace and joy. We think, mistakenly, that it is by fulfilling our desires that we will attain joy. However, it is the opposite. Fulfillment of desire leads to temporary happiness *not* because the object of desire was attained, but simply because the desire has now temporarily disappeared! If I am craving a new car and I get a new car, then my desire for a new car has gone away. It is not the new car itself that gives me the joy, but rather it is the fact that I am now free of the desire for a new car. The diminishment of desire is what brings joy to us. But the way to diminish our desires is not to rush around and try to fulfill them. There are always more. They are like weeds in the garden of our mind. No matter how many we pluck, there will always be more . . . For a short while we are satisfied, and then the fire of desire begins burning again, even more fiercely.

CHAPTER FOUR

Founding of the Hindu-Jain Temple

TRAVEL TO CANADA AND THE UNITED STATES

OVER THE YEARS, IT BECAME CLEAR THAT PUJYA SWAMIJI'S VISION, ABILITY, AND COMMITMENT WERE UNPARALLELED. ALTHOUGH PUJYA SWAMI SADANANDJI WAS OFFICIALLY THE HEAD OF PARMARTH, HE RELIED ON PUJYA SWAMIJI FOR innumerable decisions, policies, and programs. It was not surprising, therefore, that he chose Pujya Swamiji to accompany him on a trip abroad, beginning with Ottawa, Canada, followed by the United States, in September 1980.

The first place in the United States that the saints visited was Malibu, the luxurious oceanfront community of California's wealthiest businessmen and Hollywood stars. Their purpose, of course, was unrelated to sightseeing or vacationing. They had been called by a prominent Indian living in the area, Dr. Amarjit Singh Marwah, a successful doctor filled with piety and humility. Dr. Marwah was eager to have his home, his family, and the Sikh/Punjabi community blessed by enlightened saints from India. Pujya Swamiji recalls his trip to Hollywood.

I remember when I was on my first trip to the United States, over thirty years ago, and I was staying in Malibu, California. One day, one of the Indians who lived there said to me, "Swamiji, can I take you to see Hollywood?" I had no idea what Hollywood was. I had never heard of it. The fact that it rhymed with Bollywood did not occur to me at the time, and I simply assumed it was some type of forest, a woodsy, jungle area. We spoke frequently about the "holy woods" of the Himalayas, and thus I thought it must be something like this. Therefore, I acquiesced and we went the next day to see Hollywood Boulevard and Universal Studios. Needless to say, it was a jungle, but of course a different type of jungle than I had been imagining! However, on the way

OPPOSITE *Pujya Swamiji at the Hindu Jain Temple summer camp.*

Bhoomi puja *of Hindu-Jain Temple.*

something remarkable happened. We were driving down the freeway in a Rolls-Royce car, when in the middle of our discussion he stopped me and urgently exclaimed, "Swamiji, look, look, do you see that car?" The man frantically pointed out a car driving next to us on the freeway. He kept turning his head to make sure I knew exactly which car he was showing me. As we had been deep in the middle of a serious conversation on spiritual topics, he did not elaborate further. As soon as he was sure I had seen and registered the car in my mind, he changed the topic again back to the spiritual discussion. Later, when we returned to Malibu, before he left Dr. Marwah's home, he said to me, "Swamiji, I need your blessings. Do you remember that car I showed you as we were driving? That is the model of Rolls-Royce I want. Please bless me that I can get that model of Rolls-Royce." I was amazed! Here we were sitting in a Rolls-Royce and he is dreaming about a different Rolls-Royce! But, the truth is, life is always like that.

The days of mobile phones were still far off, and calls between India and the United States had to be connected by an operator. A "lightning call," referring to faster service at ten times the cost, still required a wait of at least several minutes and occasionally hours. In spite of the delays and innumerable minutes spent shouting "hello, hello, hello" with *sevaks* in the office at Parmarth Niketan, Dr. Prakash Srivastava, an Indian doctor living in Pittsburgh, Pennsylvania, managed to locate Swami Sadanandji and Swami Chidanandji in Malibu. He had been to Rishikesh earlier in the year during his trip to India, and he

OPPOSITE *Pujya Swami Sadanandji and Pujya Swamiji outside a devotee's home in America.*

had gone to Parmarth Niketan. Although he had not met Pujya Swamiji personally on that visit, he was told that he would be ideal for the role of inspiring and uniting the Pittsburgh community as well as guiding the creation of a Hindu temple. When Prakashji found out that the saints were in the United States, he decided they must come to Pittsburgh.

Pujya Swami Sadanandji refused Prakashji's requests on the grounds that their itinerary had already been finalized and there was no time available to add an extra program in Pittsburgh. He assured Prakashji, however, that his blessings were with the entire community and that on the next trip they would try to include Pittsburgh. Prakashji was not satisfied with the distance-blessings and called again a few days later to try to persuade Pujya Swami Sadanandji to amend his itinerary. For the second time his request was refused. Yet destiny was on the side of the soon-to-become Hindu-Jain Temple, and fortuitously Pujya Swami Sadanandji was not available when Prakashji called for the third time. Thus, Dr. Amarjit Singh gave the phone to Pujya Swamiji, whose mantra has always been "no problem."

Prakashji's request was simple and sincere: The groundbreaking ceremony for the Hindu temple was about to take place and they needed the saints' blessings. He didn't mention at the time their desire for Pujya Swamiji to stay permanently with the community or that he had already been told no twice. He also described the temple's struggle to unite all Indians, from all spiritual traditions, in their temple community. Pujya Swamiji was touched. He has always been committed to strengthening interfaith relations and to helping people realize the inherent oneness of all creation despite differences in culture, creed, and language. He is especially fervent about the need for the indigenous religions of India to focus more on their common roots than their divergent branches.

For these reasons and due to his generally soft heart for anyone with a sincere request,

he felt compelled to offer whatever support possible to this community. Serendipitously, the Pittsburgh temple also included a *gurdwara* for the Sikhs; thus when the discussion arose later in the day, Dr. Amarjit Singh helped Pujya Swamiji convince the elder saint that the community needed the saints' help and support. Thus, tickets were canceled and rebooked, itineraries were changed, and plans were made to spend a few hours in Pittsburgh en route from New York to Washington, DC.

That is how it came to be that on the auspicious day of Dussehra, the day symbolizing the vanquishing of evil by good, the ground was prepared, literally and figuratively, for the birth of the Hindu-Jain Temple. At the time, it was still called the Hindu Temple of North America. The name change would come later. The groundbreaking ceremony was graced by the presence of the saints as well as the consul general of India.

Although the saints stayed only a few hours, the impact was profound. After cer-

Pujya Swami Sadanandji and Pujya Swamiji enjoying nature in America.

emoniously breaking the earth for the temple and laying the foundation stone, the saints spoke a few words of blessings. Pujya Swamiji also sang three *bhajans* (devotional songs) on the occasion. As the sound of his beautiful voice floated across the grounds in the brisk autumn air, Dr. Prakash Srivastava and other temple officers immediately recognized in Pujya Swamiji the spiritual leadership they were lacking. "We knew, instantly, after he spoke a few minutes and sang some *bhajans* that he was the one we needed."

For the next many months, Prakashji and Dr. Raghunath, a professor at Carnegie Mellon University, communicated with Pujya Swami Sadanandji and Pujya Swami Dharmanandji, ardently requesting them to send the young, vibrant *sanyasi* back to Pittsburgh. In addition to writing numerous letters to Pujya Swamiji, humbly yet sincerely requesting him to make Pittsburgh his temporary home, Prakashji traveled back to Rishikesh to formally request them to send Pujya Swamiji. Raghunathji also recalls taking a special trip to Rishikesh in order to convince them. "I wasn't sure if I'd be able to do it alone," he said. "So I brought my father-in-law, who was a very well-respected person in the community."

When they requested Pujya Swami Sadanandji to please spare Pujya Swamiji for the Pittsburgh temple, he replied emphatically, "You may take anyone but him. He does everything and I cannot spare him."

The next day, Raghunathji urged his father-in-law to request him again. This second meeting bore fruit, and Pujya Swami Sadanandji agreed. However, there were three conditions. First, that each year Pujya Swamiji would spend six months in Pittsburgh and six months in Rishikesh. Second, if he was needed in Rishikesh, even prior to the end of his six months in Pittsburgh, he would be sent immediately, up to three times per year. Third, Pujya Swamiji would be given a private telephone line so he could be reached at any moment. Raghunathji agreed. Pujya

Swami Sadanandji said that Pujya Swami Dharmanandji's permission would also be required, as he was Pujya Swamiji's guru.

INTO THE LAP OF THE MOTHER

Pujya Swami Dharmanandji lovingly and immediately granted the permission for Pujya Swamiji to go to Pittsburgh to lead the creation of the Hindu temple. With the vision of a guru who is free from any personal attachment or agenda, Pujya Swami Dharmanandji knew that his disciple was meant for a mission much larger than overseeing the growth and expansion of Parmarth Niketan ashram in Rishikesh. He knew that, as Pujya Swami Brahmaswarupji had said so many years ago, even Brahma could not stop him!

In the days and weeks leading up to Pujya Swamiji's scheduled departure for Pittsburgh, work at Parmarth took on a frenetic pace. As Pujya Swamiji oversaw everything, and as he was to be away for nearly six months, all pending items needed to be completed before his departure. This included the construction of a new *bhandara* hall in which hundreds of saints, priests, *brahmacharis*, *rishikumars*, and pilgrims could sit for their meals. Pujya Swamiji had personally finalized the designs with the architect and contractor, poring over drawings for dozens of hours with meditative attentiveness. Only he knew where every brick, every pound of cement, every nail, and every knob was meant to go. From morning to evening he supervised the work to ensure that all aspects of the construction were up to par and to address any issues as they arose.

On the eve of his departure, Pujya Swamiji was sitting at the feet of his beloved guru. Pujya Swami Dharmanandji was emphasizing that, although the work was excellent and although Pujya Swamiji was clearly more gifted with vision and capability than anyone at Parmarth, nonetheless he should be sure not to lose the stillness of his *sadhana* in the midst of the busy *seva*.

"Guruji," Pujya Swamiji replied. "I am 'mast.' When I am doing *seva*, I feel that I am meditating. My outer eyes may be looking at concrete or bricks or files or drawings, but my inner eye is always beholding the Divine. My hands may physically hold a pen or a phone or a file, but my *mala* is always there and the

"If you never want disappointment in your life, then never miss your daily appointment with God."

japa is always on." Pujya Swami Dharmanandji could see deep within his beloved disciple and he knew that the words were true. He knew that Pujya Swamiji had a unique ability to be fully engrossed in work on the physical plane while remaining fully engrossed in meditation and prayer on the spiritual plane. He also knew that his young disciple was about to undertake a serious and crucial task—the creation of one of the first major Hindu temples in America—and that he was about to leave the shores of India for a world where he would spend his life carrying people from every country, every culture, and every walk of life across the ocean of the material world. He knew that his beloved child would be the vessel that would transport millions of others to the far shore of peace, bliss, and divinity. In order to be that vessel, his own anchor would need to be unshakable.

"My child," his guru said. "I know that what you say is true. However, please do not forget your days in the jungle, your intense, deep *sadhana* of solitude in your yearning to help and serve humanity. Please do not get attached to the service or to those whom you are serving. Your inner silence is your greatest strength. You must do more *anushthan* (special, extended meditation)."

"Guruji," Pujya Swamiji replied. "With your blessings, I feel that my life is *anushthan*. I am serving with full heart and full sincer-

ity, but my attachment is only to the Divine. You know this. However, if you feel that more time should be spent withdrawn from this world, I am also ready for that. I will follow whatever you say."

Swami Dharmanandji wanted to test his disciple, to make sure that he really was as unattached as he said. "You will sit in *anushthan* from tomorrow. For seventeen months."

Pujya Swamiji's test was unnecessary; his attachment—from the moment that Pujya Swami Brahmaswarupji laid a hand on his head and touched his third eye and he beheld the *darshan* of Lord Krishna—has only been to God. The service is *seva* to the Beloved. When one is in love, one brings the beloved breakfast in bed, or roses, or chocolates. One massages the beloved's feet and prepares the beloved's favorite meals. These actions are not due to attachment to the acts or a preference for chocolate or flowers. They are due to attachment to the beloved. In the same way, after spending years in the jungle, after lying in the lap of the Divine, his urge to serve the Divine has been ardent.

However, his attachment is to the Divine Himself rather than to the service. Hence, his response to his guru's unprecedented and unimaginable pronouncement less than twenty-four hours before he was due to leave for America was only two words. "Ji, Maharajji." He bowed at his guru's feet before departing to prepare for the long months of silence, solitude, and meditation before him.

Pujya Swami Dharmanandji, in that moment, had forgotten that the following day his disciple was scheduled to begin his role as the spiritual head of the Pittsburgh temple. He knew the trip was imminent but had forgotten it was immediate. He had forgotten that international tickets were booked and all arrangements were made. Further, he had simply wanted to test the veracity of Pujya Swamiji's detachment. Once Pujya Swamiji demonstrated that he was prepared to undergo intense austerities, the test had

Pujya Swamiji with his image of Ma Gayatri, upon whom he meditated continuously for seventeen months during the extended anusthana.

been passed and there was no need for him to actually continue. Thus, his guru called him back and said, "My child, don't worry. I have seen the depth and breadth of your detachment from the world and the ardor and invincibility of your connection to the Divine. It surpasses even my own understanding of you. There is no need, now, to cancel your plans for the United States. The people of Pittsburgh are waiting eagerly for your arrival. You may go as scheduled."

Pujya Swamiji was resolute. His mind, once set, is firm. He had given his word and taken the vow for a seventeen-month *anushthan* at the insistence of his guru. There was no turning back. The *bhandara* hall at Parmarth, the temple in Pittsburgh, and everything else in the outside world would wait. God would take care of them. His promise to his guru and his vow for the *anushthan* would not be rescinded.

As the winter cold began to descend upon Rishikesh, and the frigid winds began to blow across the waters of Mother Ganga, Pujya Swamiji withdrew into a small room of the ashram, which would be his meditation cave for the next seventeen months. Rather than a mat for a bed and a brick for a pillow, he had a thin mattress and a cotton pillow. Rather than having to brave the jungles at night, he had a room with its own toilet. This time his *anushthan* focused on a divine image of the Mother Goddess, of Ma Gayatri, rather than the image of Dhruv being blessed by Lord Vishnu. The rules were just as strict. For seventeen months he maintained complete silence. Once a day, an ashram *sevak* would come into the verandah outside his room to leave a tiffin of simple boiled lentils and two dry chapatis. In the evenings, as the sun's last rays danced on the waters of Mother Ganga, he would walk along Her banks. It was the only time of day that he left the confines of his room, under the blanket of sunset, eyes always lowered to the ground. For seventeen months, he spoke not a

Compassionate and benevolent Maa
Pranaam . . . Pranaam . . . pranaam . . .

Oh Maa . . . those few words you have written are full of the essence of your heart and yet so grave . . . I felt intrigued and overwhelmed . . . Not once, twice, or three times but I read it again and again and again . . . Oh, how do I express my overwhelming feeling of delight? How impotent and insufficient are all words! Maa, you have given wings to my joy and I dance in ecstasy and bliss.

Your words ended any trace of confusion and affliction that was lingering in my mind. That unknown twinge which used to bother me some times indeed was crushed on the stage of your unbounded love and motherhood! I am very happy! . . . full of bliss!!

Maa, you wrote,

"Sometimes I think of your peril . . . how difficult it must have been to manage yourself within the confines of truthfulness and principles . . . how many times you must have choked your ambitions . . . I feel very distressed and some unstated pang surrounds me from all directions . . ."

But my loving Mother! There is no trace of any pain, regret, or sorrow in my heart as to why I accepted this life . . . I have never had such thought in my remotest dreams . . . what to talk of my conscious mind . . . Yes, it is a fact that when I accepted this lifestyle I was merely a child. Without knowing, without understanding, I plunged and chose this unknown destination . . . If I say I was made to plunge and that I did not do anything myself, that will be a correct statement! As a child, I was inspired and carried by an unknown force. Neither did I know the path nor did I know the destination. But there was always a unique and uncanny longing and thirst for the Divine. Then, He took me in His arms and brought me to the destination . . . Sometimes I wonder how it all has happened . . . such a divine, inexpressible mystery . . . how do I write about it? . . . how will I describe it these golden years? . . . Maa, you are the only witness to all these occurrences. Indeed you are the one whose blessings and love have given me this infinite strength and courage!

My Pujya Maa, I am happy . . . beyond happy . . . I am truly blissful. I am thrilled, I am enchanted, I am enthralled and ecstatic by my path and destination . . . there is no room in my ecstasy for any sorrow or disappointment . . .

Oh Maa, what else do I want? I would love be born like this again and again . . . subject of course to the condition that I have the same divine mother, the divinity of the land of Uttarakhand, the caring lap of the Himalayas, and the everflowing love of the Mother Ganga and Her holy banks . . . Only if I am to receive the same limitless love of God and if I can spend every moment in sadhana from my childhood . . . If the Beloved is willing to give me this, I am all ready to come on the Earth again and again . . . JUST TODAY I HAVE SENT MY SIGNATURE ON A BLANK PAPER TO HIM!

My cup is overflowing with joy; my heart is full with ecstasy in the presence of God . . .

Tell me now, Maa, is there any possibility of sadness? Is there any scope for anguish? Maa, my destination itself is my path. It walks with me.

Maa, do not worry about any trouble I may face in this life. I know it is not an easy life or a soft path. But, Maa, no path of roses has ever been helpful on the spiritual path. Strife and struggle are what pave the way for awakening and a Divine life!

Maa, the sweat of a hardworking person makes the path green and beautiful for others. The road to the Ultimate is always adorned by the bloody footsteps of those who have walked the path of sadhana, heedless of the thorns along the way. Let all difficulties, miseries and problems come . . . I am ready to take everything in my stride . . .

Maa, whenever there were flowers on my path, my pace not only reduced, but at times it stopped altogether. These thorns have awakened me, put me on the track and helped me progress. Maa, one who faces the storms of life with a smile, he alone is able to leave his footprints on the sands of time.

My Divine Mother, all my efforts are concentrated on enduring these blows of the illusory world in order to fortify myself . . . and I am ready to welcome all storms and tempests with one of my most enchanting smiles! I believe that if one is hardworking and sincere, and receives failure as success, then ever defeat sows the seeds for a greater victory, every betrayal becomes a gift, each raging storm evokes a new challenge, opening wide the doors to Samadhi . . . Every thorn becomes a rose, and each hurdle teaches the art of living!

"What if I hurt myself by a boulder?
that piece of rock has shown me the way to my destination . . ."

The letters on these pages are actual correspondence between Pujya Swamiji, his mother, and devotees, written during his times of deep meditation and afterwards.

Dearest Divine Soul,

I send you much love.

Remember, my dear, . . . we must become a perpetual traveler on this path of life and take even the destination to be the path . . . We must become one who never thinks of halting, who will not even be bothered if he reaches the goal! This traveler never is bent by difficulties . . . and, my dear, it is not merely that flowers make a path easy. If there are only flowers and no stones or obstacles on the path of life, there can be no progress or growth . . . if there is no challenge, there is nothing to rise above . . . struggle and strife are inherent and crucial parts of life . . .

Haven't you seen flowers being pierced by the thorns or other pricks and yet blooming and giving off divine fragrance? Oh, I wish you would ask the flowers the meaning of life . . . ask those flowers which bloom with fragrance and make the entire garden fragrant!!

My dear, you are meant to be just like those flowers, and nothing less . . . this is what I expect from you . . . enrich yourself with service for humanity; toil, love and spread the fragrance of devotion in the world.

"in the face of difficulties, when it seems impossible to smile . . . smiling is your dharma!

When life is impossible, living it with purpose is your duty . . . The only need is to bend down and

lift those who are weaker than you, those who are broken and befallen . . ."

"A single moment spent in the serve of the needy is more valuable and will lead to greater ultimate treasure than centuries spent in material pursuits ."

If you make service to the needy your ultimate goal, not only that which you long for but the heights of the Himalayas will fall at your feet!

Make the most of the each moment you have . . .

My Dear Divine Soul,

In loving memory of the Divine Lord . . .

. . . the sincere curiosity of your letter compelled me to write you . . .

I am glad to know that you have been worshipping Maa Durga since childhood. Your faith will surely carry you to the shore of the Infinite Ocean . . . you will be filled with divine love, I am sure . . .

You have asked about my experiences with the Divine Mother . . . it is a divine blessing that you are curious about these types of experiences . . . without God's grace it is not possible to have such pure thoughts in one's mind.

But what do I write . . . how do I write? I cannot express the bliss of life that I experience in every moment . . . each minute, each moment, each breath I am intoxicated by the divine joy of sadhana . . . My dear, I am enveloped in infinite love . . . it is an indescribable experience . . . There is only one way for you to truly understand . . . surrender at Her feet . . . Call out to Her: "Maa! . . . Maa! where are you? Please come fast . . . or I will be lost in this chaotic world . . . Please come and carry me to you . . . Please answer my prayers . . . show me the path to you."

My dear, you must call out again and again from the depths of your being. Cry. Wash Her feet with your tears. Tell her, "Maa, please remove all the dirt of ignorance from the screen of my mind that veils

vision of You. . . . Please bless me with the vision of Your loving and all-compassionate Self. Maa, I am unworthy of Your grace . . . I have neither wisdom nor knowledge, neither strength nor devotion . . . in this darkness I am falling . . . my body and my mind are reeling in the pain of separation . . . please nurse me with Your love, heal me with Your divine ointment . . . Maa, You are always full of care and compassion toward Your children, especially those who are weak and unworthy . . . Maa, please come please come, please come."

My dear, you must call out to Her like that. Tell Her: "Maa, I don't want anything at all except your blessings . . . Maa, I know you have so many devotees, so many like me. But I only have You. Please come to me."

That's it, my dear . . . then, when you have surrendered to Her and called out with true devotion, you feel Her take your hand in Hers . . . rest assured . . . you will feel Her presence in your life.

My Dear Divine Soul,

What is the secret to life, you ask. If someone asked a flower, "What is the secret to staying fragrant and sharing fragrance with others, even during the turn of the seasons?" the flower would surely reply: "Just keep blossoming. Keep unfolding. Worry not about the rain or the snow or the seasons. Worry only about your own duty to blossom." The secret to life is the same. Just keep blossoming, keep doing good work, keep bringing fragrance to those around you. Yes, prayer is wonderful. But one hour spent in sincere service of others is worth days of prayer. It matters not how much you have in the mate-

rialist realm. Neither mansions, nor Mercedes, nor money can bring you as much happiness as when you heal and nurture someone else's heart. My dear, the time to be sure to smile is when it's the hardest to smile. The time to be sure to stand up and do your duty is the time you feel the most broken and shattered. Look at that yonder flower, blossoming in the garden. Every petal of hers is pierced by thorns. Yet she worries not. She continues—tattered and pierced—to bring her divine fragrance to the world. What a great lesson! That is the secret to life.

word, nor made eye contact with any person, nor went anywhere other than the pathway from Ganga back to his room.

After the jungles, it was the most divine time of my life. The silence one obtains in a state of meditation is not empty silence. It is not a passive silence, which is simply the absence of noise. It is not silence devoid of feeling or knowing. Rather it is a full silence, an active silence. It is a silence in which the voice of God can be heard as clearly as the waves of Ganga crashing on the rocks. It is a silence and a seclusion in which God's presence is as palpable as the mala *in your hand.*

I remember that in the very beginning, to sit erect eleven hours a day is very difficult. That was the niyam *(rule) of the anushthan I had undertaken— eleven hours a day of* japa. *The rest of the time could be spent doing* yogasanas, pranayama, *walking on Ganga, reading scriptures, or writing in my diaries, as well as resting a few hours each night. So, on the first day, I was very erect for the first hour or two. But then, slowly, I began slouching. My string of prayer beads was still in hand, but rather than sitting erect in* pad- masana *(lotus posture) I sat in whatever way I was comfortable—knees bent into my chest, leaning on one side, lounging against the wall, even lying down! As my body ached from the long hours, unmoving, in lotus posture, I gave myself great freedom in shifting about, in whatever position was comfortable, as the days wore on. There were times I lay, legs outstretched, one arm propping my head up and the other doing my* japa.

However, the moment I heard the gentle tapping on my door of the boy who brought me lunch, I immediately jumped back into perfect padmasana. *He wasn't supposed to see me. He was supposed to just leave my food on the verandah, give a gentle knock so I would know that lunch had arrived, and depart quietly. However, curiosity is universally prevalent. I was sure that he must be peeking inside the room to see what I was doing, to verify if I was really engaged in full and complete meditation. Hence, the moment I heard the sound of the verandah door opening, or the metal tiffin being placed on the table, I immediately assumed perfect lotus posture—back erect as a wall, left palm placed gently upward on the knee, right hand turning the beads of the* mala, *beatific smile upon my lips. I was sure that he must be going back and reporting proudly, "Maharajji*

sits as still as a statue, erect as a tree, all day long. He is really deep in meditation."

The moment the door closed softly behind the sevak, so did the door close upon my diligence. Once again, I would slouch or lie or lean against the wall. Until, of course, he came in the evening with the milk, at which point again I would assume impeccable dhyan mudra.

On the third day of my anushthan, *the boy had left my lunch on the table and closed the door behind him when I heard a voice. I had begun to relax my legs and was about to stretch them out fully when, from the divine image of the Mother Goddess, Her voice came. "You take perfect care of yourself in front of a servant,*

"Put the reins of your life in God's hands. Let him be your charioteer. Let Him be your chauffeur. Let him drive your life!"

but you don't care about me? He comes to leave your lunch and you assume beautiful posture, full of love, awe, and respect. I sit here all day and all night before you, and you don't even notice? Is it for him or for Me you are doing this anushthan?"

My legs shook and my fingers trembled, threatening to lose the mala *from their grip. My heart pulsed frantically and powerfully as though shouting "Om, Om, Om, Om, Om" into my chest. Her eyes bore deeply into mine. Were Hers filled with tears, or was it only my own? I had been caught—completely unaware of She who was before me. I had been performing* japa *to the Mother Goddess without opening my eyes wide enough to realize that She sat before me. My mantra called out to Her, and She had arrived without my awareness.*

From that moment no image or murti *has ever seemed to me to be just a painting or a picture or sculpture. From that moment, I can hear the voice and feel the presence of the Divine in every representation.*

Several months into the *anushthan,* in which he now sat motionless, lost in divine, ecstatic connection nearly twenty-four hours a day, a pain developed in his calf muscle. Since the day the Mother Goddess had spoken, every moment became one of complete union with

Her. Now, there was no need to lay the physical body down, for he lay continuously in Her divine lap.

Regardless of the strength and flexibility of one's limbs, sitting motionless in *padmasana* for eleven or twelve hours a day, every day for months, impairs and impedes the proper flow of blood throughout the body. After several months, young Swamiji felt the physical consequences of his ecstatic trances. Not that he minded. He would have cut off his limbs if it were required. Yet he knew that his life was meant to be in service of the world, and to do so, he would have to keep his body healthy and strong. Hence, as the pain refused to subside despite *yogasanas* and relaxation, he gave a note one day with the boy who brought lunch, requesting medicine from the ashram's homeopathic doctor. Along with his evening milk, the medicine arrived and he began to take it faithfully. However, it was of no use. His calf continued to pain him, and there was no posture he could find to alleviate the discomfort. As he sat before the Mother Goddess, saying his final prayers before sleep, She spoke to him: "You ask for medicine from the doctor, but why not ask from the Source of all healing? You have asked the doctor for a preparation, but you have not asked She who verily per-

vades all cures and treatments." Instantly, as he lay in *dandavat pranam*—face, arms, legs, torso on the ground in complete supplication—the pain disappeared, never to return.

RETURN TO PITTSBURGH

Finally, in the late summer of 1982, the Pittsburgh community members' prayers were answered and Pujya Swamiji returned to Pittsburgh. Dr. Jitu Desai, a renowned neurologist, describes his impact on the community: "The lack of a powerful leader among the self-made professional immigrants did not help matters. This led to arguments and ill feelings among the community. Instead of remaining a cohesive minority dedicated to building an authentic Hindu temple . . . divisive forces gained momentum . . . Two groups of Indians left the fold. This was a low point in our minority Hindu community . . . The arrival of Shri Swami Chidanandji gave a great boost to the religious activities in the temple as well as raising funds for the construction. His unwavering belief in the unique multidenominational temple encouraged everyone, even those who had lingering doubts and misgivings about the temple. The community responded vigorously and redoubled its efforts in supporting the construction."

Dr. Sudhakar Reddy, head of cardiology at Pittsburgh University, described Pujya Swamiji's arrival as "tantamount to infusion of life into an otherwise lifeless temple." Dr. Inder Pandit agreed: "The arrival of Pujya Swamiji provided the spark and ignited so much enthusiasm in us that the temple progressed beyond our imagination."

Long before he had any impact on the community or had created the temple, on the very first day of his arrival, an event took place that many remember nearly three decades later. "I remember," Dr. Raghunath recalls. "I received a call one day from an Indian in Pittsburgh whom I knew but who was not a close member of the community. This person

Pujya Swami Dharmanandji comes to the Hindu Jain Temple.

Pujya Swamiji picks tomatoes from his garden at the temple.

asked me whether our temple was expecting any swami to come. I told him, 'Yes, of course. Our Swamiji from Rishikesh is arriving today. Why?' The man replied, "Because he's here in front of me and it doesn't seem like he knows where to go or what to do." When Pujya Swamiji got on the phone, he said that he was waiting in the arrival area but no one was there to pick him up. Somehow, due to a miscommunication, the person who was supposed to receive him at the airport was not there. "How long have you been waiting?" Raghunathji asked. "About four hours." Raghunathji was stunned. "Why didn't you call sooner?" The reply came simply, "I don't have any money."

In accordance with traditional laws of *sanyas*, Pujya Swamiji does not carry money. Thus, he had traveled from Rishikesh to Delhi,

Delhi to London, and London to Pittsburgh without even a dollar in his bag. Not wanting to ask anyone for money, he had waited until an Indian passed by in whom he could confide his dilemma. It was fortunate that the wait had been merely a matter of hours. Given the tiny population of Indians in the area at the time, it could have been days.

SADHANA IN THE HILLS OF MONROEVILLE

At the time that Pujya Swamiji returned to Pittsburgh in 1982, the temple still consisted only of the single church-cum-temple building. Construction was under way for the new temple on the hill, but progress was slow. Initially when he arrived, the devotees all requested him to stay at their

homes. After a month of spending one week in different devotees' homes, Pujya Swamiji refused to continue. As he explains, "I realized that I had come to serve the temple, to get the temple built. In order to do that, I needed to live on site, to become one—twenty-four hours a day—with the temple." Thus, Pujya Swamiji made his residence in

"One of the keys to a spiritual path is to annihilate the ego, to become humble, to surrender oneself to God."

one of the small, spare rooms in the temple building. This decision was met with much dismay on the part of temple members and devotees.

Pujya Swamiji was not worried: "I had lived in the Himalayan jungles. I had lived amid wild animals, snakes, and scorpions. I knew when I came to Pittsburgh, as I had known in the jungles, that God's protection was with me, that I was fulfilling His mission and nothing would injure me."

The difficulties he had to face in the early days were not those of violence or crime. Rather they were issues such as where to take a shower! In Pujya Swamiji's room in the temple, there was no bathroom. The building, which had previously been the church and now served as a multifaith temple, had public toilets for men and women; the planning committee naturally assumed he would use those. They overlooked the fact that in addition to a toilet and a sink, he also needed a place to bathe.

Pujya Swamiji—born into an affluent family in North India, raised in the jungles and mountains of the Himalayas, head of an elaborate ashram on the banks of the Ganga—has lived by the lifelong motto of "Accept whatever God gives you as *prasad*, be happy with whatever you get, and never ask for more." Thus he told no one of his predicament and lived in the small temple-community center for more than six months before anyone

realized he had no shower or bathtub. Each morning, he would lock the main door of the temple building and fill a bucket from the sink in the communal kitchen. Then, he would stand on the floor of the kitchen bathing himself ever so carefully with water poured delicately from the bucket, jugful by jugful. After his morning bath, he would mop up the floor of the kitchen, lest anyone discover his method of bathing.

"Sometimes I would even have my bath in the kitchen sink. I'd scrub it out until it sparkled and then I could sort of sit down into it and pour the water over myself directly from the tap with a jug."

One morning, Pujya Swamiji forgot to lock the door, and one of the devotees arrived just as he had finished bathing. He found Pujya Swamiji, draped only in a towel, mopping up the floor of the kitchen. Thus, inadvertently, the community realized the one thing they had forgotten in carefully planning his accommodations: Their divine guide had no way to bathe. A proper bathroom with shower was immediately constructed.

"They did it in only a few days," Pujya Swamiji says. "I remember the incredible love of the community, with them all coming over and personally breaking walls and installing a sink, toilet, and tub. Donations were very scarce, then, at the *mandir*, so we couldn't simply call in a contractor and have a bathroom built. Everything had to be done by our own hands in those early days. So, they broke down walls, drilled holes for plumbing, and made me a proper bathroom in just a weekend!"

Another thing forgotten at the beginning was someone to help with cleaning the temple. Pujya Swamiji's arrival invigorated the community, and he encouraged frequent meetings and events in the evenings and on the weekends. During or following the events, there was always a service of tea and coffee and sometimes even snacks. When everyone left the premises—with dirty cups and plates strewn about—they assumed, understandably,

TOP *The Hindu-Jain Temple under construction.*
ABOVE *The original building that was used as a temple before construction was complete and in which Pujya Swamiji lived for nearly ten years.*

that someone would come in after them and clear away their cups, dishes, and napkins, wipe the tables, and sweep the floors. That assumption was true; however, they never imagined that the person who did it all was their revered and beloved Pujya Swamiji.

Taking this as just another *sadhana*, another brick in the temple of his own spiritual *tapasya*, he would clean up each Saturday night after the meetings in order to ensure that the hall was impeccable for the morning yoga classes he led. "It wouldn't look nice to have people come in, fresh for yoga on Sunday morning, and see dirty cups or dishes lying around." So, either before sitting for his nightly meditation or long before dawn, after having bathed and completed his morning meditation, he would clear away all the dishes, sweep the floors, and tidy up the room before the yoga students arrived.

This aspect of his *sadhana* was discovered, again coincidentally, by a devotee who caught a glimpse of Pujya Swamiji—his saffron dhoti tied up at his waist—carrying a large, black plastic bag of trash out to the Dumpster in the parking lot. "Maharajji," he exclaimed. "What are you doing? Aren't there cleaning people?" "Mein hoon na? (I am here)," Pujya Swamiji said. "I am the Swamiji. I am also the yoga teacher. I am also the cleaning people." The devotee's eyes filled with tears, and the temple committee immediately hired a cleaning person.

More than two decades of intense *sadhana*, including extended periods of fasting, prepared Pujya Swamiji to graciously accept whatever food arrived, or didn't arrive, for him at the temple. One day when Drs. Naval and Nila Kant examined the printed schedule that listed who was to bring Pujya Swamiji's food each lunch and dinner, she noticed something particular. On seemingly random occasions, random days of the week, Pujya Swamiji had crossed out the name of the meal provider and had written "Upvas" ("fast"). Nilaben stared at the calendar, trying to figure

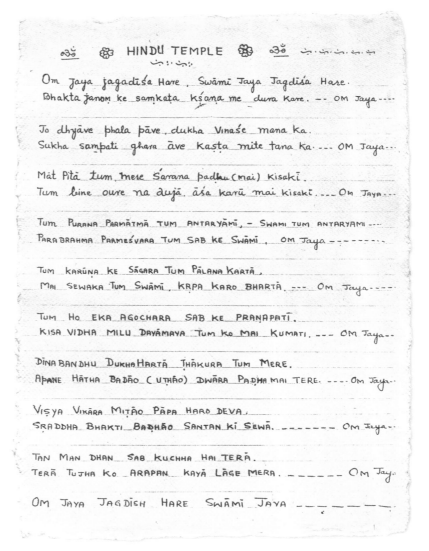

Pujya Swamiji personally handwrote the words to the aarti to distribute to everyone.

out the rhythm of his fasting. It was not every Monday, nor every Tuesday, nor every Ekadashi, nor every full moon. There seemed to be no sense at all to his fasting system. When she asked Pujya Swamiji, he answered, evasively, "I fast whenever God tells me to fast." She pressed him until he finally admitted that he fasted on those days when the people forgot to bring his food. He knew that when they finally came and saw their names on the calendar, they would be overcome with guilt for having forgotten their duty. To prevent any feelings of remorse on the part of the negligent meal providers, he wrote "fast" on the calendar; they would be relieved to know that the day they forgot to bring his food had, anyway, been his fasting day.

Despite these difficulties, whenever Pujya Swami Sadanandaji or Pujya Swami Dharmanandji called to find out how everything was going, he always told them, "It's wonderful." "Everything is super." He never even insinuated that the arrangements were anything less than perfect. Further, as one listens to Pujya Swamiji describe the early days of building the Hindu-Jain Temple, these difficulties are not the memories that come to his mind. He recalls only glorious days of erecting

"Expectation is the mother of frustration. Acceptance is the mother of peace and joy. Never expect. Always accept."

an abode for the Lord and bringing together a scattered community into a cohesive whole. He recalls turning intolerance and aggression into understanding and love.

These stories of forgotten bathrooms and missing cleaning people are found only by speaking with temple members who were there in the early days. Only then, when one confronts Pujya Swamiji with the details of such a story, does he say, "Oh, yes, that was also there. But it was no problem. The saints come to Earth to clean out the minds, hearts and souls of the people. If we also have to clean out a room occasionally, it is no problem. We are sent here to dispose of people's ego, greed, lust, attachments, and obstacles. If we also have to dispose of a trash bag, it is no problem. We are sent here to sweep out the hearts of the devotees, so that their hearts become pure homes for the Lord to come and sit. If we must also sweep out a hall, it is no problem. It is all *sadhana*; it is all Prabhu *seva*."

COMMUNITY MEANS "COME UNITY"

Harilal Patel, in the official inauguration souvenir book, describes the impact of Pujya Swamiji on the community.

The news of Pujya Swamiji's return to Pittsburgh in 1982 spread in the community like wildfire. Everyone was very enthusiastic to have his darshan and soon people were packed in his room from early morning to late night. What used to be a deserted place now became thronged with life . . . He united the entire Indian community in the Pittsburgh area. The community became very vibrant, and everyone was talking with joy about him . . . Even though Pujya Swamiji came to serve the community in the Pittsburgh area, the news of his good nature and devotion started spreading in the neighboring communities. Soon he was being invited to almost every state in the United States and in Canada. He realized the needs of Indian communities in various cities and helped them build temples . . . Shri Swamiji became an instrument in bringing unity among various sampradayas. Now he was not limited to only the United States and Canada but was sought out by many communities abroad.

Pujya Swamiji was adamant in his commitment to not only build a temple but also unite the community. "Community means 'come unity,'" he would remind everyone. "We cannot be a community until unity has come. We must be united."

Where the temple had previously been used for spiritual programs only on weekends, he began a program of bringing it to life seven days a week. After moving permanently into one of the small rooms in the building, he began making phone calls every day to various members of the community, inquiring as to how they and their families were and inviting them to come to the temple for *aarti, bhajans,* or *puja*. Drawn by the call of the Divine and Pujya Swamiji's magnetism, people slowly began to come to the temple on a regular basis.

Kalpana Jambusaria remembers one time. "Shortly after Swamiji came to America, I remember coming to the temple for the holiday of Navratri. My husband and I brought along our two daughters, Anokhi and Aneri, who at the time were two years and just a few months old. Swamiji, knowing that many of the attendees were Gujarati, took out his harmonium and invited us to do *garba* dance while he played and sang. This was an unusual

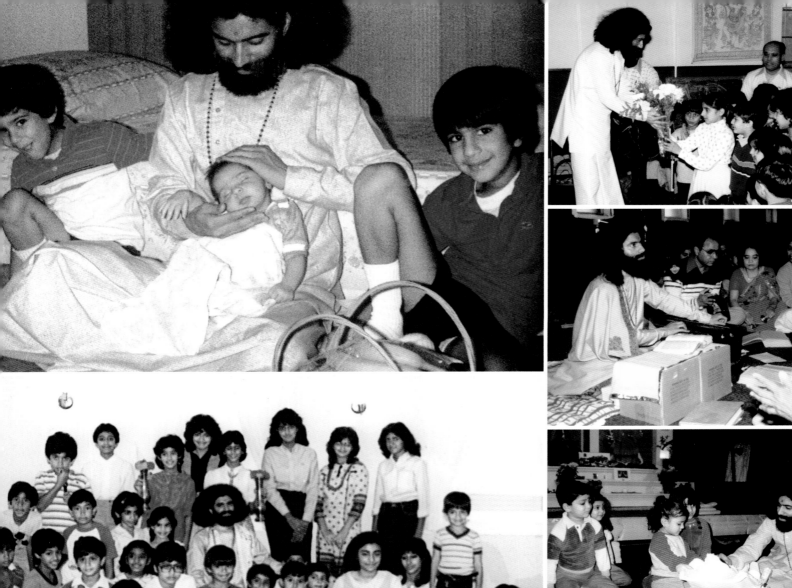

offer by a Swamiji, but nonetheless we were excited about the opportunity. As many of the other young men and women began to dance, I initially declined, explaining to Swamiji that I had to watch my baby daughter. He offered to keep an eye on her instead, if I would just move her rocker next to him on stage. I took Swamiji up on his offer and danced with the others while he watched my daughter in her rocker on the stage." To Pujya Swamiji, baby-sitting was a small price to pay to promote

"Perform your duties diligently and piously, but without any attachment to the result."

participation in temple activities that reconnected the community with their Indian culture and heritage.

Additionally, to reach those whose phone numbers he didn't have or who were not already associated with to the temple, Pujya Swamiji gave regular *bhajan/kirtan* and *satsang* programs at people's homes throughout the area. Singing the name of God and listening to uplifting and inspiring spiritual discourses reignited the sparks of piety in many of the community members.

As Vasviben Patel says, "We don't go regularly to India and don't take our children there. It is only through Pujya Swamiji and this temple that I have been able to stay connected to our culture, and for my children this is all they have! Typically, one is supposed to go to the guru, but we were especially and uniquely blessed. The guru came to us."

Shortly after his arrival, Pujya Swamiji led a special Gayatri *yagna* for the community, to restore their optimism and to seek the blessings of the Divine Mother in bringing the temple to fruition. He personally conducted all the *yagnas* and *pujas*. According to Dr. Radhu Agarwal, "He did everything. He was a swami but he worked as a priest, as a yoga teacher, as everything."

"Sorry, Wrong Number"

The local community of the area was not enthusiastic about having a Hindu temple built in its residential area, even though the Monroeville borough had finally granted permission. Those were days at the very beginning of the great influx of Indians into the United States, and prejudice was common. The Indian temple was opposed vehemently by many members of the community.

In February 1983, when attempts to block the temple through legal recourse failed, a few of the more racially prejudiced people of the local community took to vandalizing the temple and its grounds. Windows were smashed, tar was smeared on the walls, *murtis* were defaced and broken, and defamatory slogans were scrawled everywhere. The vandalism was, however, a dark cloud with a silver lining. While it discouraged and disheartened temple members, it also brought them together.

Concerned for Pujya Swamiji's safety as well as the security of the temple property, the committee hired an armed security guard for a few days, but funds were not sufficient to keep him for long, and Pujya Swamiji adamantly refused the continued protection. "We are here in the home of the Lord. He will protect us." Later, when the new temple had been built, but before the strong doors had arrived from India, nights found Pujya Swamiji asleep at the door of the temple, using his feet to hold the doors closed from inside. "I was not afraid," he says. "I knew I was sent on a mission and I had to protect God. Once, as a young child living in the jungle, I had dropped His image on the ground out of fear of the ghosts and monsters. I knew I could not let fear of vandals make me forsake Him again."

That he slept with his feet holding the temple doors closed remained a well-guarded secret, as he did not want anyone to know that there was any possibility of violence from the local community. His goal was to keep spirits high and hearts filled with devotion. "If I told everyone that vandals came at night to try to spray-paint the walls or to break the building, people would become afraid and disheartened and their faith would suffer." One day, a family of devotees came in the very late hours of the night.

"For some reason I could not sleep. I just had to see Swamiji," the wife said. So they came, and when they did not find him in his room in the lower temple, they began to search the grounds of the new temple, on the hillside. As they pushed open the doors, they felt a slight resistance. That's when they saw him, outstretched and asleep, with his feet pushing the temple door, oblivious to the howling wind and the potential of danger, with only a flashlight by his blanket.

"I took it all as a bouquet of *sadhana* that God gave me. Just as a flower garden would not be as beautiful if all the flowers were the same type, so he was giving me a vast array of different experiences in order to make the fragrance of my *sadhana* even sweeter," Pujya Swamiji says. Not only was there a threat of physical violence against him and the temple he was giving birth to, but Pujya Swamiji was also the target of occasional verbal harassment. "I learned so many new types of English words," he says laughingly of the profanities hurled at him over the telephone by people prejudiced against anyone who was not white and Christian.

One night in the middle of the night I received a phone call. The youth must have been out drinking and enjoying themselves. They called the temple's phone number, and when I answered they started saying such amazing things on the phone. I had never heard most of the words they used, but I understood the gist. On and on they went, first one boy, then another, then another, until they had all said every profane word in their vocabularies. Finally they stopped their litany, perhaps they thought I had hung up, and they said, "Hello?" They wanted to know if I was still on the line. I answered, very sweetly, "Sorry, wrong number." They hung up immediately and the obscene calls ceased.

This "Sorry, wrong number" has become a beautiful mantra Pujya Swamiji teaches people across the world. He explains that we do not have to accept the insults that others may throw our way. Just as an incorrectly addressed letter may reach our doorstep but bears no relation to our well-being, so an insult hurled at us by those filled with anger, fear, and misunderstanding should fall on deaf ears.

We are not like lightbulbs. We should not allow ourselves to be switched on and off by the whim of another. Many times I hear people say, "Oh, I was in such a good mood, but then Robert called and told me what Julie said about me," or "Oh, that phone call just ruined my day." And the same works the other way. Sometimes we are sad or depressed and we get a nice phone call or letter in the mail or we eat some good cookies. Then we feel better. How is that? How can one phone call or one rude comment from a person have so much control over us? Are our emotions so volatile and are we so impotent over them that others have more power to control our moods than we, ourselves, do?

It should not be like this. We, as humans on the spiritual path, are bigger, more divine, and deeper than this. There is so much more to this human existence than the law of action and reaction. We must learn to keep that light switch in our own hands and to give it only to God. Otherwise we are switched on and off, on and off, all day long, and the only effect is that the lightbulb burns out!

Instead, let us take whatever comes as prasad (blessing) and as a gift from God. Let us remain calm and steady in the face of both prosperity and misfortune. We must not lose our vital energy in this constant action and reaction to everyone around us.

Despite Pujya Swamiji's internal peace and equanimity, the prejudice and negativity in the local community continued to spread. Just as some members of the community had earlier tried to prevent the Monroeville borough from granting permission to build, now several neighbors tried vehemently to thwart the construction. The local church as well as local furniture stores, which had previously allowed the temple to use their parking lots for overflow parking, suddenly rescinded their standing offers.

Realizing the severity of the situation, Pujya Swamiji, whose motto in life is "If someone is nasty to you, be nice to them; if someone tries to hurt you, heal them," embarked on a friendship campaign with the neighbors. That Christmas, he and devotees prepared beautiful fruit baskets that they carried, personally, door to door. Slowly the neighbors came around, and today the neighborhood is a harmonious blend of American and Indian, Christian, Jew, Hindu, and Jain.

PREPARATIONS FOR THE NEW TEMPLE

To raise funds for construction, Pujya Swamiji used to travel throughout Pittsburgh as well as to neighboring cities, including Morgantown, West Virginia, and Erie and Johnstown, Pennsylvania. He led *bhajans*, *kirtan*, prayers, and sacred *puja* in order to raise consciousness, awareness, and funds for the temple.

Pujya Swamiji has always been a pastor of unity, nonviolence, inclusiveness, and acceptance. He explains this, in part, by the example he saw in his childhood. In the neighborhood where he spent his early prejungle childhood, there was a Hindu *mandir* that had a *gurdwara* on the first floor. The ground floor was for Hindus and just above it was for Sikhs. Next door was a Jain temple. Thus, this concept of unity had been with him since childhood.

Hindu Jain Temple basic structure in the mid-1980s, prior to completion of elaborate architectural designs.

He led the Hindu-Jain Temple with this firm commitment, and it has served not only the Pittsburgh community but also the world community. As Dr. Sethi explains, "Ours was the first Jain temple in the whole world to give equal status to the two lineages of Jainism Shwetambar and Digambar, but now our example has been taken up, and many of the new temples have both. We became a leader in the Jain community. Our temple was written up in England, India, everywhere."

Has there been any criticism? Have any of the Jain communities around the world felt that some sin has been committed? "No, not at all," both Dr. Sethi and Vinod Doshi are quick to explain. "There has been absolutely no dissension, no criticism at all, from anyone."

In fact, when Pujya Sushil Muniji and Pujya Chitrabhanuji came in May 1984 for the Prana Pratishtha, they had tears in their eyes. During the program, they said, "We had this dream, and you came and made this dream come true. Pittsburgh is a small community, compared to New York, Chicago, or Los Angeles, but in this small community, you are the first to realize this dream of ours."

It was not easy in the beginning. From 1980, when he performed the groundbreaking ceremony with Pujya Swami Sadanandji, until long after both the *sthapana* (installation of deities) and the inauguration of the final building, Pujya Swamiji ardently preached the importance of unity within the Jain tradition and between Hindus and Jains. Wherever he traveled in the world, he shared, with great joy, the courageous step toward unity taken by the Monroeville temple. His courage, conviction, and dedication turned dissenters into believers. Slowly, due to Pujya Swamiji's tenacity and resolve, and with the assistance and great support of Pujya Acharya Sushil Swamiji Maharaj and Pujya Shri Chitrabhanuji and others, Jain communities around the world began to accept a newfound unity among themselves as well as with their Hindu brothers and sisters.

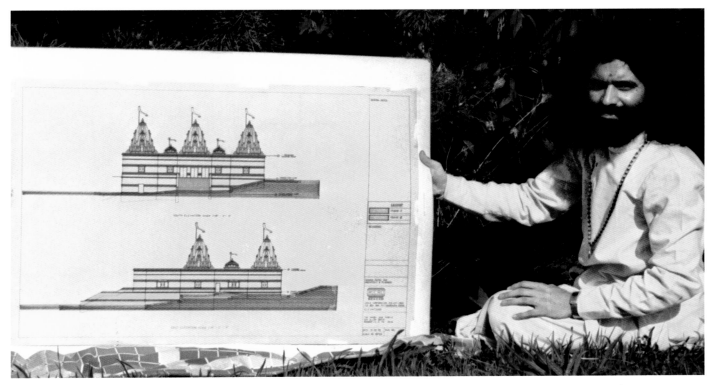

Pujya Swamiji holds the drawings, over which he pored for many hours, days, weeks, and months with architects in India and America, for the Hindu Jain Temple.

STHAPANA

By late 1983, enthusiasm was at its peak. All could see that their dream of bringing forth a temple of unity was turning into reality. After the foundational phase of the five sanctoriums had been completed and the second phase of walls and a roof was well under way, the trustees knew they were nearing the moment when the temple would be ready for deity installation, and they began to make plans for a *sthapana* ceremony.

Under Pujya Swamiji's leadership, the Hindu Temple Society began preparations for the grand *sthapana* celebrations. The *murtis* had arrived, their special garments and accessories carried from India personally by Pujya Swamiji, and the final touches were made to the individual temples that would house them. Excitement and piety filled the air as the community members readied themselves and their temple to house the divine deities. The temple would be a home not only to framed images, conch shells, incense sticks, oil lamps, and the devotion of hundreds, but also to actual deities, images carved from stone by India's best sculptors after deep meditation and brought to life by the forthcoming *prana pratishtha* ceremony.

Sthapana celebrations began officially on Ram Navami day of 1984. For nine days during the most sacred days of the Hindu calendar, Pujya Swamiji led the community in the recitation of millions of *japas* of each *yantra* for each deity. Children from the temple's Sunday school filled notebooks with tens of thousands of mantras, lovingly and devotedly written over many days. These notebooks, carrying the piety of the temple's children, were later placed in the foundation below each *murti*.

May 12–13, 1984, were the actual *prana pratishtha* ceremony days, the days in which the "Divine Breath" was brought into the beautiful stone statues, transforming them from *murtis* to deities. More than two thousand people attended from several neighboring states and even from India! The *sthapana* ceremony was graced by the presence of Pujya Swami Sadanandji, Pujya Acharya Sushil Muniji, Pujya Acharya Chitrabhanuji, Pujya Sant Keshavdasji, and, of course, Pujya Swami Chidanandji (Pujya Swamiji).

HINDU
TEMPLE
STHAPANA
CELEBRATION
MAY 5 TO 13 1984

The *sthapana* celebration included inspiring and uplifting discourses from the saints and beautiful *bhajans* from renowned singer Shri Anup Jalota, who flew in especially from India for the occasion. He recounts the event: "Typically I have conditions for performing somewhere, but as soon as I heard that Pujya Swamiji was involved, I dropped all the conditions and I told them I was coming. For me, Pujya Swamiji is my guide and also my brother. We have a very special relationship."

The councilman for the local area, Thomas Schuerger, also came and conveyed personal congratulations from the mayor of Pittsburgh, Michael Lynch. The *Pittsburgh Post-Gazette* reported, "The dedication of the new Hindu Temple of Pittsburgh, located in Monroeville, is a milestone in a unique experiment in bringing different religions of India together under one roof. It also represents a triumph in human relations within the larger community . . . It is a valuable message not only for the many groups involved in the Hindu Temple but also for other divided religious communities."

NAME CHANGE

After the *sthapana*, in which the temple name was still the Hindu Temple of North America, the Hindus and Jains felt that their lasting relationship should be officially solemnized. On June 1, 1986, the Hindu Temple of Pittsburgh officially became the Hindu-Jain Temple of Pittsburgh.

The decision to change the name was not intended to highlight the differences between these faiths, but rather to proclaim to the world that the two traditions were united. One of the Jain leaders in the community explains: "We wanted the name so that whenever people drove by on the turnpike, they would see the sign and know that there was a Jain temple nearby where they could worship. We wanted all the neighboring cities to know that Jains weren't merely being allowed to worship in a Hindu temple, but rather that the temple building actually included full Hindu temples as well as a full Jain temple."

They sought Pujya Swamiji's guidance on the matter. He encouraged them to make the name change official, as he felt it would give the Jains even more of a feeling that the temple was equally theirs, and that they were united not only in spirit but also in name. Civil engineer and one of the leaders of the Jain community Vinod Doshi explains that it all was "only due to Pujya Swamiji's vision and blessing. I've never come across any saint who is so open and broad-minded. That has kept us united."

The addition of the name "Jain" brought added prestige as well as uniqueness to the temple. However, in every community, as in every family, there are differences of opinion, character, and nature. Although the majority of temple members supported the

OPPOSITE *(clockwise from top left) Sign for* Sthapana *celebrations.* ✤ *Community children clean and prepare the temple.* ✤ *Pujya Acharya Sushil Muniji, Pujya Shri Chitrabhanuji, and other saints join Pujya Swamiji for the event.* ✤ *Pujya Swami Dharmanandji speaks at the temple.* ✤ *Pujya Swamiji adorns the deities in the lower, temporary building, prior to construction of the new temple.*

TOP *Inside hall of the Hindu-Jain Temple.*
ABOVE *Pujya Swamiji performs* aarti *in the Jain* mandir, *to the Shwetambar and Digambar divine images.*

PRANA PRATISHTHA CEREMONY: ITS MEANING

A Hindu temple is a sacred place, endowed with divine energies and powers. At the heart of each temple lie the deities, to whom we bow and pray in worship. Why is it, though, that these statues, these "idols," are worshipped as God? How did they come to be infused with divine characteristics? The answer is the *prana pratishtha* ceremony. *Prana* is the sacred breath, the force by which we are kept alive. What is it that escapes in the last moment of our life, turning us from a person to a "body"? The *prana*. On our deathbed, we are still a man, or a woman, or a father or mother. But the moment the *prana* has departed, we become a "body." *Pratishtha* means "to establish." So, *prana pratishtha* is the sacred ceremony through which life force is established in a statue, bringing it to life.

People say that Hindus are worshippers of idols. We are not. We are worshippers of the ideal. It is not the plaster and marble and stone we revere; rather it is the presence of God that has been transmitted into these otherwise lifeless statues. Our human eyes cannot behold the image of the Divine; thus, God is kind and merciful enough to infuse our deities with His Divine Presence and allow Himself to be worshipped through these deities.

The deities in the temple serve as a window to the Divine. Through fixing our eyes upon the image, we are able to catch a glimpse of the Supreme Reality. Just as looking through a telescope, we are able to behold planets in outer space, through looking at the deity, we are able to behold the Divine.

The rites and rituals of *prana pratishtha* are followed strictly according to the Agamic texts. Prior to installation, priests who have been well trained in Vedic rituals perform specific mantras and *pujas*

Pujya Swamiji performs the official and sacred opening of the eyes of the deities at the Prana Pratishtha ceremony.

that have been shown to endow an inanimate object with divine life and energy.

One may wonder how it is possible that the Divine could enter into a slab of marble or stone or clay. However, even if the entirety of the Supreme Reality doesn't inhabit the statue, even if only a tiny, infinitesimal fraction of the Supreme Reality gets established in the stone, it still becomes Divine. A fraction of infinity is infinity. Thus, even a tiny fraction of the infinite divine is still infinitely divine.

These mantras and rites begin with the artist who sculpts the stone. He is not an ordinary artist. Rather, he is one who has been blessed with the ability to create a physical manifestation of God. He performs *puja* and prayer prior to and during the sculpting. He maintains, in his mind, the vision of the deity he is sculpting. He meditates upon the image of the Divine. He prays for God to come to life in his statue. His work area looks more like a temple than an art studio. So, from the very first moment, the stone is treated with reverence and piety, preparing it to carry the force of God.

Then, when the *murtis* are finished and taken to the temple, the special *prana pratishtha* ceremony typically lasts for five days. During this time, numerous special rites and rituals as detailed by the ancient texts are performed and sacred mantras are chanted. It is after this complex set of sacred rituals that the *murtis* become infused with divine power and truly embody the God whom they represent. At this point, they are no longer *murtis*. They are deities. After this, we no longer refer to the stone or other materials of which they are constructed. For they have become sanctified and are now only a physical manifestation of aspects of the Supreme

Reality. They are no longer marble. They are now Divine. Lord Krishna tells us, "Whatever form of Me any devotee worships with faith, I come alive in that form. Whenever one develops faith in Me—in My manifest form as the Deity or in any other of my manifestations—one should worship Me in that form. I exist within all created beings as well as separately in both My un-manifest and manifest forms."

When the *murtis* become infused with Divine Life, the temple becomes alive. The deities form

ceremony and through our own faith and piety, this image of Him truly comes alive and becomes Him. So, by worshipping His image with faith and love, we arrive at His holy feet.

When we want electricity for our homes, we plug the appliance into an outlet. That outlet is connected to the main powerhouse. We do not have to go all the way to the powerhouse to plug in our blender or computer. The electrical lines have been laid; our individual house has been hooked up to the

Pujya Swamiji performs puja *(worship ceremony) for the Radha-Krishna deities in the temple.*

the living soul of the temple, and the building is the body. Some people may ask why we need deities if God exists everywhere. It is very difficult for most people to envision the un-manifest, ever-present, all-pervading Supreme Being. It is easier for us to focus our attention and our love on an image of Him. It is easier to express love, affection, and devotion to a physical deity than to a transcendent, omnipresent existence. Through the *prana pratishtha*

main powerhouse; now we only have to plug our appliance into the socket in order to receive electricity. The *prana pratishtha* ceremony is the equivalent of hooking up the *murti* to the Divine. The sacred rituals, *pujas*, and mantras are the "expert techniques" through which the connection lines are laid. Then, when we want to connect to the Divine, to receive that divine "charge," we simply go to the temple and connect to the Divine Powerhouse.

official name change, a few dissenters in both communities continued to feel, despite more than a decade of sharing and worshipping together, that the two faiths did not belong under one roof. A temporary sign was erected, while the permanent sign was being commissioned and prepared, which stated "Hindu-Jain Temple." Early one morning, when Pujya Swamiji went outside for his walk, he discovered that during the night someone had knocked down the "Jain" part of the sign, leaving it to read "Hindu Temple." He repaired the sign himself before the first worshippers arrived, lest anyone should know what had happened. A few days later, he found "Hindu" on the ground and once again, quietly, he restored the sign.

It was important to Pujya Swamiji that no one should know about these occurrences. A few isolated incidents, a few dissenters, and a couple of people unable to see beyond barriers and boundaries should not cast a shadow over the glow of unity in which the entire community was basking. Thus, he mentioned the events to no one.

Pujya Swamiji's goals were to create a beautiful monument to Indian culture and spirituality and also to unite the community. He knew that if he allowed the community to focus on difficulties and disagreements,

"If we set the divine example, others will follow."

it would undermine the project and prevent achievement of these goals.

Pujya Swamiji remained quiet but clear and focused on the goal, never giving importance to the obstacles or allowing them to block his way.

However, Pujya Swamiji found himself wondering why these events were taking place and why there was dissension among even a few in the community. If the Hindus and Jains were each devotedly worshipping their own forms of the divine manifestation, how

could anyone be going astray? In response to his inner queries, one night at midnight, after everything had been closed and locked up, he went to the temple doors and peeked quietly in to the sanctum through the keyhole. He found everything peaceful. The deities were all silent and still in their respective temples. Another night, shortly thereafter, he went at 1:00 a.m., again peeking into the darkness of the temple sanctum through the keyhole. Again, all was quiet and peaceful. Several times during the course of the next few weeks, he went at various times throughout the night to check on the *mandir*. Always he found nothing but the stillness of harmony.

At the next large function in the community, during his lecture, he mentioned his investigation.

I thought that, perhaps, when everyone went home, when the doors were locked and the lights shut off, Lord Krishna and Lord Mahavir got down off their pedestals and started fighting on the floor of the temple. I thought that perhaps they yelled at each other, called each other names, and vandalized each other's stands. However, I can tell you today that no matter what time of night I went to check, our deities were sitting quietly, peacefully, and lovingly in the temple. Even when the lights were out, even when no one was watching, they sat peacefully together. If our Gods can live in peace in one room, why cannot we live in peace in one community? If our Gods are sitting together calmly and lovingly, then why are we criticizing, slandering, and hurting each other? Are we not supposed to live our lives as our Gods dictate?

Like the head of a family who promotes harmony among family members, Pujya Swamiji served the community, quelling any sparks of dissension before they became fires of discord. With no breath to sustain them, the sparks of dissension were gradually extinguished. For more than twenty years, there has been nothing other than love, brotherhood, and harmony between the Hindus and the Jains. This may be the first temple in the world where Shwetambar and Digambar worshipped together, and it served as the model for Hindu-Jain temples all over the world.

Pujya Swamiji with his image of Bhagawan Sri Krishna.

One time, a well-known spiritual personality came to the temple. Pujya Swamiji was in Rishikesh and hence unable to receive her personally. As she stood in the center of the temple, surveying first Laxmi-Narayan, then Radha-Krishna, then Rama Parivar, then Shiva-Parvati, then the Jain temple, then the *yagna kund*, she began to complain of intense dizziness and nausea. "I am going to faint," she said during her lecture. "This temple is making me sick. We have on one side the incarnation of *rajo-guna* (the quality of passion), then over here is the incarnation of *tamo-guna* (the

quality of darkness), and over here is *sattva-guna* (the quality of purity). They cannot all be together in one place. Whoever designed and created this temple will go to hell for sure!"

When this event was recounted to Pujya Swamiji, he responded by saying, "If I have to go to hell for building a temple of unity, I am prepared to face that. I am worried about prejudice. I am worried about barriers and boundaries between brothers and sisters. I am worried about discrimination. I am not worried about hell. If we go to hell, don't worry. We will build a Hindu-Jain temple there also!"

ANUSHTHAN

The summer of 1985 was a record cold year. It was the first time Pujya Swamiji had seen so much snow. Although his childhood had been spent in the Himalayas, and he had experienced severe cold, frost, and even snow, and although he had now spent several winters in Pittsburgh, he had never seen snow the way it came down in the winter of 1985. In a letter to a devotee he wrote, "There is snow everywhere and nothing but snow! Snow on the rooftops, snow on the cars, snow on the trees, snow on every bit of land . . . I wonder, if it is snow on the earth or the earth of snow . . . snow on the trees or are they snow trees . . . I am really enchanted by these snow-covered trees! Pittsburgh ashram looks adorned like the mighty Mount Kailash situated in the marvelous snow-white ranges of magnificent Himalayas . . . how wonderful! Surrounded by this glorious snow-white purity, this ashram emerges to be an incredibly blissful experience. Peace and harmony everywhere . . . oh, how beautiful! . . . Inspired by this perfect peace within and without, I have decided to undertake *anushthan* of forty days' silence from January first week to February."

And he did. In January and February of 1986, Pujya Swamiji undertook a forty-day silent Gayatri *anushthan* in the temple. Seeing no one, speaking to no one, he spent forty days engrossed in nothing but the Divine. Community members commented on the incredible vibrations one could feel during the time of his *anushthan*. "Although we did not have his *darshan* for forty long days," one member said, "and we missed him terribly, the spiritual vibrations were amazing. Merely upon entering the temple compound, one could sense that something truly remarkable was taking place inside."

Upon his emergence from the *anushthan*, as he was greeted lovingly by the crowd of devotees waiting outside his room, eager for the first *darshan*, he looked at Haribhai Patel and said, "Kem cho, Haribhai? (How are you, Haribhai?)" Pujya Swamiji's native tongue is Hindi. He was schooled in Sanskrit, and he spent much of his youth in the mountains and villages of Punjab. He also had a long association with many people of Marwar background from Rajasthan. Thus, Hindi, Sanskrit, Punjabi, and Marwari flow natively from his tongue. But Gujarati? In the decades since 1986, he has spent a great deal of time in Gujarat and has thousands of Gujarati devotees. However, in 1986 his physical connection to Gujarat was limited;

"If you never want to be cornered in your life, be sure to have a spiritual corner in your heart and in your home."

he had traveled there fewer than half a dozen times. Yet, upon emergence from a forty-day silence, the first words that fell from his tongue were in Gujarati.

Stunned, the Gujarati devotees told him "Thoke raakho (Keep speaking)." Keep speaking he did, and his Gujarati today is so fluent that many people actually think he is natively Gujarati. "In some past life I was definitely Gujarati," he says. "It took this particular *anushthan* for the language to come back. It just came to me during the *anushthan*. In my room there was a Ramcharit Manas book by Pujya Morari Bapu in Gujarati. During the periods of the day when I was not doing *japa*, I would read the scriptures. One day I picked up this Ramcharita Manas and just began to read it, fluently and with no difficulty, as though it were my native tongue."

As Pujya Swamiji became more involved with supervising humanitarian projects and guiding devotees around the world, he could no longer take off for months or years of silence. Nevertheless, the forty-day *anushthan* became a staple of his annual routine, and he regularly undertook them in the United

The Hindu-Jain Temple, on a snowy winter day.

States and later in Australia, when he was living there as the visionary creator of the first underground temple in the world, a Hindu temple in Sydney.

SACRED THREADS

The Hindu-Jain Temple is a place where people come for daily *puja* and *aarti*, for weekly events such as Shivabhishek or Hanuman Chalisa, for holidays and festivals, and for celebrations of major life events and rites of passage. In Indian culture, there are sixteen main rites of passage, referred to as *sanskaras*. They include a child's first haircut and culminate in the ash immersion or final rites. One of the most important *sanskaras* is the sacred thread ceremony, or *upanayana sanskar*, traditionally performed for young boys at the beginning of their Vedic studies. It is comparable to a Jewish boy's bar mitzvah or a Christian boy's communion and is typically performed only for boys of the Brahmin caste, even if they are not preparing to read the scriptures. As

playful childhood to serious scriptural study and also symbolizes the divide between castes. Brahmin boys, even those having no intention of becoming priests or studying the scriptures, undergo the sacred ceremony, marking them with a physical reminder—in the form of three interwoven threads—of their caste.

One day, a devotee of the temple approached Pujya Swamiji to ask if it was okay to have the *upanayana sanskar* performed for his daughters. Pujya Swamiji, of course, said "no problem." Along with several young girls, a young boy of a lower caste also received the sacred thread in the same ceremony. The boy actually belonged to another temple where he had not been encouraged to undergo the *sanskara*. Sensing the lack of support, he opted out of the ceremony at the other temple but enthusiastically received his sacred threads at the Hindu-Jain Temple. This is the gift that Pujya Swamiji's presence brings wherever he goes. Under his vision and guidance, the Hindu-Jain Temple has become a place where God is worshipped by the letter and also by the spirit.

SUMMER CAMP

In the early days, temple committee members were discussing the need for a place where their children could go during summer vacations, where they could not only learn about Hindu culture but also actually live, breathe, and imbibe it, a place where learning would be educational, entertaining, and enjoyable. They decided to start a summer camp for the temple children and chose a beautiful location on the banks of Lake Erie with log cabins, a dining hall, and sports facilities.

Pujya Swamiji graced the camp with his presence and filled the atmosphere with joy. He immediately became one with the children, leading them in prayers and chants and teaching them to sing the *aarti*, as well as inspiring and guiding them as they all enjoyed the beautiful natural surroundings.

girls did not become priests, they did not go through this rite of passage, nor did boys from other castes. As the priest class was made up entirely of Brahmins, with other castes fulfilling the other professions, traditionally, young boys of other castes did not have any reason to undergo the *upanayana sanskara*.

As fluid systems of logistic arrangement based on individual temperament became static, rigid hierarchies based on birth, the *upanayana sanskar* has taken on ever greater significance. It signifies a boy's passage from

*U*panayana sanskar is also referred to as the *yagno pavit*, or sacred thread ceremony. It is a significant initiation ritual and is said to mark a new birth. Traditionally, the ceremony marked the time when the child left the comfort of his home with his parents and went to the home of the guru to study. During the next several years, under the tutelage of the guru, children would learn the ancient science of the scriptures as well as essential components of a dharmic life, including meditation, *pranayama*, and *yogasana*. *Upa* means "near to" and *nayan* means "to take (him) to," so *upanayana* is literally the rite of taking the child near the teacher.

The *upanayana sanskar* typically takes place around the eighth year of a child's life; however, some receive it as early as five and some as late as twelve. The sacred thread ceremony is considered such an essential rite of passage that most traditions concede that the *sanskar* should always be performed, however late in the child's life it may be.

The ritual marks a rite of passage. A carefree, unfettered child passes into the serious and profound world of scriptural study. The student bids farewell not only to the home of his parents but also to his frivolous and immature childhood ways and enters the world of responsibility, sincerity, and devoutness.

The donning of the thread is an intricate, ancient ceremony, and the thread itself also has deep significance. There are actually three thin threads, tied together in a knot and worn across the body from shoulder to hip.

Thread binds and unites. If we need two things bound together, we use thread and sew them to each other. In the same way, the sacred thread ceremoniously and ritually ties the child to God. The Vedic ceremony is performed to open the child's

Whispering of the sacred mantra.

heart and anchor it to the Divine. Every time the child looks down—while changing, while bathing, and throughout the rest of the day—he will see the thread and remember, "Ah, yes, I am tied to the Divine. I am His. I must, therefore, behave accordingly." Just as a prince, the son of a king, is constantly reminded that he must always live in such a way as befits royalty, so the child who has received a *janoi* (thread) is constantly reminded that he is the son of the Divine King, and as such he must live a divine, dharmic life.

The threads themselves have several meanings. One meaning is that they symbolize the three debts; everyone has in life: to the seers, saints, and *rishis*, to one's ancestors; and to God. They remind the wearer that one's life is not merely something to throw away decadently. Rather, that I exist at all is due only to God and to my ancestors. That I have attained any knowledge is due only to the saints and *rishis* who made wisdom available. Therefore, if I am alive and if I have any understanding, any knowledge at all, I am indebted. The only way to repay my debt is through living a righteous, honest life and utilizing the breath in my lungs and the knowledge I've been given to serve humanity.

The three strings of the *janoi* also denote the three *gunas*, or qualities of life—*sattva* (balance and purity), *rajas* (passion), and *tamas* (darkness). The wearer must be above the three *gunas* and must transcend the bondage of the three qualities of life.

The three strings are tied in a knot called the *brahmagranthi*, which symbolizes the united trinity of divinity: Brahma (the power of creation), Vishnu (the power of sustenance), and Shiva (the power of dissolution).

Upanayana sanskar of the rishikumars at the Parmarth Gurukul.

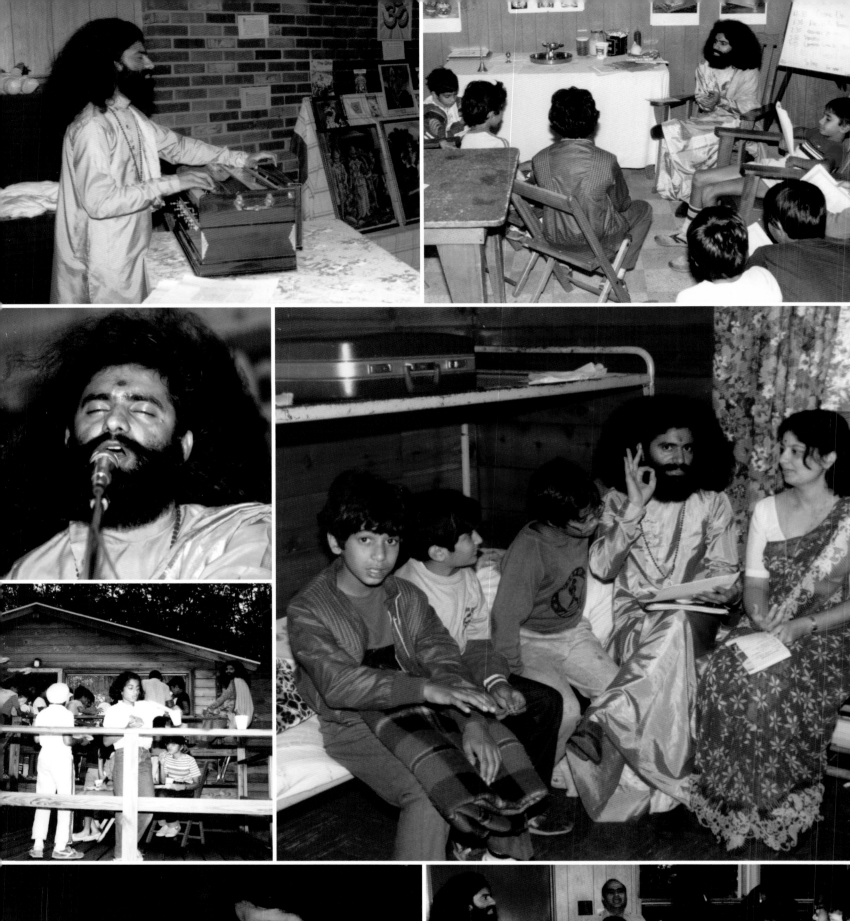

Dr. Rohit Agarwal remembers, "I will never forget that first Hindu-Jain Temple summer camp when Swamiji arrived. He was a young, charismatic, vibrant, and energetic man. He was different from all the previous spiritual leaders we had seen. He was one of us, down-to-earth, and a friend. He made the religious teachings enjoyable and brought smiles to our faces. We loved him . . . he was our hero and our leader."

Vasviben Patel describes the way Pujya Swamiji taught all the children how to do *japa*: "It wasn't only *japa* of Krishna or Shiva or other forms of God. Rather the *japa* Pujya Swamiji taught everyone was 'no problem.' All the children still remember their 'no problem' mantra. In fact, today, decades later, whenever anything happens with my own children, they always say, 'No problem, Mom,' or 'No problem, Dad.'"

One of the highlights of Sunday school, just like summer camp, was always Pujya Swamiji. Whenever he was in town he would take part in the Sunday school, leading the children in prayers and *bhajans*, teaching the words to *aarti*, telling stories from the scriptures, and giving lucid, logical, and compelling answers to their innumerable questions. Devanshi Patel recalls: "I remember during Sunday school, as Pujya Swamiji's schedule grew hectic and eventually we saw him only a few times a year, whenever we were told he would be there, all the kids and parents would be so excited. Kids would show up that day who I didn't even know were in Sunday school."

Like human beings, buildings need regular maintenance. As the years go by, certain parts may need to be repaired or replaced. Further, as the temple community has grown in numbers and in funds, they have been able to undertake additional projects on the land. For example, the original church building that had served as the old temple and Pujya Swamiji's residence became a makeshift community center when the new temple opened on the hill. It had long been a dream of the com-

Bhoomi puja *for new community center.*

munity to have a proper community center including classrooms, a library, and a large hall with kitchen and dining facilities. This dream was fulfilled in 1998 when the new community center project began.

On January 23, 1998, as the winter rain poured down on the temple, members gathered for the occasion. Pujya Swamiji performed the *bhoomi puja* for the new community center. Nearly twenty years after he had shoveled the earth and broken the ground of the temple's foundation, he raised the first shovelful of dirt on the site of the new center. A few feet outside the window of the room in which he had lived for years, the room that he had made his own despite protests from the community members who wanted him to stay comfortably in their own houses, just outside what had served as the temple for so many years, he broke the earth to lay the ground for a center of education and culture.

OPPOSITE *Pujya Swamiji leading and guiding the youth at the Hindu-Jain Temple summer camp.*

How to Walk on the Path of Life

DURING MY EARLY YEARS AT PARMARTH, AN OLD, REVERED SAINT CAME TO RISHIKESH TO GIVE his satsang at our ashram. However, rather than staying in the comforts of the ashram, he used to stay in a small hut on the banks of the sacred Ganga, up past the marketplace.

I was given the special *seva* (divine duty) of going to pick him up each morning and bring him to the ashram. As we walked through the busy marketplace, I would try to push everyone and everything out of his way so that this revered saint could walk comfortably and unimpeded to the ashram. I asked everyone along the way, "Side please. Please give us the way to walk." I would gently push all the wandering cows and donkeys out of his path. I moved standing bicycles and fruit carts out of the way so he could pass.

Finally as we reached the gate of the ashram I was feeling very glad that I had been able to bring him so safely and smoothly to the ashram, and that I had been able to clear such a nice path for him to walk.

This saint, however, looked at me lovingly and said, "Beta, kis kis ko hatate rahoge? Aur kab tak hatate rahoge?" ("My child, how many people, cows, and donkeys can you push out of the way? For how long can you move other people and things out of your path? That is not the way.") "Apna rasta banate jao aur apna rasta banake nikalte jao." ("Do not try to move others; rather find your way between the others and around them. Make your own path, but do not worry about moving others. Find your own way in the midst of the chaos.")

We frequently get frustrated and broken by the feeling that others are blocking our way and thwarting us on our path. We blame their presence and their actions for our own failure. We explain to ourselves that we would have been able to succeed if only they had let us, if only they had moved out of the way for us. We try to push people and obstacles aside to clear a way for ourselves in life.

But obstacles never stop coming. People who are jealous never stop trying to block our path. For how long can we try to move them aside? How many obstacles, how many enemies can we try to push away? The answer is simple—we must find our own way around them and between them. If they are blocking the path on the right, we walk on the left. If they are blocking the path on the left, we walk on the right.

For those who are pure in mind, thought, and deed, there will always be a path in which to walk. The path may be narrow at times and it may seem that obstacles and enemies line both sides. But we must humbly and sincerely make our own way on the path of life. We must just keep walking the path of our dharma, the path of righteousness, the path of honesty, purity, and piety, without worrying about those who try to block our way.

So much of our precious time, energy, and focus are wasted in the futile task of trying to remove obstacles and other people from our path. It is not necessary. Find your own path around the obstacles. Find your own path around the enemies. Do not try to push them aside, push them down, or fight them for the right of way. Rather, carefully examine the situation and see where the path is clear. Then, choose that path and continue on your way.

The more attention we give to those who are trying to sabotage us and thwart our progress, the less time and energy we have to walk the right path. In that way, then, the enemies win, for they have stolen our peace of mind, our tranquility, our joy, and also our time. Instead of trying to drive them out of the way, we must remain humble, pure, and focused on the goal. If we can see our destination clearly, we will always be able to find a path in which to walk.

CHAPTER FIVE

Major Changes

PRESIDENCY

IN 1986 PUJYA SWAMIJI WAS IN EUROPE WHEN HE RECEIVED AN URGENT CALL FROM PARMARTH THAT PUJYA SWAMI SADANANDJI WAS UNWELL AND HENCE HIS PRESENCE WAS IMMEDIATELY REQUIRED. HE TOOK THE NEXT FLIGHT TO DELHI AND REACHED

Rishikesh the following day to find Pujya Swami Sadanandji's health continually declining. Witnessing a great soul prepare to leave his body is a beautiful and also uncanny experience. The spiritual energy is as bright and strong as ever. The health of the spirit is as complete and infinite as ever. Yet the container of this spirit, the vehicle that it has chosen to ride for a period of years, is visibly tattered. As Pujya Swamiji sat by Pujya Swami Sadanandji's bedside, he told Pujya Swamiji that he wanted him to take over officially as president of Parmarth. For many years, despite traveling around the world to inspire, guide, and lead the formation of temples, Pujya Swamiji still oversaw all the day-to-day running of

Parmarth. Whether in person or via telephone and telegram or later via fax, he was involved in every decision, from the most major to the most minute. Now, Pujya Swami Sadanandji wanted to formalize that role. As his health deteriorated, he knew that his days in the physical body were numbered, and, rather than having confusion after his passing, he wanted to ensure that the transition was smooth.

That year Pujya Swamiji became the official president of Parmarth Niketan.

One of the first major decisions he made was to renovate the guest rooms by adding attached bathrooms. Previously, except for a few select rooms, none of the rooms

OPPOSITE *Pujya Swamiji on his regular walk along the banks of Ganga in Rishikesh.*

TOP *Pujya Swamiji speaking at the* mahasamadhi *of Pujya Swami Sadanandji.*
ABOVE *Shri L.K. Advani visits Parmarth for the first time in the 1980s.*

had attached bathrooms. Between 4:00 and 6:00 a.m., one could see a steady procession of pilgrims and guests carrying canisters of water as they headed behind the ashram into the jungle or onto the banks of Ganga. Pujya Swamiji's motivation for adding attached bathrooms was twofold. First, after spending extensive time abroad, he realized that both foreigners and Indians living in metropolitan cities were accustomed to attached bathrooms. Therefore, for their comfort and convenience, he felt that bathrooms should be added to the rooms.

Second, since he arrived on the banks of Mother Ganga in 1969, at the tender age of seventeen, She has been his divine Mother. It is to Her that he rushes, first thing in the morning, long before sunrise, to bathe in Her presence and waters, just as a young child crawls into his mother's bed in the early morning, to begin the day in her arms. As he watched people regularly performing their morning bathroom duties upon Mother Ganga's banks, he knew he had to find an alternative. Attached bathrooms solved two problems—the inconvenience and discomfort experienced by visitors to the ashram and the morning exodus to the banks of the Mother to empty bladders and bowels.

The other major change he instituted was in the basic cleanliness routine at the ashram. Trash cans were ordered and placed in numerous common locations throughout the grounds, an additional team of sweepers was hired, and signs were erected in Hindi and English, urging people to use the waste bins and not to drop litter on the ground. Within a short period of time, Parmarth Niketan had become one of the cleanest places in Rishikesh.

As positive as these changes may seem in retrospect, they caused significant protest when they were implemented. "He is trying to turn Parmarth into America," staunch traditionalists complained when sweepers and garbage collectors appeared in every corner of the ashram. "Itini gundi baat (What a dirty, filthy idea)," they said, regarding the concept of having a toilet in such close proximity to one's sleeping quarters. However, Pujya Swamiji knew that, throughout his life, his duty was to move forward in spite of the criticisms he would encounter or the obstacles he would have to overcome. His job was to serve God's creation as much as possible and in whatever way possible. The motto for his life has been "Maanaa ki is zamin ko gulzar na kar sake. Kuchh khaar to kam hue guzre jidhar se ham." It means "We may not have the power to make flowers blossom in all the gardens of the world, but at least wherever we go, whatever path we walk on, we can remove the thorns we pass on the way."

"You Are Not This Pen"

In 1988, Matashri and Pitashri followed in their divine son's footsteps and undertook a sacred pilgrimage in the Himalayan mountains. The purpose of their journey was not to delve into a life of renunciation, nor did they intend to remain forever in the Himalayas. Rather, they undertook the journey to a specific location, a sacred pilgrimage area known as Badrinath. The Badrinath temple is one of the four sacred Char Dham *yatra* locations. It is a place unparalleled in its religious significance for Hindus, particularly Vaishnavites (worshippers of the Divine in the form of Vishnu and His incarnations). The traditional way that one visits the holy temple is first to bathe in the fresh, hot, natural mineral springs of *tapt kund*, located just beneath the temple's main doors. Cleansed and purified by the waters, one then enters the temple for *darshan* of Lord Narayana.

The road between Joshimath and Badrinath, the last stretch of the long, mountainous journey, is only wide enough for one-way traffic. Hence it is run on a gate system with specific timings of gate openings for those headed north into Badrinath or south to Joshimath. After Matashri and Pitashri had had their baths and *darshan* in the temple, they headed back to the car to catch the late gate out of Badrinath.

As his foot stepped on the bridge that would take him across the Alakananda, away from the *mandir* and back toward the parking lot, Pitashri stopped. "I want to have one more bath," he said. There was still some time before the last gate, so Matashri acquiesced and they returned to *tapt kund*. He lowered himself into the pond and sank blissfully into the steaming water. Eyes closed—not merely the eyelids but the organ of the eye itself, shutting out all visual perception from within or without—he stood in the sacred waters, the temple of Narayan towering overhead. He folded his hands in prayer, bowed his head,

and said quietly to his wife, "I need to have *darshan* one more time."

She replied, "Okay, but please be quick, as we don't want to miss the gate." Silently, he emerged from the pond, dried himself half-heartedly, and walked steadfastly toward the temple. "It was as though he were being pulled, as though an invisible hand were drawing him up the steps and back through the doors of the temple," Matashri describes. Typical *darshan* is a matter of moments. With queues that wind around and around the marketplace and streets of Badrinath, the priests are sure to move people along quickly. "Chalo, chalo (Keep moving, keep moving)," they exhort, as worshippers linger as long as possible in front of the Divine.

A full twenty minutes passed before Pitashri emerged from the *mandir*. Time for the closing of the gate was near, and if they missed the gate, it meant staying the night in Badrinath, for which they had neither reservations nor preparations. As he exited the *mandir*, his wife urged him to hurry back to the car. "Just one more bath in *tapt kund*," he replied, and she knew from the tone of his voice that there was no room for negotiations. He returned to the pond, where he stood with steam rising in vapors around him, the night dark except for the stars and the dim fluorescent light above the main door of the temple. Immersed in the bath up to his chest, his hands together in prayer, eyes closed to the world, shrouded by the steaming mist, Pitashri's lips moved in prayer. Matashri watched as he opened his eyes, turned to face the *mandir*, gently lowered his head, and—with his hands held together in prayer and lips moving with the names of the Divine—began to tilt and fall into the water. By the time she reached the pond, his body was fully submerged, and by the time passersby helped her remove him, his heart had beat its last. It is believed that his heart stopped as his lips chanted God's name, as he stood upright in the *kund*, and that it was the departure of his *prana* as he united with the Divine in prayer that caused his lifeless body

When Pujya Swamiji was not leading the ashram and its innumerable activities, he was on the banks of Ganga, meditating, contemplating, and planning.

"THE 'I' is the cause of all our problems. It is a wall, a barrier between us and others. Learn to bend the 'I' and make it a bridge."

to descend into the waters. In short, there is no one—neither doctor nor onlooker nor family member—who believes that he drowned. From detailed accounts of the events, it is clear that Pitashri's life departed while he was fully conscious, engrossed in meditation, and that it was his lifeless body that fell and which they tried, unsuccessfully, to resuscitate.

Parmarth has a sister ashram in Badrinath—Parmarth Lok. Therefore, word spread very quickly that the father of the "Parmarth Swamiji" had passed away, and soon the news had reached Pujya Swamiji in Rishikesh. "We

"Just stay focused. Don't react. Just be a witness and you will see the magic of it."

are bringing the body to Rishikesh for his final rites," his mother told him on the phone from Badrinath. Pujya Swamiji discouraged Matashri from performing Pitashri's final rites at Parmarth. In 1975, when Sant Narayan Muniji entered Ganga, clad in the yellow robes of a *brahmachari*, and emerged, naked, into the saffron robes of a *sanyasi*, he was reborn. Sant Narayan Muni, son of Matashri and Pitashri, had entered Ganga. Swami Chidanand Saraswati, son of Ganga, came forth from Her waters. On that day, the world became his family. The knot that held him bound to his family was untied, and the connection was severed. He emerged, unfettered, from the rushing current.

Performing the final rites for his father would unnecessarily evoke feelings of family ties in his relatives; they would expect him to feel and behave in ways that were not genuine. His special feelings toward Pitashri included deep gratitude and appreciation for what his father had imparted to him at a young age, and for the rich spiritual environment he created in the home. Even today, Pujya Swamiji's heart is full of love for this man who held his hand and sat him at the feet of his guru. However, these feelings do not include attachment or that singular affection which most people have toward their parents. He could not manufacture the feelings of loss or despair expected of a son upon his father's death. It would be impossible for him to play the role of a grieving child at his father's funeral. He told his mother that they should perform the final rites in the town where all their relatives and friends could come and pay their respects.

Matashri was not to be assuaged so easily. She called Pujya Swami Dharmanandji in Haridwar, exasperated by his disciple, her son, who would not even acquiesce to perform his father's final rites. Pujya Swami Dharmanandji told her to bring Pitashri's body to the Haridwar ashram and he would make all arrangements for the sacred cremation and ash immersion. Pujya Swamiji then received a call from his guru. "How could you refuse your mother? You will come to Haridwar to perform your father's final rites," Pujya Swami Dharmanandji admonished him.

"Maharajji, is she any more my mother than every woman who walks through the ashram? Is he any more my father than every man I meet? Am I any more their son than the son of the Himalayas?" Pujya Swamiji asked.

His guru realized the depth of truth in what he said, yet still could not believe that the boy who had been Muniji could so truly and completely embody the essence of *sanyas*. He instructed his disciple, "At least go and meet the procession across the Ram Jhula bridge as they travel from Badrinath to Haridwar."

So it was that Pujya Swamiji met his mother for the first time in years. Their car was followed by a long caravan of devotees who, coming to know that the deceased was the father of Pujya Swamiji, came along to be present at the cremation, hoping to receive final blessings from the soul of the man who had fathered such a great saint. As her car stopped, she got out and fell, weeping, into her son's arms. Soon they were surrounded by a growing crowd of onlookers—those who were part

The sacred temple of Badrinath, dedicated to Bhagawan Vishnu, high in the Himalayas of Uttarakhand.

of the procession from Badrinath and those who were joining from Rishikesh. Matashri lifted her head from Pujya Swamiji's shoulder, looked him squarely in the eye, and whispered sharply, "Cry! You must cry! What will everyone think? How can you not cry? Cry! Now!" She looked at him so intently it seemed she was trying to magnetically draw the tears out of his eyes. But they did not come.

"Ma," Pujya Swamiji said quietly after some time. "It was you who first taught me the Bhagavad Gita. It was you who sang and chanted Bhagawan Krishna's words in my small ears. It was you who explained that His Sanskrit words mean the soul is never born and never dies, that it can neither be cut nor burned nor dried nor injured in any way. The soul is eternal, unlimited, and infinite. This is

the time you must remember that. The Gita is not just for *satsangs* or for teaching your children. It is for your life."

Matashri bowed her head and realized that God had truly taken her child for His own. He was no longer her son, if he ever had been. She got back into her car, and the procession continued on its way to Haridwar.

The term *vairagya* is one used frequently on the spiritual path, particularly in the Hindu tradition of renunciation. It refers on a basic level to "detachment" and is commonly translated as such. However, it is not synonymous with "apathy" or "indifference." Rather it is a "reattachment" of the self to that which is eternal, infinite, divine. That "reattachment" to the Divine can either precede or succeed a detachment from all that is fleeting, finite, and material. According to Indian philosophy, it is our innocent yet ignorant identification with the physical body—its pleasures, pains, desires, and aversions—and with the emotions generated by the physical brain that leads to misery.

"You are not this pen," Pujya Swamiji frequently exhorts disciples as he holds up a plastic ballpoint. They laugh. Of course they are not pens. How obvious. "There will come a time," he continues quite serious, "in which it will seem equally absurd to you for me to tell you that you are not your body. Today you understand you are not the pen but you still think that you are your desires, your fears, your hunger and thirst. Someday you will realize that you are no more your yearnings than you are this pen."

So *vairagya* is an identification with what is described in the Bhagavad Gita as that which cannot be cut by a knife, nor burned by fire, nor dried by the wind. It is an identification with the eternal, infinite Self that resides, temporarily, within the vehicle of the body. But just as no one would identify deeply with their car and say "I need a new paint job," when it is clearly the car that needs painting, similarly it is falsehood to say "I am distraught" or "I am

Pujya Swamiji sending inspiring letters to devotees around the world.

tired" when it is only the body and mind, not the Self.

When Pujya Swamiji met Matashri and the caravan from Badrinath, he was not indifferent to the passing of Pitashri or to his mother's pain. Rather, he had so completely identified with the eternal nature of the Self that he was able to see, in the words of Paramhans Ramakrishna, that his father had simply "moved from one room to another room." He knew that his mother's connection to Pitashri far transcended the physical—it had been decades since they'd had marital relations—and he wanted her to focus on what was everlasting rather than to sink into despair over the loss of the temporal body.

OPPOSITE *Pujya Swamiji on a walk through the forests of Rishikesh.*

The Time for a Spiritual Life Is Now

THERE WAS ONCE A DISCIPLE WHO WAS LIVING A DIVINE LIFE OF SADHANA AND SEVA IN HIS *guru's ashram. One day, he went to his guru and said, "Guruji, I want to live a spiritual life. I want to live in the service of God. I want to go beyond the binding chains of this mundane, materialistic world. But, I feel that I am not quite ready. My desires for*

a family, for material possessions and enjoyment, are still too strong. Grant me some time to fulfill these wishes, and then I will return to your holy feet."

So the guru said, "No problem, my child. Go. Get married, have a family, and acquire possessions. In ten years I will come for you. My blessings are with you."

With the blessings of his guru, the man went out and quickly found a beautiful girl to marry. They had three beautiful children, and the man become financially successful.

After ten years, there was a knock on the door of their home. The man's wife opened it to see a haggard-looking beggar standing on the doorstep. The beggar asked to see her husband. At first she started scolding the beggar, thinking that he was just there to beg for money. But, the husband realized that the beggar was his guru, so he lovingly invited him inside.

"I have come to take you away from this world of illusions now that you have fulfilled your desire of having a wife, family, and earnings. Come with me, my son, let me show you the way to God."

But the man looked at his guru and he said, "Dear, Beloved, Guru. Yes, you are right. You have given me my ten years ever so generously and with your blessings I have prospered. But, my children are very young and my wife would not be able to handle the burden of them alone. Allow me to stay another ten years until the children are old enough to care for themselves."

A true guru will guide you to the path but he will never force a disciple—against the disciple's will—to follow a particular path. Thus, the man's guru compassionately agreed, saying, "So be it, my son. Stay another ten years until you feel that your mission is fulfilled."

Ten years later, the guru returned to the home and again gave the call to his disciple. "My child, I am here to take you away from this world of illusion. Your children are now grown. You have given twenty years to married life. Come now and embark on your spiritual journey."

However, the man fell at his guru's feet and cried. He said, "My divine guru. Yes, it is true that ten more years have slipped by, but you see that now my children are just finishing their education and they are just getting ready to marry. I cannot leave this householder world until I marry off my children and get them settled professionally. My youngest is fifteen, so if you could ever so graciously give me only ten more years, then all my responsibilities will be complete."

"So be it, my child," the guru said. "But remember that your true path is a spiritual path. Remember to keep your aim on God. Fulfill your duties but do not become attached."

Ten years later, the guru returned to the house to find a large bulldog out front guarding the house. Immediately he recognized his disciple in the dog and saw—with his divine vision—that the man had passed away in an accident several years before, but due to his intense protectiveness over his family and wealth, he had reincarnated as a guard dog. The guru put his hand on the dog's head and said, "My child, now that you have regressed from a human to a dog due to your attachment to these worldly things, are you finally ready to come with me?"

The dog licked the hand of his guru lovingly and said, "My beloved Guruji. You are right that it is my own attachment that has driven me to take birth as a dog, but, you see, my children have many enemies who are envious of their wealth and power. These enemies are very dangerous, so I must stay here to protect my children. However, I am sure that within a few years everything will sort itself out and they will be fine. Give me just seven more years to protect them, then I am yours."

The guru left and returned seven years later.

This time, there was no dog out front and the home was filled with grandchildren running around. The guru closed his eyes and saw with his divine vision that his disciple had taken birth in the form of a cobra, wedged into the wall near the family safe to guard the money. He called the grandchildren of the house: "My children," he

said. "In the wall to the right of your safe, there is a cobra curled up in a small nook. Go there and bring the cobra to me. Do not kill it. It will not harm you, I promise. But just break its back with a stick and then bring it to me." The children were incredulous, but went to the wall where the old man had directed them. And they saw that—just as the guru had said—a cobra was curled up in the wall. Following his orders, they broke the cobra's back and carried it outside to the guru. The guru thanked the children, threw the cobra over his neck, and left.

As he walked away carrying the cobra over his neck, the guru spoke to the cobra, who was injured and aching, "My child, I am sorry for hurting you, but there was no other way. Thirty-seven years and three births ago you left to taste the material world of sensual pleasures. But the ways of maya are so alluring and so subtle that they trap us instantly. You have wasted these lifetimes in the futile pursuit of material success and in attachment to people who also are only actors in the Cosmic Drama. My child, all here is maya—Cosmic Illusion. It lures us into its trap, convincing us that it is real, permanent, everlasting, and significant. But, in reality, the only thing

that is real is Him, and the only true purpose of life is to get close to Him. These attachments merely divert our attention from the true purpose of life. I had no choice but to come to your rescue as I saw you sinking deeper and deeper into the clutches of maya."

So frequently in life we think, "Just one more year" and then I will simplify my life. "Just one more year" and I will cut back on my time at the office, and I will spend more time engaged in spiritual pursuits. "Just one more year" and I will dedicate more time to meditation, seva, and sadhana. "Just one more year" and I will delve into the divine depths of spirituality. "Just one more year" and I will cut down on indulging in sensual pleasures." But, that year never comes. Our intentions are good. We want to be more spiritual. We want to devote more time to spiritual pursuits. We want to spend less, need less, and serve more. We want to be the master over our lust, anger, and greed. Yet, we are deluded, deceived, and blinded by the power of maya. Thus, we continue to find excuses for why we must work fifty- or sixty-hour workweeks, have no time for meditation, can't squeeze in a visit to holy places, and continue to satiate our insatiable sensual urges.

This lack of willpower is frequently misconstrued as a lack of strength. It is not that. It is not actually weakness. It is the veil of maya, which intoxicates us in the allure of more—more wealth, more possessions, more sensual enjoyments. She casts her spell upon us and we follow, blindly, like the circus animal promised a reward for jumping through the hoop.

When we read spiritual literature, when we listen to the holy ones, when we spend a few moments in meditation and prayer, that veil is temporarily lifted and we can see where we need to go. Just as the disciple was able, whenever his guru was present, to realize that ultimately he needed to leave the world and follow the guru. However, the moment his guru departed, the curtain of

maya dropped down again and the next act in his life unfolded as though there had been no intermission.

We are the same. We see where we need to go. We see what we need to do. Yet, the changes rarely come, we continually get carried out on the waves of maya back into the tossing, turning, cresting, falling, tumultuous ocean of samsara.

We can break free. We can live in truth. The very nature of our existence, the purpose of our human birth, is to realize our ultimate divinity, to reunite with the Divine and break the chains of maya.

But how?

The way to break free from the blinding veil of maya involves a twofold practice. First we must surrender to God and ardently pray for Him to take our lives in His hands, guiding us and giving us strength. Second, we must make and stick to concrete vows as to how we are going to be better people. Rather than saying "I will find time to meditate," we must say "I will not leave for work without sitting in meditation and I will not sleep at night without doing my nightly introspection." Rather than saying "I will try to visit holy places whenever I can," we must say "I will take a spiritual holiday this year." Rather than say "I will try to cut back on my expenses so that my financial needs are less," we must say "I will not buy another jacket or pair of shoes until the ones I have are broken or torn or no longer fit me." We must commit to having daily appointments with God in which we consider the many times we allowed ourselves to be overpowered by anger and lust and greed. We must pray for strength. Daily, we must pray to remain calm, peaceful, and balanced in our lives.

If we wait for the right time, that time will never come. The time for a spiritual life is now.

CHAPTER SIX

Parmarth Blossoming

PRAYER IN ACTION

PUJYA SWAMIJI'S ROUTINE IN RISHIKESH WAS FIXED. AT 4:00 A.M. HIS EYES OPENED, FREQUENTLY SECONDS BEFORE THE ALARM RANG. IT WAS A RARE MORNING WHEN THE ALARM WOKE HIM. BY 4:15 HE WAS ON THE BANKS OF GANGA. A DEVOTEE SHARES her experience of seeing him arrive there one morning.

I remember being so surprised to see him alone. Every other time I had seen him in the ashram, he was surrounded by so many people—the devotees, his sevaks. There was always a buzz around him. However, here, he seemed to float down the steps to the water. At first I didn't even realize it was Swamiji because he was all alone, his head gently lowered so that nothing should come into his vision other than Mother Ganga. He lay down on the marble of the ghat, legs straight behind him, arms straight in front of him, nearly parallel to the Ganga Herself, but ever so slightly turned toward Her (due to the steps on the ghat, there wasn't room for him to lie down directly facing Her). He lowered his head onto the marble between his outstretched arms and lay there for many moments. Although he was several inches from

the water, it seemed, in the predawn light, to wash over him, like a mother pulls the blankets up over her child when he crawls into her bed in the early hours of the morning. It appeared as though he were lying in the water, rather than next to the water. Then, as he rose, again the edge of the water seemed to return to its previous position, several inches from where it had appeared moments before. His hair and clothes were dry—so the water had not actually, physically, risen up to cover him—and yet I am not someone whose eyes deceive her. I am not someone who sees visions. For those moments when he lay in pranam to the Mother, Her water had most definitely covered him.

After rising, he stepped into the current and walked out, calmly and gracefully as though the strength of the current had no impact on him. He walked several feet out into the water, but the level was

OPPOSITE *The Ganga Aarti ceremony each evening, led by Pujya Swamiji, has become internationally famous.*

shallow and the water remained at calf height. Gazing up at the moon as it began its descent over Ram Jhula and behind the Himalayas, to give way to the sun waiting to rise, he closed his eyes and folded his hands at his chest in prayer. At that moment there was no moon, no Ganga, no Swamiji, and no ghat. There was only child and Mother. He had come home, in the early hours of the morning, to spend a few precious moments with his Mother before beginning the day. The two merged so completely and so seamlessly that it was hard to imagine that a few moments before they had been water and man. As his dhoti floated behind him, held up by the strength of Her current, I would have sworn he had no legs. He was not standing. He was floating—immersed and merged into the Goddess Ganga.

Suddenly I felt voyeuristic. I was witnessing, as though watching a divine movie, the precious moment of Pujya Swamiji's union with his Mother. Slowly and reluctantly, I turned into the shadows and left, while his eyes were still closed.

After his morning prayers and meditation on the banks of Mother Ganga, he returned through the gates of the ashram and conducted the 5:00 a.m. morning prayers. Sometimes playing the harmonium, sometimes the cymbals, and always singing, he led the ashram residents, guests, and pilgrims in prayers to the Divine. "Sita Rama, Sita Rama, Sita Rama kahiye," his voice would call out into the sunrise. "Jahi vidhi rakhe Rama, tahi vidhi rahiye." Wherever the Lord keeps you—whether in a palace or a hut, whether in a bus or a Mercedes, whether in success or in failure—remember to be always happy, always content and to keep chanting his holy name.

The lines from these prayers have become messages Pujya Swamiji shares, to this day, with devotees around the globe.

Today we have everything set. TV set, sofa set, entertainment set. But we are up-set. Our happiness does not and cannot come from external sources. It comes only from the divine connection to God. So whatever He gives us, remember that success in life is not measured by our bank accounts or titles or degrees. It is measured by our spiritual

anchoring. It is measured by our awareness, our consciousness. This comes when we realize that whatever we are given is exactly what we need to get closer to Him, to take another step on our path to divinity. That divine awareness comes when we realize that success is not a reward and failure is not a punishment. Wealth is not good and poverty is not bad. They are the fruit of that which we have planted and sowed in the past and which we reap and harvest today. The true divine awareness, joy, and peace come when we stop bemoaning our lot or craving more and start asking ourselves how we can use what we've been given to take the next step closer to the Divine. The divine life comes when we stop saying "Why me?" to God and we start saying "Try me. I am Yours."

Another line from the morning prayers that Pujya Swamiji has carried out of the *satsang* hall, across the oceans and into the homes and halls of innumerable devotees around the world, is "mukh mein ho Rama nama, Rama seva hatha mein." ("Keep the name of God on your lips, and keep your hands engaged in selfless *seva*, in divine work.")

The end goal of spirituality is not, Pujya Swamiji teaches, individual peace. Yes, of course, he explains, internal peace is crucial, for without it one cannot move toward external peace. "If you are in peace, you will exude peace, manifest peace, spread peace, and share peace. But if you are in pieces? What will you share? Only pieces." Yet, internal peace is only the first step. It is the means, not the end. When we are at peace inside, the constant clamoring of our ego and desires begins to cease. The incessant prattling of the mind begins to quiet, and we have moments in which we are able to think and act for others. "We then become a divine vessel for God's work," he says. "When we become fully united with Him, then we simultaneously become fully united with all of humanity and with all of the creatures on the planet. Their pain is our pain.

OPPOSITE *The story of Goddess Ganga, and how Her overwhelming force and flow were held in the locks of Bhagawan Shiva, and Her waters were released slowly and gently for humanity.*

इन्द्र शर्मा.

Their hunger is our hunger. Their ailments are our ailments." So, with God's name on our lips, we engage ourselves fully in service of His humanity. It is not that the work itself is the goal. Rather the work for others is a natural consequence of the deep experience of oneness with the Divine and therefore with all of creation. Pujya Swamiji asks, "Is loving someone any different from bringing him a cup of tea? Is loving someone any different from wiping her feverish brow? Of course not. There is no way to determine where love ends and service begins. When the love is true and pure, service is the most natural outcome." Pujya Swamiji's teachings, both in word and by example, emphasize the inextricable link between the attainment of divine union, the awareness of the divine nature of the Self, and the consequent service of God's creation.

After morning prayers, Pujya Swamiji would go for his daily walk in the jungle. Out the back gate of the ashram, up the dirt paths into the forest, he would, again, years after he had exited the forests for the world he was to serve, become one with the trees, the leaves, the earth, the flowers, and the birds. "I always understood what they were saying. I don't know how but instinctively I always could hear words in the chirping and cheeping of the birds." Silently he walked, chanting his mantra, again a young boy alone in the forests but this time without any fear of ghosts.

"Forgive, forget, and move forward. This is the only way. It is not enough to forgive and forget. One must also move on."

An hour later, he would return and begin his daily duties of running the ashram—from the micro to the macro.

One time, while on his daily walk, suddenly from behind a bush a man jumped into the pathway ahead of Pujya Swamiji. He had a revolver in his hand, pointed straight at Pujya Swamiji, a few feet away. "Sign this paper, or I'll kill you," the man said. It was an official document transferring a plot of land into the man's name. "I cannot," Pujya Swamiji explained. The man then attempted to bribe him, offering a variety of financial incentives. "You have dialed the wrong number," Pujya Swamiji responded gently and stepped forward to continue his walk. Drugged or perhaps simply intoxicated with anger, the man raised his gun, steadied his hand, and prepared to shoot.

"Just one moment," Pujya Swamiji said. "Please, before you shoot me and it becomes all bloody, take my handkerchief from my hand." The man was equally suspicious and curious. Slowly, without diverting his attention away from the gun in his right hand, he reached forward with his left hand and carefully pulled the handkerchief from Pujya Swamiji's outstretched palm. "Why did you give me this?" he asked.

Pujya Swamiji explained, as matter-of-factly as if he were giving the cook instructions on how many guests to serve and what to prepare, "I will be dead. Devotees from all over the world will come to demand justice for my murderer. They will come looking for you and will not rest until you are found. They will locate the gun and they will find your fingerprints. Then you will go to jail for the rest of your life. Your two young sons and your young daughter will have no one to care for them. Your wife will have no way to support the family and she will become an outcast in the community. No one will hire your sons or marry your daughter. None of this will bring me back, but your family's life will be ruined as well, through no fault of their own. With that handkerchief, I want you to wipe off the gun very carefully after you shoot me and then place the gun in my own hands. It will look like a suicide, your fingerprints will be nowhere to be found, and your family will live in peace. Either way, I am going to die.

At Pujya Morari Bapu's katha in Rishikesh. They were both Swami Chidanand Saraswati, one the head of Parmarth Niketan, the other the head of Sivananda Ashram. It is for this reason, agreeing to a request from the elder swami, that for many years, Pujya Swamiji kept "Muniji" at the end of his name, to avoid any confusion.

But please do not take your own family's life along with mine."

Tears rushed from the man's eyes, down his cheeks, and onto the dirt path in front of him. The revolver trembled in his hand. Finally he threw the gun into the bushes and fell onto the dirt path, grabbing Pujya Swamiji's bare feet tightly. "Please forgive me," he pleaded. "I have committed a great sin. Please do not curse me. Please forgive me and take me as your disciple."

THE WORLD COMES HOME
TO PARMARTH

As the years became decades, Pujya Swamiji's impact and influence at Parmarth and in the surrounding areas began to grow. It was clear that both his vision and his ability to bring that vision to reality were

unique. Parmarth expanded and blossomed day by day, both in size and in scope, in depth and in breadth. Where the annual events had previously been limited to Sadhana Saptah and the celebration of the anniversaries of the births and deaths of the saints in the lineage, first every month and then every week brought another major event. Parmarth became a hub of spiritual activity for people from all cultures, all countries, and all walks of life.

Revered spiritual leaders of various Hindu *sampradayas* and also of all the world's religions began to arrive at Parmarth, for a few hours or days or weeks, to spend time in Pujya Swamiji's presence. Having met him abroad, in events at the United Nations or world parliaments, these religious leaders were drawn by the purity of Pujya Swamiji's teachings and message. "If you are a Jew, be

THIS PAGE (*clockwise from top left*) *Top leaders of all the different religions come together at Parmarth for a Sarva Dharma Sansad (Parliament of Religions) conference.* ❖ *Pujya Swamiji convenes the conference.* ❖ *Pujya Swamiji with Maulana Mehmood Madani, a renowned Muslim leader and member of parliament.* ❖ *Ekhart Tolle comes to Parmarth.* ❖ *Pujya Swamiji with a Buddhist leader from Thailand.* ❖ *Pujya Swami Gurusharananandji embraces Pujya Swamiji at Parmarth.* ❖ *A group of Thai Buddhist monks comes to Parmarth.* ❖ *Pujya Swami Dayanandji and Pujya Swami Avdheshanand Giriji join Pujya Swamiji for International Yoga Festival.*

THIS PAGE *(clockwise from top left)* *Morari Bapu at Parmarth.* ❋ *Pujya Swamiji welcomes Rabbi David Rosen to the Ganga Aarti.* ❋ *Pujya Swami Kalyan Deviji, comes to Parmarth at 125 years old.* ❋ *Pujya Swamiji and Pujya Bhaishri bathe in Ganga.* ❋ *Kumbha Mela 2010 graced by the presence of Pujya Maulanna Wahiduddin Khan, Pujya Morari Bapu, and Pujya Bhaishri.* ❋ *Pujya Goswami Indira Betiji comes to Parmarth.* ❋ *Pujya Naini Ma sits in Pujya Swamiji's hut.* ❋ *Pujya Vishnu Swamiji at Parmarth.* ❋ *Pujya Sri Sri Ravi Shankarji and Pujya Swamiji bathe in Ganga at Parmarth's ghat during Kumbha Mela.* ❋ *Pujya Madhavpriyadasji at Parmarth.*

Sacred puja at the feet of Bhagawan Shiva on Parmarth's ghat (platform) on the banks of Ganga.

a better Jew," he urges his followers. "If you are a Muslim, be a better Muslim. If you are a Christian, be a better Christian." From his mouth, fundamental Hindu tenets attain universal applicability. "The teachings of our scriptures do not make one a good Hindu," Pujya Swamiji emphasizes. "They make one a good human being."

Innumerable celebrities, from Bollywood to Hollywood, are also drawn to Parmarth. They come to take off their masks, shed their costumes and roles, and bathe in the waters of Mother Ganga. Perhaps, for the first time in their lives, they find themselves sitting in front of someone who sees not their body, not their face, not their hair or their voice, not the tangled web of their romantic lives, but who sees only their soul. Parmarth has also attracted many international political and social leaders who come to spend time in deep silence in the sacred atmosphere and

to seek guidance and wisdom from one who has neither prejudices nor allegiances, nor any personal agenda or goal.

The introduction of free TV, and later the Internet, brought Pujya Swamiji's international acclaim and achievements home to Rishikesh. Suddenly the tirelessness with which he was traveling, teaching, and touching people throughout the world became tangible news in Rishikesh and across India. Thus, Pujya Swamiji's role became firmly established, not only as a revolutionary young sadhu who espoused toilets and trash cans but also as an international leader, mediator, peacekeeper, and mentor.

Under Pujya Swamiji's guidance and due to the magnetism of his message and appeal, Parmarth became home to innumerable conferences, summits, camps, and festivals with emphases ranging from peace and interfaith harmony to nature cure and yoga.

THIS PAGE *(clockwise from top left) Pujya Swami addresses the Swaminarayan shibir, led by Pujya Swami Madhavpriyadasji.* ✳ *International Yoga Festival participants do yoga on the banks of Ganga.* ✳ *Pujya Swamiji addresses the festival participants.* ✳ *More than 600 people came for the 11 11 11 Peace Festival and joined together to clean the banks of Mother Ganga.* ✳ *Pujya Swamiji and Pujya Shankaracharya Swami Divyanand Teerthji at the opening of the South Indian temple at Parmarth.* ✳ *Pujya Swami Ramdevji distributes sweets during Pujya Bhaishri's katha at Parmarth.* ✳ *Katha audience.* ✳ *Pujya Swamiji performs the puja for the deities of the South Indian Temple.* ✳ *Pujya Swamiji addresses the hundreds gathered for the 11 11 11 Peace Festival*
OPPOSITE *Inauguration of Hanumanji deity during the Hanuman Jayanti celebrations at Parmarth, April 2011.*

The sunset Ganga Aarti, or lighting ceremony, has become world famous, drawing huge crowds of participants from across the world. It is the divine "happy hour."

GANGA AARTI

The evening Ganga Aarti (lighting ceremony) at Parmarth has become famous around the world. From Frommers to Lonely Planet to *Vanity Fair* to *Time* magazine to BBC and Discovery Channel, the *aarti* has received effusive and glowing acclaim. Christians, Jews, Sikhs, Jains, Muslims, agnostics, and even atheists from every country have come together for what Pujya Swamiji calls "happy hour." It is a time in which the stress and strain of daily life slip off like shawls from the shoulders as one sways and sings the glories of the Divine. Prayer, Vedic chanting, meditation, and ecstatic singing make up this evening ritual. The Ganga Aarti has become the official "cultural event" of innumerable hotels and resorts from Haridwar to Dehradun. "It is a happy hour with no hangover," Pujya Swamiji explains when asked how a ceremony can possibly have such universal appeal, cutting across boundaries of race, religion, and language. "And the happiness lasts much longer than sixty minutes." It is also, Pujya Swamiji explains, a thanksgiving ceremony. "All day long, the Divine bestows upon us the light of life, the light of grace and the light of His blessings. At *aarti*, we

offer back the light of our thanks, the light of our gratitude and the light of our devotion. One of the meanings of the word *aarti* is "remover of pain", so thanks are offered to the divine remover of pain in our lives.

But how did it start? *Aarti* is one of the most common rituals in Hindu tradition. It is routinely performed several times a day in most temples. How did Pujya Swamiji think to turn the marble steps leading down to Ganga into the site of such a sacred ritual? The genesis of Ganga Aarti tells more about Pujya Swamiji than about either Ganga or *aarti*. The unrelenting use of the banks of Ganga as a toilet began to wear on him when

he first came to Parmarth as a young sadhu. However, at that time the population was minimal. The aesthetic and ecological affront was also, therefore, minimal. Over the years, the population increased. Unfortunately, along with the burgeoning population of Rishikesh, there was no corresponding civic planning or environmental awareness. The banks of Ganga remained a toilet—now for a large population of both permanent residents and seasonal tourists. Each morning, before the sun began its ascent over the Himalayas, the exodus to Ganga's banks would commence with the earliest risers and continue until late in the morning when the sun's rays

OPPOSITE *(top and bottom) Pujya Swamiji performs Ganga havan yagna and aarti.*
THIS PAGE *(clockwise from top left) Mukesh and Nita Ambani.* ❋ *Bollywood celebrity Sanjay Dutt.* ❋ *Pujya Shankaracharyaji of Kanchi, Jayendra Saraswatiji.* ❋ *L.N. Mittal.* ❋
Pujya Swami Kalyan Deviji at 125 years old. ❋ *Sushma Swaraj, leader of the opposition party (BJP) of India.* ❋ *Najma Heptullah, vice president of the BJP.* ❋ *Bollywood celebrity Hema Malini.* ❋ *Kokilaben Ambani, mother of Mukesh and Anil Ambani.* ❋ *Hollywood celebrity Uma Thurman.*

Pujya Swamiji dancing to divine music on Holi, the festival celebrating the life of devotee Prahlad and the coming of spring.

were strong overhead and the last stragglers had conducted their business alongside the flowing river. Those bathing in the river, filled with piety and devotion, and those bringing handful after handful of water to their mouths seemed unaware that the morning toilet ritual was probably taking place upstream.

The use of Ganga as a toilet posed not only aesthetic issues. The river irrigates the farms that feed more than a third of India's population. Hence, any pollution, any toxicity that may enter the water in Rishikesh, could potentially affect those as far away as Calcutta, and of course all those living along the 1,500-mile stretch of Ganga's banks. Pujya Swamiji had, unsuccessfully, tried various means to convince the people of Rishikesh not to use the river's edge as a toilet. By nature, he is not one to argue or shout or complain. "Action above *andolan*" (agitation) is his motto. Hence, rather than aggressively trying to ban a long-established habit, he simply searched for an alternative. Even the most irreligious Hindu would never wear shoes into a temple, let alone foul temple premises. Thus, Pujya Swamiji realized, he must turn the banks of Ganga into a temple; automatically people would cease defecating in the morning on the same ground where they prayed in the evening. Further, if he could instill a distinct, specific, and deep reverence for Ganga—in addition to the ubiquitous adoration held by all Hindus—he hoped people would restrain themselves from defiling the area with their personal and household waste.

Once the sand and rocks lining the banks of Ganga became a marble ghat, the site of the world-renowned Ganga Aarti, the image of people using the water's edge as a toilet became a distant memory.

OPPOSITE *Dev Prayag, the confluence of the Bhagirathi river from Gaumukh (Gangotri), the Alakananda from Badrinath, and the Mandakini from Kedarnath. The true beginning of the river called Ganga.*

Forgiveness—The Only Answer

ONE OF THE GREATEST ABILITIES GIVEN TO HUMAN BEINGS AND ONE OF THE MOST IMPORTANT on the spiritual path is the ability to forgive. Forgiveness is not condoning someone else's hurtful behavior or saying that no mistakes were made. Forgiveness does not mean that the perpetrator should not be punished.

Forgiveness means that we, as human beings on the path of spirituality, must release the pain, anger, and grudges that act like a vice on our heart, suffocating us in their grip and wrenching out our vital energy and life force. Forgiveness removes the vice from our hearts and allows us to breathe, live, and love freely.

When someone hurts us—knowingly or unknowingly, purposely or accidentally—we have three ways of dealing with that hurt.

1. EXPRESSION

The first way is expression. We can express our anger, hurt, and pain. Sometimes this is useful, particularly if we can express our feelings calmly, articulately, peacefully, and in a productive way. However, typically the expression of anger quickly degenerates into shouting, tantrums, and revenge. Our vision becomes blinded and we can see only the hurtful act. Years or decades of love—as well as our inner calm, balance, and peace—get left by the wayside of our consciousness as the steam engine of fury plunges ahead.

Further, expression of anger becomes a habit. We become accustomed to immediately giving voice to our wrath and rage. Slowly, we become the slave of our intractable anger. We become unable to contain it, restrain it, or reign it in, and it becomes the greatest hurdle on our spiritual path. Each time we express it, we deepen the groove of anger in our own psyche, making it more likely that we will lose our temper in the future. Just as river water flows into the channels carved through years of erosion, so our emotions and behaviors flow in the pathways laid down by our own life's patterns.

2. SUPPRESSION

Another way of dealing with anger is suppression. We feel the pain and anger but—due to societal, cultural, or psychological factors—we do not express it. The pain is real. It lives within us, feeding on every thought of vengeance, playing and replaying the wrong that has been perpetrated upon us over and over again on the screen of our consciousness. We are able to squeeze our lips shut, preventing the venomous words from spilling out, but we continue to seethe inside, and our ire festers within us.

Suppressed anger causes depression, anxiety, and stress as well as myriad physical illnesses. Further, it distances us, day by day, from our deep, inner Self.

3. FORGIVENESS

The only other option is to forgive. Many people misunderstand forgiveness to be a pardoning or exoneration of the act committed. It is not.

Forgiveness is more for ourselves than for the person who committed the act. Every wrong act and every evil deed will be punished by the law of karma. Isaac Newton discovered that "for every action there is an equal and opposite reaction." This was hailed as a groundbreaking scientific discovery, and to this day Newton is regarded as one of the greatest scientists of all times.

Newton was a brilliant scientist. His precision, method, vision, and discoveries were unprecedented. However, our ancient scriptures had already given the law that is today known as Newton's third law of motion. We simply call it karma. Every action you perform is like a boomerang. It comes back to you—if not in this life,

then in later lives; if not directly, then indirectly. Whatever pain we cause to another, we will experience ourselves. No one is free from the law of karma.

It is crucial to understand that forgiveness does not mean we absolve someone of their karma. That is God's role, and it is not one that we have the power to play even if we wanted to.

Forgiveness means that we are able to separate the person from the act. It means that the act may be deplorable, but the person who committed the act is still human and therefore has strengths as well as weaknesses, good points as well as negative points. Forgiveness means that we are able to tap into the well of compassion that flows in our hearts and offer some of it to those who have wronged us.

Forgiveness means that we are ready to move forward, that we do not want to stagnate and freeze in the moment of the inflicted pain. When we hold on to our anger, it immobilizes us, precluding us from blossoming into the people we are supposed to become and achieving all that we are supposed to achieve.

WHEN WILL YOU DRAW THE LINE?

So many people come to me, their identities determined and lives plagued by wrongs that have been wrought upon them sometime in the past. Sins of commission (e.g., the abusive parent), sins of omission (e.g., the absent or indifferent parent), sins they can recall, sins they cannot recall, sins committed by those who are still living, sins committed by those who have long since passed away, sins by those they knew, sins by strangers, sins upon them personally, sins upon the collective consciousness of which they are a part.

Their lives, their paths, and their decisions have been shaped by the enduring pain of these past wrongs. They may not remember details of the sin itself, but they are vividly aware of how this sin has ruined every day of their lives since. They are stuck, unable to move forward, held prisoner by acts long ago committed, crying over abuse lashed onto skin cells that have long ago perished.

The abuses, the wrongs, and the betrayals are all very real. The stories are heart-wrenching, and my eyes fill with tears for each person who has had to endure pain. I am confident that the perpetrators have all received or will receive in the future the bitter fruit of this karma they have committed.

However, just as tragic as the stories of abuse and betrayal, of stolen childhoods and shattered dreams, are the stories of these people today: broken adults unable to cut the chains that bind them to events of the past, unable to take a step without the shackles of yesterday.

I ask each of them the same question: "Are you going to take this pain to the grave?" They all emphatically reply "No!" or "I hope not!"

I then ask them, "Are you going to release the pain on your deathbed? How about a week before your death? Two weeks before your death?" These people are usually decades away from old age, and their answers unanimously reflect their wish to be free of the pain long before the end of their lives.

Then I ask the crucial question: "But when? When will you release the pain? You are waiting for someone to come and draw the line, to come and say, 'Now you are free.' No one will draw the line for you. You must do it yourself. But today I tell you, 'You can be free. Just draw the line.'"

We hold on to our pain because it identifies who we are, it gives us an excuse for behaving the way we do, it has become such a familiar feeling that—regardless of its self-destructive nature—we cannot let it go. Yet let it go we must if we want to move forward.

The best way to release the pain is to honestly and deeply forgive the person who has wronged you. We must see the perpetrators as fallible human beings and allow the love in our heart to flow toward them. When we are able to feel compassion for the circumstance (either physical or mental) that they must have been in to make this mistake, the chains that bind us are loosened and we are free to take a step forward into today and tomorrow. It is not an easy task, but it is an essential task if we want to live full, joyful, and peaceful lives.

There are innumerable examples of how saints and seers have forgiven those who wronged them, the most famous being Jesus Christ's last words of "Forgive them, Father, for they know not what they do." There are divine, beautiful stories of how vast the ocean of forgiveness can be. Let us fill our cup from the infinite ocean of compassion and forgiveness so that we can step freely, peacefully, and joyfully into the future, leaving the shackles of the past behind. Let us fulfill our unique purpose, our divine mission here on Earth, rising to our greatest potential—academically, professionally, emotionally, and spiritually.

CHAPTER SEVEN

Turning Pieces to Peace

MY WAY OR NO WAY

IT WAS 2002, AND THE SWELTERING HEAT OF BANGKOK IN JUNE WAS FURTHER HEIGHT-ENED BY THE TENSION IN THE LARGE CONFERENCE ROOM. THE FULLY FUNCTIONAL AIR-CONDITIONING POURING THROUGH THE VENTS DID LITTLE TO MITIGATE RISING

temperatures, and the secretary general presiding over the conference wiped his brow. Two years after the Millennium Peace Summit of Religious and Spiritual Leaders at the United Nations in New York, a follow-up summit was held at the UN in Bangkok. This summit was focused primarily on the preparation of a unanimous declaration through roundtable discussions. However, the dialogue had reached a stalemate. A renowned religious leader and legal expert did not agree with certain aspects of the declaration. He responded to every effort to move the discussion forward with a caustic remark or a critical retort. Although his arguments were sound, his manner left no room for

negotiation or compromise. His message was clear: "My way or no way."

The secretary general of the summit called for a break and privately asked Pujya Swamiji how to solve this issue. One obstinate participant was obstructing the preparation of a unanimous declaration and threatening to derail the entire conference. Pujya Swamiji assuaged him. "Don't worry," he said. "I'll take care of it." He invited the cleric to sit with him and sent one of the helpers to bring tea. "I am so impressed by the clarity of your thought and understanding," Pujya Swamiji said. "Tomorrow, I would like you to take my session in the main assembly hall." Receiving time to speak in front of the entire gathering in the main assembly hall was a unique honor, one granted only to a very small handful of the most respected leaders of each tradition. However, Pujya Swamiji was not interested in the honor or glory. He was interested only in achieving unanimity so the declaration could be signed

"If we want to be torchbearers of peace, we must first become rivers of love, dousing all flames of discord in the waters of our own compassion and serenity."

and presented to the world. Sacrificing a speaking opportunity was a small price to pay.

The leader was shocked but immediately warmed to the idea. "Sure, I would be honored to speak tomorrow to the main assembly. Thank you for the opportunity."

Soon the tea came, and along with it Pujya Swamiji ordered some cookies for his new friend. Feeding him tea and cookies, Pujya Swamiji proceeded to find points of similarity between them, and he spent the tea break engaging the other leader on these points of similarity and mutual agreement. When it came time for the session to begin, Pujya Swamiji pulled an extra chair to the front row, where he was sitting, for the cleric. Originally, this leader had been seated toward the back, and the simple act of giving him a seat

of prominence and importance softened him immediately. As the discussion commenced, every time the man started to criticize or condemn another speaker or to thwart progress in the declaration, Pujya Swamiji gently reached down below the table and lovingly squeezed his knee. Pujya Swamiji's gentle touch and the implicit signal to be calm and quiet restrained him from hindering the progress, and the declaration was nearly signed.

Only a few points of disagreement still remained, and so the secretary general called a meeting in his hotel room later that night. Pujya Swamiji again called this other leader to sit next to him in the meeting and continually stroked his arm and squeezed his hand whenever tension arose. "Let's do one thing," Pujya Swamiji suggested. "Rather than talk about the issues with which you don't agree, let's go through all the ones upon which we *do* agree. Then we can come back to the troublesome points later on." As Pujya Swamiji read out point after unanimous point, the animosity in the room dissipated. Each time a point of contention arose, he said, "No problem. Put this aside for now." At the end, there were only a small handful of discordant points, which were easily solved in the conciliatory, amiable environment. The following day, a unanimous declaration was passed.

Millennium World Peace Summit of Religious and Spiritual Leaders at the United Nations, New York, 2000.

TOP ROW (left to right) Chief rabbi of Israel, Yona Metzger. ✦ Dr. Djibril Diallo, head of the UN office for Sport, Development, and Peace. ✦ Cardinal Gracias, the archbishop of Mumbai and Cardinal Quintana, the Vatican's ambassador to India. ✦ Pujya Swami Agniveshji. SECOND ROW (left to right) Pujya Shankaracharyaji Swami Jayendra Saraswatiji. ✦ Pujya Dadi Janaki, head of the Brahmakumaris. ✦ Mustafa Ceric, grand mufti of Bosnia. ✦ Archbishop Desmond Tutu. THIRD ROW (left to right) Hamad Bin Khalifa Al Thani, emir of Qatar. ✦ Maulanna Wahiduddin Khan Sahib. ✦ Pujya Asaram Bapu. ✦ Mother Teresa. BOTTOM ROW (left to right) Rabbi Moshe Garelik, founder of Rabbinical Center of Europe, from Brussels. ✦ Kumbha Mela 1998 at Rishikesh with Pujya Swami Gurusharananandji, Pujya Swami Avdheshanand Giriji, Maulanna Wahiduddin Khan Sahib, and other saints. ✦ Turn of the millennium in Varanasi, December 31, 1999, with H.H. the Dalai Lama and Pujya Dada J. P. Vaswani. ✦ At the Parliament of World Religions with Siri Singh Sahib, Yogi Bhajan, and Dr. Manjit Singh, then Chief Jathedar of the Golden Temple.

Whether through a soft, gentle hand on a muscle tense with agitation, a sacrifice of personal speaking time or front-row seat, or simply the willingness to let the ultimate goal of harmony trump any personal agenda, Pujya Swamiji has been successful in healing rifts between fractious religious groups, political leaders of international repute, and divorcing spouses.

He is a frequent speaker and delegate at the world's most prestigious international conferences and summits, including the United Nations, the Parliament of World Religions, the World Economic Forum, and the World Conference of Religions for Peace. He also has served as a mentor to various international youth organizations and youth representatives, including the United

Pujya Swamiji speaking in a panel on tolerance at the World Economic Forum with the Chief Rabbi of Israel, the archbishop of Canterbury, and other renowned leaders.

Nations Global Youth Peace Summit and the Tony Blair Faith Foundation Youth Fellows Training.

THE LANGUAGE OF LOVE

In 1990, as President Gorbachev prepared to dismantle the Soviet Union, Pujya Swamiji was one of the spiritual leaders he invited to spend a week in the Kremlin for the Global Forum on Environment and Development. Along with his inspiring words in the conference, Pujya Swamiji also presented President Gorbachev with a string of sacred *rudraksh* beads, to protect him and give him wisdom and inspiration. Further, as Pujya Swamiji's favorite language is the international language of love, he had learned how to say "I love you" in Russian. As he placed the *malas* over the heads of president and Mrs. Gorbachev, he looked each in the eye and said, "Ya tebya lyublyu."

After a moment of trying to fathom what exactly this Hindu monk was saying, they both spontaneously burst into huge smiles.

Love is a force as powerful and fundamental as gravity. As gravity pulls us toward the Earth, love pulls us toward each other. If gravity didn't exist, we would all be floating, spinning, spiraling through the atmosphere, disjointed, disconnected, ungrounded, and unanchored. Gravity centers us, pulls us down, and plants us firmly on the Earth. Love does the same, but on an emotional and spiritual level. Those who do not love are disconnected and ungrounded. They exist physically and may even be successful on a logistic and mundane level, but emotionally and spiritually they are spinning and spiraling, unable to connect. Gravity not only pulls objects toward the Earth but also changes the very nature of those objects. An object being acted on by gravity is different—if one is an expert physicist and knows where to look—than an object not being acted on by gravity. In the same way, love not only pulls us closer to each other and closer to the very core of our own beings but also changes our very nature. A person in love is

OPPOSITE *Pujya Swamiji leads, organizes, and participates in a variety of national and international interfaith events, including the Parliament of World Religions, Tony Blair Faith Foundation Fellowship Training, Guru Sangamam, and private roundtable meetings between Muslims and Hindus in India.*

TOP ROW *(left to right)* Hon'ble Pratibha Patil, president of India. ❖ M. Hamid Ansari, vice president of India. ❖ Governor general of Australia at the opening of the Shiv Mandir, which Pujya Swamiji founded near Sydney, Australia. ❖ Atal Bihari Vajpayee, then prime minister of India, at the ceremony for the Encyclopedia of Hinduism in New York. MIDDLE ROW *(left to right)* Former U.S. president Bill Clinton. ❖ Former prime minister of the U.K. Tony Blair. ❖ Pujya Swamiji brings Ganga water to fasting activist Anna Hazare. ❖ Pujya Swamiji is greeted at the home of Shri L.K. Advaniji. BOTTOM ROW *(left to right)* Chief minister of Gujarat Narendra Modi. ❖ In Jerusalem with Israeli president Shimon Peres. ❖ Former president of India APJ Abdul Kalam. ❖ Members of the British Parliament, Paul Boateng and Barry Gardiner.

alchemically different than a person not in love. Of course, it does not matter if the object of one's love is a spouse, a child, a parent, or a tree. As long as the love is deep and pure—untainted by lust—the nature of the lover's being will change. Once one has experienced true

> *"If you cannot be huggy-huggy (full of love) here on Earth, do not expect that hugs will be waiting for you in heaven, learn to be huggy-huggy here on Earth first and then this Earth will become your heaven."*

love, one becomes love, and then one carries this love, carries this flowing, melting, uniting quality wherever one goes.

We call so many things love today. We tell the lady who checks us out at the supermarket "I love you" when

she gives us a discount on carrots. We gush to the airline agent "I love you" when he manages to squeeze us onto an oversold flight. We casually and lightly tell friends and acquaintances "I love you" every time they do us a favor or whenever we hang up the phone. However, "Thank you, I appreciate it" or "Good-bye, it was nice to speak to you" and "I love you" are vastly different concepts and should not be interchanged frivolously.

We also call our lust love. Yet lust and love are nearly opposites. Where love is expansive, lust is contracting. Love is about merging and melting; lust is about fulfilling our own desires. Love is about the beloved; lust is about the self. With love, our vision— not just the vision of our eyes, but the vision of our heart and our spirit—becomes vast. With lust we develop tunnel vision.

So, how to develop true love? How to plant it and nurture it so it grows and blossoms within us?

The first line of the Upanishads *says isavasyam idam sarvam / yat kinca jagatyam jagat / tena tyaktena bhunjitha / ma gridhah kasya svid dhanam. This means that everything on the Earth, everything in the universe, is pervaded by the Divine. So the first step to true love is to develop love for the Divine. It doesn't matter how one envisions the Divine, by what name or form one worships. The Divine is equally available by the name of Krishna or Christ or Adonai or Allah or Buddha or Grandma! It really doesn't matter. What is important is that we connect. Once we develop love for the Divine, then we take this line from the Upanishads and we realize that if we are connected to God and if God pervades everything on Earth, then whatever we see is also a form of God. If, for example, I worship Krishna in my temple, and I develop—through the practice of devotion, prayer, and meditation—true love for God in the form of Krishna, then wherever I go, whomever I meet, I should see my Krishna in them. Thus, that same overflowing love that fills my heart in my temple should fill my heart all the time.*

As difficult as this teaching is to implement, Pujya Swamiji has mastered it. His heart naturally melts for all, and love flows forth from his words, his actions, and the simple light in his eyes wherever he goes. At a large interfaith conference in Kyoto, Japan, the registration documents asked for "languages spoken," with boxes to check next to

a dozen different international languages, including a box next to "other." After ticking Hindi and English, he also checked the "other" box and wrote "the language of love" in the blank space provided.

THE UNITED NATIONS GOES VEGETARIAN

At the United Nations Millennium Summit of Religious and Spiritual Leaders, he was the leader of the Hindu delegation, charged with heading the largest delegation of more than 108 religious leaders from India, many of whom had never been out of India and didn't speak a word of English. At times, tact and guidance proved to be necessary. "You cannot wash your underwear and hang it to dry out the windows or in the hallways of the Waldorf Astoria," he exhorted the saffron-clad members of the delegation. "In America, they are not used to this. They will not appreciate it."

Always looking for ways to spread messages of peace and nonviolence, and undeterred by the possibility of criticism, Pujya Swamiji and Dr. L. M. Singhvi, the former high commissioner of India to the United Kingdom and one of the senior advisors at the summit, suggested to the secretary

At the United Nations Millennium World Peace Summit, speaking outside with Amritanandamayi (Ammachi) and late Dr. L.M. Singhvi.

"WE MUST LEARN
to be noiseless amid the noise."

general of the summit, "Why not make the entire summit vegetarian?"

"But is it possible?" the secretary general wondered. "We have so many non-vegetarians, so many meat-eating religions and cultures here. What will they think? I love the idea, but is it feasible?"

Pujya Swamiji was persuasive and allayed any concerns the secretary general may have had. "It is a peace summit, not a gastronomy summit," he emphasized. "How can we dis-

> *"'I want peace,' everyone says. Simply remove the 'I' and remove the 'want' and you will have 'peace.' Peace is not something to search for. It is 'I' (our egos) and 'want' (our desires) that make peace elusive."*

cuss peace in the hall and then eat meals of violence? The food we serve should reflect the spirit of the summit." Thus it was that for the first time in history the United Nations went vegetarian for three days while hosting a summit of thousands of the world's top religious, spiritual, and social leaders.

Why vegetarian? Pujya Swamiji's commitment to vegetarianism has nothing to do with culinary preferences. Rather, it is a reflection of his commitment to nonviolence, environmental protection, and ser-

vice of humanity. The United Nations has declared the livestock industry the single greatest contributor to global warming. The statistics speak volumes regarding the direct and dire impact of meat production on the environment as well as on world hunger. Pujya Swamiji explains.

If we required meat in order to obtain the necessary vitamins, minerals, and calories to sustain our own lives, it would be a different situation. However, we do not. A diet of fruits, vegetables, grains, and nuts is sufficient to provide for all of our needs. Hence, the tortured lives and cruel slaughter of billions of animals a year is needless violence. It is violence due simply to our own sensory desires, our own preference for a hamburger over vegetables and rice.

The meat industry deprives millions of our starving brothers and sisters of their basic sustenance and even of their lives. The deaths of tens of thousands of children a day of starvation are preventable by us, by our choices, by our decisions. Their deaths are, rather, caused by us, by our choices and decisions.

The food supply on planet Earth is tragically limited. Food shortages and famines are prevalent and pervasive across the world. Can we afford to make choices that take the food out of the mouths of starving children with nearly every meal? More than enough grain is produced to feed every person on Earth. There is no need for anyone to go hungry, let alone starve to death. However, the vast majority of this grain is not being fed to hungry humans. It is used as feed for the cows, pigs, and chickens who become our breakfast sausage, our lunchtime turkey sandwich or hamburger, and our evening roast chicken or steak.

Tens of thousands of farmers across the "developing" world are collapsing on their desiccated fields. There is no water for their parched mouths or withered crops. Many commit suicide, unable to face the prospect of a tomorrow with no means to feed themselves and their families. Many others are taken by sickness and death. Others abandon the fields of their ancestors and flood the already overpopulated cities to eke out a meager existence in a slum on the muddy outskirts of a third-world metropolis. A typical family consumes the equivalent of 2,600 gallons of water during one meal of hamburgers.

The world of the twenty-first century cannot remain in ignorance of these facts. We don't have to be quantum physicists to understand the way that our personal choices and actions directly impact the rest of the planet. If a loved one needed an expensive operation, we all, immediately and instinctively, would make whatever financial sacrifices were required to ensure that he or she could get that treatment. We would forsake regular pleasures, whether movies or massages or bottles of fine wine. These sacrifices would not even feel like sacrifices, and we certainly wouldn't pat ourselves on the back as martyrs. We would simply be making choices based on our priorities and values—keeping the loved one alive is obviously more important than a massage or movie or bottle of expensive wine.

Every religion of the world exhorts us to view the world as our family. Can we make the "sacrifice" of giving up meat so that our starving brothers and sisters may be fed and farmers' lands be irrigated and trees continue to grow in the Amazon? So that the rate of global warming and environmental devastation may be checked, and so that Mother Earth may continue to have fertile land for growing crops? Can we truly feel the same oneness, the same sense of family, for those who do not seem to be "us" as we do for those living under our own roofs or within our circle of friends?

The world today is suffering not so much from a food shortage as from a consciousness shortage. Today's tragic situation of poverty, hunger, and environmental destruction requires not that we connect on Facebook and Twitter or that we count our global presence in the number of "friends" or "followers" we have, but that

we truly and deeply take the world into our hearts. It is not easy. The suffering is vast and seemingly infinite. We naturally feel helpless and overwhelmed; we shut ourselves down and narrow our circle of kinship so that we do not have to be face-to-face with this global pain. We can no longer live like this. Politically, environmentally, socially—the world requires us to be present and aware of even those things that seem out of our control and beyond our reach. We will find that it is within our power to change so much more than we thought. Perhaps we can't change entire industries or government systems, but every choice we make about where to shop, what to wear, what to purchase, and what to eat has a direct and powerful impact on children dying of starvation, prepubescent girls and boys working eighteen- or twenty-hour days in toxic sweatshops, cotton pickers suffering from pesticide-induced cancers, farmers contemplating suicide, and the health of Mother Earth.

TOP *At the first interfaith meeting of the Tony Blair Faith Foundation in New Delhi, hosted by Tony Blair.* BOTTOM *Pujya Swamiji with Pujya Pramukh Swamiji Maharaj, the head of the BAPS lineage of the Swaminarayan tradition.*

You Are the Ambassador

In 2006, at the World Youth Peace Summit at the United Nations, delegates were present from each of the UN member nations. By policy, no religious or political leaders were invited, for the summit was focused uniquely on the youth as the leaders

The United Nations World Youth Peace and Leadership Summit.

of tomorrow and as the only possibility for true peace. Despite the lack of a niche for religious leaders, Pujya Swamiji was requested to serve as a mentor for the youth. He urged them, "You are not the Next Generation. You are the Now Generation." During the three-day summit he guided the young delegates in panels, in question-and-answer sessions, and, after hours, in informal gatherings.

At a two-day retreat prior to the summit, organized in the woods of upstate New York by the Global Peace Initiative for Women, he met many of the most active and prominent youth leaders, helping them to focus their thoughts, ideas, and attention for the upcoming summit. One of the youth leaders, a dynamic young woman from Africa, began each session at the mountain retreat with a rousing call-and-response clapping routine. She would give forth, in a voice rich with spirit and emotion, a tribal-sounding call that had a corresponding clap, once, twice, or three times in rapid succession. By the end of the first day of the retreat, all the youth had quickly learned the routine—each call warranted a different clap—and prior to each session, the large mountainside hall would burst forth in traditional African chants and claps.

Two days later, away from the safety and familiarity of the woodsy upstate New York retreat center and down in the official assembly hall of the United Nations, the youth's spirit had grown self-contained. Where there had been dance in their steps, now they would tread carefully, frequently on well-balanced tiptoes. Barbara, the young woman who led the chanting at the retreat, had been selected as one of only two or three youth to give a presentation on the main stage of the General Assembly Hall on the day not only when the secretary general of the United Nations was in attendance but also when dozens of ambassadors from countries around the world were seated on the dais.

Her hands trembled visibly as she reviewed and reviewed her typed speech, waiting for her name to be called. She approached Pujya Swamiji's seat and knelt down at his feet. Grasping his hands she said, "Pray for me. I am *so* nervous."

Pujya Swamiji held her quivering hands in his own and said, "You must begin with your chanting. Then give your talk."

The sharp intake of her breath was audible several feet away. "What?" she gasped. "I could not possibly. It is not appropriate in such a gathering. My own ambassador is sitting on stage."

Pujya Swamiji bent down and looked straight in her eyes. "My dear, you *are* the ambassador. This assembly hall and this world need your spirit much more than another typed speech. You must bring that spirit into this hall and inspire everyone. That is what this summit is about. Just *do* it."

She hung her head down, gathering strength from some inner resource, and a few moments later raised her head, her hands still locked in his. "Okay, I will do it. But you must pray for me that I don't embarrass myself, my country, and my ambassador. Please bless me." Pujya Swamiji put his hand on her head just as her name was called from the stage.

She rose gracefully and walked up the stairs to the top podium, the highest seat, the one from where the secretary general typically addresses the United Nations. He and the ambassadors were seated on the lower platform of the dais. She closed her eyes, and as she opened them, she focused directly upon Pujya Swamiji, who gently nodded his head with a smile. He closed his hand into a fist and discreetly made the "go for it" signal with his arm. Her first call was gentle and tentative, but the microphones were powerful and the call was clearly audible. Immediately, all of the youth who had been at the retreat responded loudly with the corresponding claps. She felt encouraged, and the second call was louder, and more of the youth clapped along. The third and final call echoed through the hall of the General Assembly of the United Nations and was met with the youth ambassadors of the world clapping the response with all their might. Pujya Swamiji silently wiped the tears from his chin.

Later, Barbara ran to him excitedly, "My ambassador wanted a picture with me!"

A full awareness and embrace of the Self, that Self that is not just one with the Divine

"Do not wait for miracles. You are the miracle! Never forget the miracle of yourself!"

and hence, in essence, the same as all humanity, but that Self that is also unique, that has come into this world with its own package of strengths and talents, and that has its particular dharma to fulfill—a deep acceptance and embrace of that Self is what Pujya Swamiji encourages and teaches. "If you are a rose, be the best rose you can be. Don't try to be a jasmine. Don't bemoan the large size of your petals or their redness. Don't bemoan the thorns on your stem. You have been put on Earth to give the divine fragrance and beauty of a rose. And if you are a jasmine, long not for the velvety softness of the rose nor the bright crimson of her petals. Spray the world with the scent of the jasmine." Similarly, when he is meeting with, dialoguing with, or guiding world leaders of any age, he is insistent in the respect and reverence that must be given to differences. Each religion, each culture, each faith, and each leader have unique gifts to share with the world and to help lead the world to a positive future. The goal is not for roses to become jasmines or jasmines to become roses, or for someone to self-appoint as the Divine Gardener and determine who should be planted where. Rather, the key to a peaceful future is to utilize the strengths, wisdom, teachings, experience, and expertise that each has to offer.

I Want Peace

THE MANTRA OF TODAY SEEMS TO BE "I WANT PEACE." "I WANT PEACE." EVERY DAY PEOPLE TELL me this. They all say, "Swamiji, I want peace. Tell me how to find it."

The obstacle and the solution are buried in the statement. Listen: I want peace. I want peace. What do we have in that statement? An "I," a "want," and a "peace." If you remove the "I" and the "want," what is left? Peace. You do not have to look for peace, find peace, or create peace. All you have to do is remove the "I" and remove the "want." Peace is then unencumbered and unobstructed. It is the "I" and the "want" that obscure this treasure from our view and prevent us from reveling in the truth of our own peaceful natures.

The key to internal peace, then, is not to go out in search of it, not to try to purchase or create it, but rather to quietly, sincerely, and devotedly work to remove the "I" and the "want" so that peace can be unearthed.

There is a beautiful story of an elderly woman who was outside in the evening searching on the ground, under the light of a bright streetlamp. A wise man was walking and saw her. "Mother," he asked. "Can I help you? What are you searching for?"

The old woman replied, "I have lost my key and I am searching for it." At this, the man too bent down and began to look in the street for the key alongside the old woman. After many minutes of searching, however, he stopped and asked, "Mother, where exactly did you lose your key? Do you remember?"

"Yes, of course," she replied. "I lost it in the house."

"Then why are you searching outside in the street for it?"

The woman looked at him and said, "Because in my house it is dark. There is no light. Here there is a bright streetlamp, so I am looking in the light of the street lamp."

The wise man gently responded, "Mother, if I may offer you some advice. Go back inside. It may be dark, but eventually you will find the key. Even if you had an army to help you search, you would never find your key out here because—no matter how light it may be—the key is not here."

For this old woman the key was, perhaps, the key to a dresser or a safe or a door. For us, it is the key to peace. We search and search outside for that key when really we have lost it inside. We look in the shopping malls, in retreats, in courses, in possessions, in other people. But the key is within us. The answer is simply to remove "I" and "want," which keep peace elusive.

REMOVING "I"

"I" is one of the greatest obstacles to peace. I is our ego, our sense of doer-ship and pride.

WE ARE ONLY THE TOOLS

Our ego thinks, "Oh, I am so successful at my job. I am so good. No one could do what I do as well as I do it." But, the truth is that we only go to work; God works. We can do nothing without His grace. One minute we may be at our desks, acting like kings of the world. The next minute, if one nerve, just one microscopic nerve in our brain fails, we will no longer be able to speak, write, or even feed ourselves.

So the truth that we all must realize is that we are merely pawns in His hands. We are clay in the hands of the Divine Sculptor. As long as He wants us to succeed, we will continue succeeding. As long as He wants our hearts to continue beating, they will beat.

Of course this realization does not exempt us from working diligently. It does not release us from responsibility. We must fulfill our duties to the best of our

abilities. We must be sincere in every undertaking. However, the sincerity and assiduousness with which we work is our own duty, our own *sadhana*. The fruits of that labor are in His hands alone.

When we truly surrender our lives, our actions, and our work to God, then our little, individual I becomes merged in the big I, the universal I, the divine I. Our lives become like drops of water that merge into the Divine Ocean. The tension, stress, arrogance, and separateness melt instantaneously and we become bathed in the great Ocean of Peace.

Bending the I

When "I" stands vertically, it is an obstacle, a barrier. But if we take this "I" and turn it to the horizontal, then it becomes a bridge—between our families, our communities, and our nations.

What does it mean to bend the "I"? It means to become humble. It means to sacrifice.

There is a saying in Hindi:

Jhukataa to vo hai jisamein jaan hoti hai
Akard to murde ki pahachaan hoti hai

It means you can tell if a man is alive by whether he can bend. A corpse is rigid. A living man is flexible. However, the saying implies something deeper and more profound. It means that if we want to be truly alive, we need to be flexible. We need to bend ourselves in humility. Otherwise, we are no better than corpses.

Removing "Want"

What is "want"? Want symbolizes our needs, our desires, our cravings, our insatiable appetite for more and more. Look around you. All the advertisements, the magazines, the movies, the TV shows, the entire culture aims to convince us that the deepest joy, the most meaningful experiences, the surest peace can be found in owning the right car, wearing the right brand of jeans, living in the right type of home in the right area of town, or by vacationing in the right resort.

The insidiousness of this indoctrination is that it is not only false but also contradictory. Not only won't possessions provide peace and joy, but also the constant struggle for more and more actually leads us further and further down the road to anxiety, restlessness, anger, and frustration.

It is not that possessions themselves breed unhappiness or unrest. There is nothing inherently wrong with being wealthy or owning luxury items. Rather, it is the incessant and unrelenting drive to obtain more and more that steals our peace and disconnects us from our Divine Self. It is our discontent with what we have and our craving for what we don't have that are at the root of our chronic dissatisfaction.

These days so many people are talking about "manifesting abundance" or "enlightened abundance." I always remind them that

abundance is not what we have. It is how we feel about what we have. If we feel that our cup is overflowing, and our instinct is to give and share, then we are rich. If we feel that the grass is greener across the street and our cup is half full, if our instinct is to grab and hoard, then we are poor. True enlightenment, true spiritual awakening, the true manifestation of divinity within us is not about materializing mountains of money. In fact, the greater our attraction to accumulating material prosperity, the more our spiritual practice is lacking. The true indication of spiritual awakening is "Thank you, God," not "Please, God." The more awakened we are, the less we need and the more we want to share.

We have everything these days. We have tea sets, TV sets, sofa sets, video sets, but we, ourselves, are up-set. Everything is set and we are up-set. Why? Because no TV or sofa or material possession can bring us happiness. As we dedicate ourselves to accumulating things that have no connection to our inner peace, the less time, energy, and focus we have for true spiritual discipline. Hence, the more up-set we become.

I always say, "Expectation is the mother of frustration, and acceptance is the mother of peace and joy." If we live without expectations, we will always be in peace. The key to being in peace is to expect nothing, crave nothing other than God. As long as our hopes are pinned on material pleasures and achievements, we will be forever miserable. Only by attaching ourselves to God alone will we be able to attain the true state of bliss.

Chapter Eight

Giving Is Living

Mother of the World

FOR PUJYA SWAMIJI, THE WORLD IS HIS HOME AND THE WORLD IS HIS FAMILY. JUST AS A MOTHER—PERHAPS SLEEPLESS, PERHAPS EVEN UNFED—RUSHES INSTINCTIVELY TO THE CRY OF HER CHILDREN, SO HE RUSHES TO THE CRY OF THE WORLD. THE MOTHER thinks only, immediately and instinctively, how to care for her baby. And she does it joyfully, her heart overflowing with love, tenderness, patience, and affection. Pujya Swamiji, having taken to a life of renunciation and celibacy long before typical instincts of nature even begin, has never biologically fathered a child. However, he sees every child with pangs of hunger as his starving son. Every girl abandoned, neglected, discarded, abused, is his daughter. Every patient, ailing with disease, too poor to seek treatment, is his own. The broken, the bereaved, the impoverished, the confused, the lost, the oppressed, the hopeless—these are his children, and he serves them as a mother tends her newborn throughout the day and the night.

"Giving is living, living is learning, learning is knowing, knowing is growing, growing is giving, and giving is living." Biologists refer to the cycle of life as encompassing the growth, death, and birth of species. The dry foliage of autumn falls to the ground, and winter's frost melts to reveal a new layer of rich, fertile soil in which the flowers and trees of springtime will grow. The annual desiccation and death of leaves and regular, natural fires that sweep through forests create fertile soil for new growth. To Pujya Swamiji, the cycle of life is not related to biology. His cycle is one of giving. "To give is to live," he is frequently heard exhorting devotees. "Our scriptures have no prohibition against earning money or becoming wealthy," he explains.

OPPOSITE *A meeting in Pujya Swamiji's jyopadi (bamboo hut) with Ram Boojh, the head of UNESCO in India, and other scientists and environmentalists, planning for how to make the river Ganga declared a World Heritage Site.*

"Even Bhagawan Krishna was king of a city of gold. However, although one may earn with one hundred hands, one must give with one thousand hands."

Wherever Pujya Swamiji walks, whatever he sees, inevitably there is a project waiting to be undertaken. Schools, vocational training programs, orphanages, medical clinics, rural development projects, environmental and ecological programs—there is neither limit nor limitation on the breadth, scope, or number of projects to which he says yes. Nor is there ever any advance planning. "Whatever falls in my lap must be sent there by God" is Pujya Swamiji's way of explaining the ever-expanding scope of needy people, polluted rivers, poorly managed holy pilgrimage areas, and general despair taken under his wing. Those close to him smile as they explain that regular people go for *yatra*, perform *puja*, have *darshan*, and return home. Pujya Swamiji, on the other hand, goes for *yatra*, performs *puja*, has *darshan*, adopts the entire area, and then returns home. "He never comes back from any holy place without having adopted the entire area," they explain.

"Giving is living, living is learning, learning is knowing, knowing is growing, growing is giving, and giving is living. That is the cycle of life."

"What else should I do?" Pujya Swamiji asks if one ever dares to question the feasibility of taking on yet another project. "My life is not for just sitting idly. My life is to serve. Once you see God in all, then you realize that to serve humanity is prayer to God. It's not men or women or children we are serving. It's not rivers or forests we are protecting. It is *puja* to the Divine in the form of these men or these women or these children or this river. That awareness of the Divine as present in everyone and everything is the ultimate vision our *sadhana* gives us. It is for that reason

that true *bhakti* yoga and true *gyan* yoga lead so directly to karma yoga."

Miraculously, or perhaps not, as Pujya Swamiji refers simply to "God's blessings," the means to accomplish and fulfill any project appear nearly as soon as the word "yes" has escaped his lips.

WAVES OF DESTRUCTION AND WAVES OF REHABILITATION

On December 26, 2004, a tragic tsunami devastated the coasts of South India, Indonesia, and Thailand. Three days later, when the news reached Parmarth, Pujya Swamiji immediately decided to leave the ashram, despite a large function taking place at the time. Five *rishikumars* and Sadhvi Bhagawati traveled with him down to Chennai, where Vivek Oberoi, the Bollywood heartthrob who had organized Pujya Swamiji's trip into the tsunami area, was waiting. Vivek had already begun collecting information as well as supplies for the villagers. Together, they traveled to the ravaged beachfront areas of Tamil Nadu.

Originally, they had planned to have a huge, sacred *yagna* ceremony on January 1, praying for the souls of all those who had departed and for peace and strength for those left behind, and to adopt all the tsunami orphans, either building an orphanage locally or bringing them back to Rishikesh to the Gurukul, depending on what the government preferred. When they arrived and saw the complete devastation and destruction of the lives that had been torn apart as easily as thatched roofs, Pujya Swamiji realized that a lot more was needed than a *yagna* and an orphanage. With nothing more than a handbag and two sets of clothes, they stayed for nearly a month, establishing seven community kitchens where thousands of people received hot meals twice a day; repairing and replacing boats; and distributing thousands of shoes, clothes, food items, blankets, stoves, and other necessities to those who had lost all their possessions.

THIS PAGE *The tsunami relief work ranged from immediate, emergency measures of providing water and hot meals to thousands of villagers to the construction of hundreds of homes, an orphanage, a school, and a medical clinic. The governors of Tamil Nadu, Pondicherry, and Uttarakhand all came for the inauguration of the orphanage complex.*

On the first day, they selected the coastal village of Devanampattinam as the place to begin work, as it was the largest and one of the most severely affected. Standing in a huge, parched field where even the memory of thirty feet of water had receded, Pujya Swamiji was speaking with the district collector of Cuddalore (in which Devanampattinam falls) and the relief commissioner about building houses for the tsunami victims. Five days had passed since the disaster, and most of the victims sat motionless and stone-faced on the rubble that used to be their lives, staring without blinking at the waves, which now seemed so innocuous. In a land that had never heard of post-traumatic stress disorder, it left no one untouched. "We must rebuild their homes immediately," Pujya Swamiji said. "These women need a place to change their clothes." The authorities explained that the official land distribution policy had not been determined, and it would probably be several weeks before anything was finalized. "At least, then, let us build temporary homes," Pujya Swamiji said. "They lived in thatch before. They can live in thatch again until the land is allocated for their new permanent cement homes."

The question then arose of where to build these temporary homes. "How about here?" Pujya Swamiji asked, standing in the barren, dry field. "This field is government property. It's empty. It's flat and we could probably easily put one hundred thatched huts here." The district collector granted the permission and sent a local contractor to meet with Pujya Swamiji to find out exactly what should be built.

A few hours later, under the baking sun of the South Indian afternoon, Pujya Swamiji communicated via translator with the contractor. "We want at least one hundred homes, as many as can be put here. They should be good quality, as one doesn't know when the permanent allocation will be made; hence they need to be constructed well. And I want them up within thirty-six to forty-eight hours. These people have been without shelter for five days.

We need to get homes built immediately." The contractor agreed upon the stipulation that half of the payment—coming to several hundred thousand rupees—should be given up front and the other half immediately upon completion. Pujya Swamiji nodded in agreement.

Sadhvi Bhagawati looked at the five young *rishikumars* who had come with them from Rishikesh and asked, "Do any of you have any money?" Together they had fewer than five thousand rupees. She looked at Vivek Oberoi. He said it would take a couple of days to get sufficient cash from Mumbai. Funds were available, but not immediately. There was no ATM there for any bank with which they had an account. A tsunami had just ravaged the area, and basic utilities were still significantly substandard. How in the world, they wondered, would they possibly get enough funds for this contractor by sundown so that his work could begin first thing tomorrow morning? He wouldn't take a check, and a bank draft would have to be sent by courier from Mumbai or Rishikesh and would take at least until the next afternoon to arrive.

A few hours later, as the scorching sun began to show signs of relenting, from across the decimated landscape, a hired taxi approached, carrying with it a billowing cloud of dust. The car pulled up just outside the shed that they had turned into the Project Hope headquarters, losing its wheels

"Do divine! Be divine! It is not enough just to be divine; one must also do divine."

immediately in the deep sand. From the back doors emerged familiar faces, devotees of Pujya Swamiji. As Sadhvi Bhagawati and the *rishikumars* welcomed them, bewildered as to what they were doing so far from the comfort of Delhi, the couple explained. They had arrived at Parmarth Niketan yesterday, planning to spend New Year's with Pujya Swamiji, on the banks of Ganga. Upon arrival they had learned that he had gone down to the

tsunami-affected areas. Taking a chance, they drove back to Delhi, flew to Chennai, hired a taxi, and drove south, inquiring along the way for Swamiji and Vivek Oberoi. A revered saint and a well-known Bollywood celebrity feeding thousands of people in a village on the coast do not go unnoticed. Hence, news had spread, and it was easy for this couple to find out where they had set up headquarters. As

"We should live our lives like gardeners in God's divine garden carefully tending each flower and each tree, but never becoming attached to what will blossom, what will flower, what will give fruit, and what will wither away."

they drank cold lemon water, the man reached into his handbag and held out an envelope. "It is a donation for the new year," he explained. "We had planned to offer it to Pujya Swamiji in Rishikesh, but when we found out he was here, we decided to come and see if it can be of use in your work here." The sum in the envelope was exactly 50 percent of the payment for the houses. It was exactly what was needed to hand the contractor an hour later.

Pujya Swamiji was not surprised to know that this couple had miraculously appeared and given the donation for the contractor. "When you do God's work, He always takes care" was his matter-of-fact reply.

JAI GANGE!

The *yatris'* morning had begun in the dark; the generator at the guesthouse in Bhojwasa was turned on only after 7:00 a.m., by which time they were already on the way. They carried light bags with water, some snacks, and an extra set of clothes as they walked the final few miles to Gaumukh, the source of Mother Ganga. The glacier towered overhead, and dawn broke behind its peak. Slowly, shadows lifted from more and

more of the face of the mountain, and as they approached, the entire glacier shone in the yellow light of morning. The final stretch was pathless, simply boulders that had fallen from the surrounding mountains, and they scrambled carefully over boulder after boulder, following in Pujya Swamiji's agile, graceful steps and pulled by the glacier Herself.

Icy water rushed out of the mouth of the glacier, white and frothy, as they fell to the ground in reverence and awe. "Are you really going to bathe? It's freezing!" Whispers could be heard among the group. And freezing it was. A few seconds of filling one's hands with water from the frigid stream were sufficient to render them numb. However, the flow of grace is a completely separate stream from the flow of freezing water. A bath in the latter may have been impossible; a bath in the former was essential. Thus, one by one and then in groups they dipped their bodies into the rushing, flowing, freezing, burning river of Divine Grace. Throwing themselves—some hesitatingly, some with abandon—in the path of the Mother, they were swept up in Her arms and carried on the waves of melting ice into divine bliss.

With Ganga pouring from their eyes, they emerged from the river and bowed at Pujya Swamiji's feet, adding their tears to the water still glistening upon his toes.

Moments of meditation felt like days as the *yatris* sank into the ocean of stillness upon rocks bathed in morning sunlight. The typical instruction of "withdraw the senses" was unnecessary, as the senses themselves were swept away by the sound of the rushing current and the cool wind.

The sun was high overhead, and its rays warmed their still-damp bodies as they finished drying off and changing for the twelve-mile trek from Gaumukh back to Gangotri. They began the ascent in silence. There were no words; there was no place for language. The experience had touched them all in prelingual parts of their beings.

Sarva Dharma Sansad • Save Ganga Movement
India Heritage Research Foundation

"THE WATERS of Mother Ganga
are always *pavitra* (pure),
but we must pledge and work to keep
them also *swatcha* (clean)."

Pujya Swamiji says that cleaning Ganga is cleaning ourselves. Our minds, hearts, and lives become as clean as we can make Her waters.

The silence was broken only by a young *rishikumar* exclaiming, "Maharajji rukiye, mein utha lunga isko (Please, Maharajji, stop. I will pick it up)." Pujya Swamiji had stepped off the track and down the steep, bush-covered mountain in order to retrieve an empty potato chip package stuck on a low branch approximately ten feet below the path. As the *rishikumar* scrambled down the path to pick up the package, Pujya Swamiji suddenly directed the attention of another boy to an empty water bottle tossed casually in a bush up ahead. The *rishikumar* understood, and, with his poorly tied yellow dhoti flying in the wind behind him, he ran to retrieve the bottle.

Suddenly all the *yatris* began scanning the ground on the path and off the path for any trash. Pujya Swamiji reached into his own handbag where, with his typical foresight, he had packed several large, black trash bags. Unrolling the bags, he distributed them to the *yatris*, the type of *prasad* one receives from a

guru who wants not only to make the receiver's life sweet but also, through the receiver, to make the world sweet.

The coolies looked on incredulously as for the entire trek back revered saints, renowned international doctors, high court justices, Beverly Hills millionaires, Hollywood actresses, and brahmin students studying the Vedas bent down, over and over, to collect trash discarded along the route. By the time the group returned to Gangotri, as the sun was setting quickly over the mountain range, the black bags had been filled with empty chewing tobacco pouches, potato chip bags, water bottles, biscuit wrappers, and a variety of other items deemed unnecessary by the thousands of visitors who had walked the trail in recent years.

"You picked up all the trash between Gaumukh and Gangotri?" People were astonished. "Don't you pick up the trash in your own house?" Pujya Swamiji responded gently. "To me, the source of Mother Ganga is my home. It is only natural that I should keep it clean."

In the years since that *yatra*, as Pujya Swamiji's projects to keep the waters and banks of Mother Ganga *aviral* (free-flowing) and *nirmal* (clean) have expanded significantly, he frequently exhorts people: "We must see not only our *ghar* (house) as ours, we must also see the *gulli* (street) as ours. As much attention and care as we give to keeping the *ghar* clean, that same attention must be given to keeping the *gulli* clean."

So, the multifaceted, multiarmed ecological and environmental projects have, at their root, spirituality rather than science. The science has come in later, as engineers and experts in the fields of horticulture, waste water management, solid waste management, solar energy, and river ecology have joined hands with Pujya Swamiji and become members of his Ganga Action Parivar (family). The foundation of the project and the fervor with which he works are based in his experience of the world as one. We all ensure that our beds are made, dishes are clean, floors are swept, countertops are wiped, and trash

is taken out before any guest arrives. Even without guests, these tasks are undertaken on a daily basis. Instinctively everyone understands that the floors of one's home should not be strewn with garbage. The problem, according to Pujya Swamiji, is where we think the boundary of our home ends and the "rest of the world" begins. If that boundary is at the physical threshold of our residence, it means our spiritual practice is lacking.

Therefore, he has undertaken numerous projects dedicated to environmental protection and preservation and founded the Ganga Action Parivar in 2010. Pujya Swamiji, who never completed traditional high school, who never took even an introduction to biology class, is spending his days working with expert scientists on enzymes that clean river water. He who never has taken a class in chemistry or physics is discussing, in intricate detail, how a new model of solar cell can provide hundreds of times the energy for a fraction of the cost.

When the work began, e-mails started arriving from various scientists and engineers whom he had inspired to get involved in the project. The e-mails would typically consist of

Picking up trash on the trek from the Gaumukh glacier back to Gangotri.

Pujya Swamiji inspires visitors, guests, and devotees from across the world to come together and help clean Ganga.

THIS SPREAD The rishikumars of the Parmarth Gurukul spend their days receiving both a standard as well as Vedic education (culture to computers), engaging in meditation, yoga, and ancient rituals, and traveling on sacred journeys with Pujya Swamiji.

TOP *Pujya Swamiji and young child over-looking the Atlantic Ocean, in Tenerife, Spain.*

ABOVE *Pujya Swamiji with young devotee Avani.*

a reverential letter in which the author paid his or her respects to Pujya Swamiji and long PDF attachments of complex and esoteric scientific research or engineering feats. His secretary innocently printed only the e-mails for him, believing that the attachments would be a waste of paper, as Pujya Swamiji surely wouldn't go through them anyway. After a few days, he asked her, "Weren't there attachments with this e-mail?"

She stammered "Well, yes, Maharajji, but I assumed you didn't need them. After all they are detailed scientific papers."

His reply was simple: "Print the attachments." Soon his tables and couches became covered with articles relating to technology by which wastewater circulates from a toilet, through a filter, and into agricultural fields; the possibility of using corn products as an alternative to polyethylene (plastic); and trees whose roots prevent erosion.

The ease and fluency with which he was able to read, understand, discuss, and even improve on the ideas in the articles were incredible at first to those around him, until they began to understand that he was simply accessing the universal storehouse of knowledge. Most people are limited to the knowledge they personally attain, whether through their own direct experience or vicariously through hearing or reading about someone else's experience. He, however, is able to access another's knowledge as if it is his own, even without specifically hearing or seeing the other person attain it.

Thus, what began as a trash cleanup at the source of Mother Ganga has become a 1,500-mile project, spanning five states and affecting 450 million people.

As Pujya Swamiji sat at the home of close devotees in London on the morning of his fifty-ninth birthday, a young child asked him, "What do you want for your birthday?" Pujya Swamiji looked down, touched the child softly on his head and said, "Nothing, my dear. By God's grace, I already have everything." Pujya

Swamiji never accepts gifts. In fact, if anyone should make the mistake of presenting him with something, and if, by chance, there is still a tag on it rendering it returnable, Pujya Swamiji will immediately tell the giver to take it back. If the giver has removed all tags or otherwise manages to convince Pujya Swamiji that the gift absolutely cannot be returned, he will occasionally accept it as an honest mistake, but on one condition: that it's the last time. "No more gifts. Promise?" he extracts from every giver. So this answer to the child was customary, and no one was surprised.

However, a few moments later, as the child walked slowly away, disheartened, Pujya Swamiji looked up and said, "Actually, if you want to give me something, I know what you can give me." Suddenly the room seemed to bristle with excitement and all side conversation immediately quieted as the boy rushed back to Pujya Swamiji. Had he really just said he would accept a gift?

"Toilets," Pujya Swamiji said definitively. "You can build toilets." The child's excitement drained immediately from his face. A toilet was certainly not a very interesting gift to give his guru. However, Pujya Swamiji was serious and turned his attention to the adults in the room. "There are more telephones than toilets in India. Every day, millions of women have to sneak out under the cover of darkness to take care of their bathroom duties, shy to do so in the light of day when anyone could pass by at any moment. Imagine. Imagine what it must be like to be pregnant or sick to your stomach or shivering in the dead of winter and have to go outside in the dark to relieve yourself. Imagine trying to relieve yourself by the railway tracks, as so many do, and then having to jump up every time a train passes. Entire schools have no bathrooms; all day long boys and girls have to run outside, down the mountain, to go to the bathroom. Imagine that an average village has a few hundred families who go to the toilet at least twice a day. Imagine how many villages there must be in the 2,500 kilometers of the

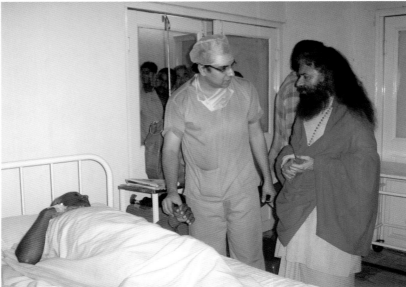

Free medical camps at Parmarth Niketan include prosthetic limbs (top), urology (middle), eye surgery, pediatrics, and much more. The vocational training center (bottom) includes computer practice and theory, spoken English, and fashion design.

Planning for cleaning the kunds (lakes/ponds) in Vrindavan and Govardhan.

Ganga basin! How many people must be using the banks of Her waters as their toilet every day! We must build proper toilets, for the people and for Ganga."

Thus was born the 3T program, including plans for toilets, taps (running water) and trees in all the villages that line the 1,500-mile stretch of Ganga from source to mouth. Despite living on the banks of the river or Her tributaries, the vast majority of villagers don't have access to water other than that which they can carry in buckets. In dry season, the river beds can run dry. Therefore, in addition to toilets, which include full sewage treatment and management systems, the 3T program includes boring wells and bringing water on tap to the villagers. It also includes a massive tree plantation program of trees that can bring income through provision of fruit, for example, or trees whose roots prevent erosion of precious topsoil.

"I'm giving you 3Ts now," Pujya Swamiji said, "and next year, when I turn sixty, I'll give you the other three, so we will have six Ts for six-ty."

Many months before his sixtieth birthday, the 3Ts had already given birth to 3Gs: *gau*

(cows), Ganga, and girls. So now the entire, mammoth Ganga program is only one arm of a divine trinity. Cleaning, preserving, and protecting Ganga (including the 3Ts), removing all stray and wandering cows from the road and giving them a safe, nurturing place to live, and engaging in multifaceted action to protect innocent girls from the scourge of feticide and infanticide have become his mission.

"Is it really possible?" Someone asked him recently.

"Yes, of course," he replied. "By God's grace."

Three orphanages/*gurukuls* (schools) with nearly five hundred children, countless free schools and vocational training programs, medical clinics, and free medical camps now span distances from coastal South India to rural Himalayan foothills to the far reaches of the Tibetan Plateau. Many people wonder how Pujya Swamiji can possibly inspire, plan, guide, and oversee so many multifaceted projects. To him, they are simply different aspects, different facets of one humanity.

OPPOSITE PAGE *(clockwise from top left) Tree plantation along the sacred Govardhan Mountain. * Pujya Swamiji is committed to cow care. * Planning for the beautification of the sacred areas in Govardhan and Vrindavan. * In Kutch after the Gujarat earthquake. * Planning with local officials for the beautification and development program in Vrindavan and Govardhan. * He feeds everyone who comes to him.*

Seva and Sadhana—The Paths to the Divine

ACCORDING TO TRADITIONAL INDIAN PHILOSOPHY, THERE ARE THREE MAIN PATHS TO THE Divine, or "yogas," described in compelling detail by Lord Krishna in the Bhagavad Gita—the path of knowledge, or *gyan yoga;* the path of righteous action, or *karma yoga;* and the path of devotion, or *bhakti yoga.*

Let us talk for a moment about the latter two: *karma yoga* and *bhakti yoga.* Are we better off sitting still and meditating upon the Divine, chanting His name and endeavoring to experience our inherent oneness with Him, or are we better off getting up and selflessly serving His creation? This question arises frequently on the spiritual path—which is more important, *sadhana* or *seva?* Will I attain enlightenment, liberation, *moksha,* or the state of divine bliss faster in lotus posture with eyes closed or with eyes open, hands working?

Or, is there really any true difference between the two? Are *karma yoga* and *bhakti yoga* really two distinct paths?

There is a wonderful story of a devoted man who spent a great deal of time each day in meditation and prayer. One day in his meditation he heard God's voice commanding him, "There is a large boulder in the field just opposite your house. I want you to push that boulder with all your might." So the man immediately rose and went into the field. He pushed and pushed, perspired and perspired, but the boulder didn't budge. Finally, exhausted under a sky long since dark, he returned home. The following morning before sunrise, eager to complete the Lord's bidding, he was out in the field again, pushing and pushing. Still, the huge boulder moved not an inch. This went on for many days, and then the days became weeks and the weeks became months. Still the boulder did not budge.

Finally, one day the man collapsed in despair. He called out loudly, his voice choking with tears, "My Lord, I have failed You. You gave me such a simple task, and even that I was unable to fulfill. I am useless and unworthy of Your favor. Please forgive me."

The Lord responded lovingly, "My child, I never asked you to move the boulder. I put it there, and thus I am well aware that it cannot be moved by human might. All I asked was that you push against it. In pushing against that boulder for the last several weeks, look at how your arms and legs have strengthened. Do you see the firm muscles where loose flesh had hung before? Look at how healthy your sallow skin tone has become. There is a shine on your skin now, strength in your step, firmness and flexibility in your body. This task was not about moving the rock. It was about molding you. If I wanted the rock moved, I would have moved it Myself. What I wanted was for you to experience physical labor. I wanted you to feel the sun on your skin to know the fatigue of a hard day's work and to see how much more potential your body has than what you had imagined."

Seva tunes us and tones us, not just the body, but also the mind, the thoughts, the ego. It is one thing to sit in meditation and feel egoless; it is another to serve in the world with no ego. It is one thing to find a state of peace and stillness of the mind sitting silently in a forest or temple. It is another to find that same state of peace and stillness in the midst of a major *seva* project. That is the goal. The joy, peace, oneness, and divine connection we feel in meditation and prayer are what we carry with us into the day of *seva*. Just as we see the Divine in the images in our temple, can we see the same Divine in everyone with whom we interact, in everyone and everything for whom and with whom we are serving?

Many times we mistake the meaning of *seva*. We think it is about the end, about the goal, about success. We see it as a task before us that we undertake with the feeling of generosity or devotion. However, *seva* is purely *sadhana* in an active form. *Seva* serves two specific purposes, aside from the actual benefit to the poor of the schools, hospitals, and orphanages we may build. *Seva* teaches and trains us to see the Divine in everything. *Seva* is not about "us" serving "them." It is not about "we" who are privileged giving to "them" who are disadvantaged. *Seva* is a practice of seeing them as us. Every religion in the world teaches us that we are all one. Hinduism says, "Vasudhaiv Kutumbakam" ("The world is one family"). Christianity says, "Love thy neighbor as thyself." This does not mean that because I love cookies I should feed cookies to my neighbor. In order to truly, deeply, and fully love another being as myself, I must see that person as myself and see myself in them.

The word *yoga* literally means "union." It is a union of the self to the Divine. Whether one walks the path of *karma yoga*, *bhakti yoga*, or *gyan yoga* or practices *mantra yoga* or *siddhi yoga* or *laya yoga* or *raja yoga* doesn't matter. The destination is the same. They are all yoga, practices of union. In each of these practices we are striving to realize the union of ourselves with the Divine. The moment we have a glimpse of union with the Divine, we immediately realize a union with all of creation. God is not partial. God would never say, "I'll be one with you and you, but not with you." The scriptures implore us to realize that we are one with God. They never say, "But only if your name is included at the end of this book." No, we are all one with the Divine, and if we are all one with God, then, by definition, we are one with each other. If A = B and B = C, then by definition A = C. So, if I am one with God and you are one with God, then you and I are one with each other.

That oneness with the Divine and through the Divine with all of creation is the fruit of true *sadhana*. So when we serve others in *seva*, when we work for the benefit of the world, on any level, through any means, the goal is not about the particular fulfillment of a project. The goal is to see the Divine in all whom we are serving—whether a child, a woman, a patient, a cow, or a river. When we see the Divine in those whom we are serving, then of course we will work with sincerity, focus, attention, dedication, and commitment. After all, we are serving God. We are serving the true Self.

So, *seva* and *sadhana*, *karma yoga* and *bhakti yoga*, go hand in hand, and—in the higher levels of awareness—merge into one. After all, is loving someone any different from bringing him or her a cup of tea or wiping his or her feverish brow? There is no way to determine where love ends and service begins. When the love is true and pure, service is the most natural expression of it. When the *sadhana* is true, *seva* is the natural extension of it. Through *seva* we attain a state of love and unity that deepens and enriches our *sadhana*. Slowly, slowly, we realize they are simply two sides of the same coin, two streams meandering and merging together into the great ocean.

CHAPTER NINE

Building a Temple of Knowledge–
The Encyclopedia of Hinduism

I N AUGUST 1987, A SPECIAL RITUAL WAS CONDUCTED AT THE HINDU-JAIN TEMPLE, A
SAHASRA SHIVALINGA ABHISHEKAM. PUJYA SWAMIJI LED THE PITTSBURGH COMMU-
NITY, AS WELL AS DEVOTEES WHO HAD COME FROM NUMEROUS NEIGHBORING CITIES

and states, in performing this ceremony dedicated to
Lord Shiva. For the event, several revered spiritual leaders were called from across the United States and even
from India, including Pujya Swami Dharmanandji, Pujya
Sushil Muniji, and Pujya Swami Sivaya Subramuniyas-
wami, founder of *Hinduism Today* magazine.

Following the conclusion of the *abhishek*, many of the
devotees (who also included, serendipitously, several
scholars on Hinduism) sat together with Pujya Swamiji
in the temple, discussing the state of Hinduism in the
United States. They shared concerns for the diluted way
in which Hinduism was being presented by schools, universities, and colleges throughout the West, and the dearth

of any available sources of reference on authentic Hinduism. Hindu youth being born, raised, and educated in the
West were coming face-to-face with misconceptions and
misinformation and, consequentially, with prejudice and
disparagement. When their American friends queried
them on various aspects of Hinduism, they frequently had
no answer and no place to turn in search of the answer.
Embarrassed, these youth would return home and express
their frustration to their parents. In many cases, the parents also didn't have the answer.

Hinduism is more of a way of life than a "religion"
in the traditional sense of religious dogma. It is inclu-
sive, expansive, and permissive of innumerable forms of

worship. Therefore, it typically manifests in day-to-day life more than in religion classes. Hence, Indians who had been born and raised in India, steeped in Hindu culture, may have lived Hindu rites and rituals throughout the day without necessarily knowing the specific meaning or significance. The rites and rituals simply were part and parcel of daily life. However, when these Indians moved to the West, and their children began questioning their religious ways, which were so different

"Engage yourself in karma (good, selfless work), under the shade of dharma (righteousness), with an awareness of Brahma (God)."

from those of their friends, these parents frequently had no sufficient way of explaining Hinduism to their children.

These concerns and dilemmas were discussed that summer afternoon in Pittsburgh, and conversation shifted to the idea that a major text should be brought out, encapsulating all the details of Hinduism. It was noted that every major religious tradition had produced one or more encyclopedias on their respective religion, as an authentic source of information and as a necessary academic tool for information and research. References were made to the *New Catholic Encyclopedia* and the *Encyclopedia of Judaica*. It was pointed out that the government of Sri Lanka was preparing an encyclopedia of Buddhism, and the Turkish government had brought out the Turkish version of encyclopedia of Islam. Further, the Indonesian government had produced its own encyclopedia of Islam. Punjabi University in Patiala was preparing the encyclopedia of Sikhism.

Yet, those gathered realized that the Hindu tradition, one of the oldest, largest, and most influential religions on earth with over seven thousand years of history and prehistory, did not have a comprehensive encyclopedia of Hinduism.

Pujya Swamiji immediately said, "We should bring out an encyclopedia of Hinduism. We should provide the children, the children's children, and all the children of the world with an authentic, informative, insightful, and inspiring source of reference for Hinduism."

He turned to Dr. K. L. Seshagiri Rao, a respected professor from the University of Virginia, and said that with Dr. Rao guiding the project from an academic standpoint, they would undertake this mammoth task for all of humanity. Dr. Rao and others looked incredulously at Pujya Swamiji. A multivolume encyclopedia of the world's oldest living religion was a huge commitment, a herculean undertaking for a young Indian sadhu. "Do you really think it can be done?" someone asked Pujya Swamiji.

He closed his eyes, entered a meditative trance, and opened them a short while later. "Yes," he replied upon opening his eyes. "It can be done and we will do it." He explains: "I needed to see if I received the green signal from God. The moment, with closed eyes, I got the signal, I knew the project could be done and would be brought to successful completion."

On November 21, 1987, Pujya Swamiji organized a meeting to form the India Heritage Research Foundation, a nonprofit organization dedicated—in its initial stages—to bringing out the multivolume encyclopedia of Hinduism. IHRF's activities have blossomed and expanded greatly in the last decades to include innumerable projects for the benefit of humanity, including free schools, orphanages/*gurukuls*, vocational training programs, women's upliftment projects, rural development, disaster relief, ecological preservation programs, and much more.

Pujya Swamiji was selected as the chairman of the board of IHRF, as it would be through his leadership, inspiration, and blessings that the encyclopedia could come to fruition. Pujya Swamiji requested that Dr. Rao serve as the chief editor of the encyclopedia. Dr. Naval Kant generously purchased the building just next to the temple, to house the office of the encyclopedia. Dr. Rao took voluntary retirement from the University of Virginia and moved to Pittsburgh to work on the encyclopedia full-time.

The board recommended that the encyclopedia should be authentic and lucid, be easily comprehended by the average educated person, informative on the rich and ancient Hindu heritage yet relevant to the modern world, profound but not abstruse; sensitive to the Hindu tradition but not narrow in outlook, and educational but without losing the spiritual substance of the tradition. It should be useful and informative to the students of humanities in general and to students and teachers of religions in particular.

It was agreed that the encyclopedia should present each sect, school, and movement of the Hindu tradition in its own terms. The approach should be holistic, ecumenical, harmonious, and spiritual. The encyclopedia should use historical, philosophical, exegetical, and critical methods appropriately, wherever necessary. Accurate data should be presented with appropriate illustrative material, such as drawings, photographic reproductions, and maps.

Conceptual work for the encyclopedia, planning the project, and the preparatory work, both academic and administrative, were all done at the office in Pittsburgh, with the enthusiastic help of many leaders and volunteers of the Hindu-Jain Temple.

SELECTION OF SCHOLARS

Pujya Swamiji spent years from 1987 to 1992 traveling around the world with Dr. K. L. Seshagiri Rao, interviewing scholars and professors from dozens of internationally reputable universities, colleges, and academic institutions. Not only did the scholars chosen for the encyclopedia have to be expert in their particular field, but also their experience had

"LIVE IN PEACE, not in pieces.
If you are in peace, you will exude peace,
manifest peace, and spread peace.
If you're in pieces, you will manifest
pieces and spread pieces."

Pujya Swamiji organized functions across the world to raise awareness of the encyclopedia project.

to be greater than simply obtaining a degree in a subject. Pujya Swamiji wanted to ensure that the authors of the articles in the encyclopedia were academic and scholastic experts as well as those who had been touched by the subject matter. The encyclopedia was not to be merely an academic exercise. Rather, Pujya Swamiji's vision had the encyclopedia filling young Hindus with both information and inspiration regarding their ancient and timeless tradition.

A project of this magnitude would require funds, a paucity of which was available. Pujya Swamiji organized dozens of international *yagnas*, *kathas*, and *yatras* throughout the United States, Canada, Africa, and the United Kingdom, as well as Australia, New Zealand, and Fiji. He invited Pujya Sant Shri Rameshbhai Oza to deliver uplifting and inspiring *kathas* on the *Ramayana* and the *Srimad-Bhagavatam*, to help Indians get more deeply in touch with their spiritual culture and to help them see the need for the encyclopedia.

Finally, around 1993, the work began in full swing, and over the next few years, offices

sprouted up around the globe—Madras (Chennai), Bangalore, Varanasi, Pune, and Delhi in India as well as a new head office in Columbia, South Carolina, courtesy of the University of South Carolina.

Initially encouraged by the scholars' enthusiasm and hyperbolic assertions of how quickly they could work, IHRF announced that the encyclopedia would be completed before the dawn of the new millennium.

Pujya Swamiji recalls:

We actually had no idea how long something like this would take. The scholars were all, of course, expert in their own fields, but that didn't make the cohesive whole come together any quicker. Those were the days before e-mail, and the vast majority of scholars didn't use computers. Therefore, most of the articles were handwritten, and that too in native languages—Telegu, Kannad, Bengali, Hindi, etc. Then, the articles had to be translated by someone not only fluent in the language but also proficient enough in the subject matter to be able to ascertain nuances of particular words and concepts. Then, round after round of editing was done. Incredibly, none of the scholars ever received an article and said, "Great. It's perfect." Inevitably they said,

ANCIENT RITUAL — Sejal and Madhavi Patel, Pittsburgh, put herbs and flowers on the ceremonial fire during the Hindu services Saturday in Paxinos. The rite attracted 500 Indian worshippers. **Additional photos, page 6**

Press-Enterprise/Keith Haupt

500 Indians gather for Hindu fire ritual

By SUSAN BROOK/ *Press-Enterprise staff*

PAXINOS — A sacred Hindu fire ritual led by a revered Indian religious leader drew 500 Indians to worship here Saturday.

As chanting and sweet-smelling incense wafted across an open field behind a motel here, the gathering drew Indian residents from nearby towns and invited guests from as far away as Toronto. It was a rare opportunity to worship together in traditional Hindu fashion.

Under a bright yellow and green tent, family groups sat crosslegged, listening as the bearded Swami projected his chants over a sound system.

With hours of prayers, chants and

fires, the group aims to release good vibrations to promote peace, prosperity and concern for the natural environment, said Dr. Naval Kant, Lewisburg, one of the organizers.

"This is sort of offerings to the God and to the planets," Kant said. He said Hindus promote universal goodwill by such observances.

"It is not only for the individual persons, but for the entire universe, in the way that good in thought in mind is spread around you," he said.

Similar outdoor rituals draw large crowds in India; this time the site was Glossers' Motel, now owned by an Indian family.

The fait...
Please se...

RELIGIOUS LEADER — Swami Chidanand Sarasv... Rishikesh, India...

Press-Enterprise/Kei...

Swami Chidanand Saraswati, seated front, led the yagna for peace and prosperity held

Saturday on the property of the Glosser Motor Inn, Paxinos. (News-Item photo)

Hindus gather for ceremony

By John Lindermuth
Staff writer

PAXINOS — The hills around Paxinos vibrated Saturday to unfamiliar chanting embracing this area and the universe in a mantle of bliss.

More than 500 Hindus gathered for a Yagnan, a spiritual ceremony invoking goodwill, held at the Glosser Motor Inn.

Led by Swami Chidanand Saraswati of the tri-state Hindu Temple of Pittsburgh, the event drew persons of Indian descent from throughout the area as well as invited guests from across the United States and Canada. Though primarily Indians, participants included a number of Caucasian converts.

Hosted by Manilar Patel, Elysburg, owner of the motor inn, and other local Indians, the sacred ceremony was held in a large yellow and white tent a... and which served as a temple creat...

The resplendent costume of these women added a colorful touch to the sacred ceremony attended by more than 500 Hindus from across the country and Canada. (News-Item photo)

...rregular basis and participants ...y a few times it has been con... ...United States. The last one was ...a, S.C.

...ligious purpose, the gathering ...y for socializing and for the ...r a major ...dation affi...

...urg, secr...
...ers of Sa...
...of Hindu...
...oldest an...
...s, cultur...
...indu is

Show of faith

Hindu religious ceremony held in Paxinos

PERFORMING THE CEREMONY — Swami Chidanand Saraswati from Rishikesh, India, pours purified butter over the flames.

■ Press-Enterprise photos by **KEITH HAUPT**

AFTER THE CEREMONY — Urns for the sacred fires are turned on top of each other until they burn out after a ceremony in which they were burned.

Over 500 Hindus gather for ceremony

...faithful removed their shoes ...they entered the tent and ...ered in family groups around ...on which they would burn ...offerings. Strict rules of con... ...were enforced within the tent ...h served as temple for the dura... ...of the Ram Katha (the spiritual ...vance).

...ami Saraswati sat crosslegged ...e altar and presided over the ...ce with other temple officials ...ding one who served as ...rator and provided an English ...lation at the beginning of each ...e for those who did not unders... ...the language.

...nubhai Patel, who came with ...family from Detroit for the ..., explained that yagna signifies ...ifice. "We must cleanse ...lives, sacrifice all evil thoughts ...ctions, and become unified in ...will before we can pray for the ...it of others," he said.

...th this in mind, Swami ...swati began by invoking

prayers to ensure noble thoughts among those participating. The chanting was taken up by the moderator and the audience, followed by the ritual sipping of water and touching of different parts of the body.

Patel explained that this was done to purify speech, mind, heart and body before the auspicious tasks to follow. This is made clear in the prayer:

"Blessed be thy name O Lord! May Thou strengthen and bless my organs of speech, my respiratory system, my organs of sight and hearing, my centres of love, feeling and heart, my throat and brain, my arms and hands both for personal ends and for the good of my fellowmen amidst whom I live."

After the initial cleansing, the katha continues with prayers for the intervention and protection of the Supreme Being and all its manifestations for the assembly and leading up to the Agnayaadhaan, the

lighting of the fires on which sacrifices of camphor incense, purified butter, coconut, fruit and flowers were made for the benefit of all.

The sweet and pungent odor of the offerings and smoke soon filled the tent. Though her eyes smarted from the smoke, Rani Dave, a young girl from Harrisburg, said she welcomed it because the discomfort made her more aware of the reality of what they were doing. "I enjoy the social occasion," she said, "but what we are doing is more important to me for the religious purpose."

Patel agreed, noting that at the end of each chant is a repetition of "idanna mama" which means the participant has no selfish motive in making his offering. "It is to remind us we are making sacrifices for the benefit of others," he said.

The fire in which the sacrifices are burned and each of the various offerings has special meaning.

The flames of the fire, for in-

stance, always rise upward toward the point of origin reminding the worshiper to seek new spiritual heights. They also consume, or purify, that which comes in contact with them, symbolizing the burning away of the impurities of life such as ignorance, greed, anger, ego, hatred and lust.

The yagna written by Swami Saraswati concludes with the Gayatri mantra, considered the greatest of all the prayers from the Rig Veda, the Hindu scriptures.

According to the Vedas, character is determined by mental disposition. It is believed the Gayatri mantra purifies the mind and enhances wisdom and its use in worship provides for long life, spiritual strength, wealth, fame and enlightenment to all.

The fervent expressions on the faces of those reciting the final verses of the short prayer showed their belief and hope that a better world is possible for all.

THIS PAGE *Yagnas, sacred fire ceremonies, were organized in various cities throughout the world to unite the Indian communities and reconnect them to their heritage and roots.*

TOP *Pujya Swamiji discusses the encyclopedia project with late Shri Shankar Dayal Sharma, former president of India.*
ABOVE *Pujya Swamiji presents a draft volume of the encyclopedia to Pujya Swami Satchidanandji of Auroville, West Virginia.*
ABOVE RIGHT *The first edition of the completed eleven-volume set of* Encyclopedia of Hinduism.

"Oh, I need to edit this." Then another several months would go by. We wanted to make sure that every article was edited by experts for both substance and copy, content and readability. Each article ended up being edited at least six to eight times before the encyclopedia was finally completed.

Because e-mail didn't become commonplace until the last few years of work, we literally used to have to send our office people around to the scholars' homes and university campuses to urge them to turn over the article. Mobile phones were not yet commonly available in India, and many people did not even have residential landlines.

Therefore, completion took nearly a full extra decade than originally anticipated. This was due to the natural amount of time the work required (which had been significantly miscalculated in the beginning) and to a variety of other obstacles, challenges, and what Pujya Swamiji terms "opportunities for *sadhana.*" He smiles as he says, "We could fill an entire encyclopedia with the correspondence that went on for the encyclopedia."

Pujya Swamiji had received the infallible green light in 1987 when he closed his eyes to ask for divine guidance before embarking on the project. Thus, it was bound to come to successful fruition. In 2010 the first volumes were launched at a function of enormous proportions during the Maha Kumbha Mela in Haridwar. Since Pujya Swamiji's first Kumbha in Allahabad in 1977, the scope of the *melas* has grown exponentially. The 2010 Kumbha Mela in Haridwar saw more than sixty million people have a bath in Ganga in a stretch of river less than twenty miles long. His Holiness the Dalai Lama, Pujya Swami Ramdevji, Pujya Swami Gurusharananandji, Pujya Swami Avdheshanandji, Pujya Sant Shri Morari Bapu, and Pujya Sant Shri Rameshbhai Oza were some of the dozens of revered spiritual leaders who launched the encyclopedia with Pujya Swamiji. Shri L. K. Advani, former Deputy Prime Minister of India and leader of the opposition party, Bollywood celebrity Vivek Oberoi, and innumerable other spiritual, national, political, and social leaders were present for the celebration.

OPPOSITE *(clockwise from top left) The published encyclopedia was launched by the hands of the Dalai and numerous spiritual and national leaders at a mega event.* ❧ *The first set of the encyclopedia presented to the Hon'ble President of India, Pratibha Patil.* ❧ *Launch of the encyclopedia by the hands of H.H. the Dalai Lama and other revered spiritual and national leaders.* ❧ *Prior to that, the first volume, ready for publication, was ceremoniously unveiled by the saints during Pujya Bhaishri's katha in Rishikesh.*

Ten Commandments of Hinduism

MANY PEOPLE ASK, "WHAT ARE THE BASIC TENETS OF HINDUISM? WHAT ARE THE RULES? What are the commandments?" Hinduism is, as our sages and seers have said continuously, not a dogma but rather a way of life. The true, correct term is actually *Sanatan Dharma*, eternal way of life.

It encompasses, not a set of strict, binding rules and regulations that are applicable and appropriate to a certain time and place, but rather the very essence of what a good, righteous, spiritual life should be.

However, despite the broadness of Hinduism's reach and despite its nearly boundless inclusiveness, it is helpful to have some guidelines, some understanding of what makes up the righteous life according to our tradition. These can be found in the *yamas* and *niyamas* of Patanjali's yoga sutras. When we think of "yoga" we tend, unfortunately and incorrectly, to think only of a series of physical postures and breathing exercises. Hence one might wonder why or how the *yoga sutras* could possibly encompass the commandments of *Sanatan Dharma*. Although yoga does encompass asana (the postures) and *pranayama* (the breathing exercises), the word *yoga* actually means "union." Union of what? Union of the self to the Divine. One-ness with the Divine is what we are striving for in our lives. The final limb of Patanjali's eight-limbed path of yoga, the uppermost branch on the tree, is *samadhi,* or divine bliss. But one has to begin at the foundation and move upward.

Oneness with God, unwavering peace, ecstatic joy, and ultimate fulfillment in life—of our external, physical desires as well as our internal, spiritual desires—can only come if we abide by the natural laws of dharma. These laws are delineated simply and comprehensively in the first two "limbs" of the yogic path: the *yamas* and *niyamas*.

What are they? What are the ten commandments of *Sanatan Dharma*? We begin with the five *yamas*—the moral restraints and injunctions that, when followed with dedi-

cation and discipline, help us become the master of our bodies, minds, and lives.

I. *AHIMSA*—NONVIOLENCE

This is the fundamental, most basic and crucial tenet of living as a good human. What does nonviolence mean? Simply it means "Do not cause pain or injury to another." However, *ahimsa* does not pertain only to our physical actions. It does not simply mean "Thou shalt not kill" or "Thou shalt not hit." Rather, it encompasses all forms of violence—violence in thought, violence in speech, and violence in deed. We must think pure and loving thoughts. We must speak pure and loving words, and we must practice pure and loving acts.

Further, *ahimsa* does not only call upon us to live peacefully with other human beings. Rather, the meaning of *ahimsa* encompasses all beings, all creatures, all life on the planet. It includes the animals as well as Mother Nature. This means—of course—that one should be a vegetarian and shun products that are made through violence to animals (either animal products or those test on animals). It also means that one must take care of Mother Nature, protecting and preserving our natural resources.

Moreover, the law of *ahimsa* goes even deeper than that which we do to others. It also includes that which we do to ourselves. When we smoke cigarettes, take drugs, eat food that we know leads to heart disease or diabetes, get involved in relationships in which we are abused, victimized, and suppressed, or when we simply waste our precious time engaged in meaningless activity—these are all ways in which we injure ourselves.

2. SATYAM—TRUTHFULNESS

This tenet also goes deeper than its surface meaning. Yes, of course we must speak the truth. But, that is not enough to say we are practicing *satyam*. We must also live the truth. Our thoughts, our values, our words, and our actions all must be aligned. So many times we say one thing in front of others, or in the temple, or to impress people, but we act in a different way. I have even heard parents tell their children, "Do as I say, not as I do." This is not *satyam*. *Satyam* means "As I say, so I do." *Satyam* means being true to our promises and vows, fulfilling our word to ourselves, to others, and to God.

3. ASTEYA—NOT STEALING

Asteya is not as simple as refraining from stealing a possession that belongs to someone else. We steal much from others without realizing it. We steal people's time by wasting it in idle gossip or complaints. We steal people's credit by claiming to have done something that actually was accomplished by someone else. We steal from Mother Earth by using more than we need—by driving cars that are too big and use too much fuel, by building homes larger than our requirements, by purchasing more and more unnecessary possessions which are made using natural resources and whose production pollutes the atmosphere. Further, if God has blessed us with prosperity and we have enough to help others, it is stealing if we do not share our wealth. We must realize the joy that comes from sharing with others. Life is for sharing and caring. Life is for giving.

4. BRAHMACHARYA— RESTRAINT OF THE SENSES

Brahmacharya is frequently translated as "celibacy" or "abstinence," but actually its meaning is more complex than refraining from sexual activity. Rather, it actually means one who is *brahma-acharya*: one whose actions are all dedicated to God, whose actions are all pure and holy. It means one whose attention, energy, and life are focused on God. These ten commandments are not applicable only to *sanyasis* or monks. Rather they were laid out by one of the greatest sages of all times, for all of humanity. Therefore, the law of *brahmacharya* also pertains to those on the householder path. What does it mean? It means restraint. It means moderation. It means realizing that the purpose of life is much greater and far deeper than continually fulfilling one's sexual urges. By overengaging in sexual activity, our minds and attention are diverted and our vital energy is dissipated. So, even if you are married, still one must try—as much as possible—to move beyond the realm of the body to the realm of the spirit.

5. APARIGRAHA—NONACCUMULATION

Aparigraha literally means "nonhoarding." It means "Don't take more than you need—in any area of life." Mahatma Gandhiji said it beautifully: "There is more than enough for everyone's need, but not enough for any man's greed." It means "Live simply. Use only that which you require. Purchase only that which is essential." It doesn't mean that everyone must live like a wandering monk, but it means that we must cultivate a sense of moderation and simplicity, regardless of our financial means, we should not live extravagantly or surround ourselves with unnecessary possession.

Aparigraha also means that there should be no sense of "mine" in life. We should realize that everything is God's and we have simply been lent a certain amount for a temporary period of time. In *yagna* ceremonies, after each mantra, the priest chants "idam namamah." It means "Not for me, God. It is for you, God." This is *aparigraha*. Nothing is mine. Everything is His. Everything is for Him.

We also have five *niyamas*—the spiritual and ethical observances that, once we have mastered our bodies and minds through practice of the yamas, will take us higher on the spiritual path.

1. SUACHA—PURITY

Suacha means "cleanliness and purity," but it does not simply imply that one must bathe each day and keep one's fingernails clean. Rather, it pertains to a deeper level of purity—purity on the inside, purity of thought and action. We must purify our thoughts through *japa*, meditation, and the practice of positive thinking. We must purify our lives by ensuring that our actions are models of integrity, dharma, and righteousness. Suacha also pertains to what we allow to enter our bodies and minds—what food we take through our mouths and also what food we take through our ears and eyes. True *suacha* means refraining from putting anything impure into our being—this includes everything ranging from drugs and cigarettes to negative gossip to violent rock-music lyrics to pornography. Practicing *suacha* is like taking perfect care of your brand-new car. If you had a $100,000 new Mercedes, you would only put the purest, best-quality gasoline in the tank. You would never fill it up with cheap, bad-quality gas, and you certainly would never dump mud into the engine! Yet, our divine selves are more valuable than the most valuable car, and we continually fill them with low-quality, impure junk!

2. SANTOSHA—CONTENTMENT

In life, the tragedy is that no matter what we have, we always want more. It is a disease of the human mind: We are rarely, if ever, satisfied. The tragic irony is that even as we earn more and more, buy more and more, acquire more and more, and achieve more and more, our hunger for possessions and achievement only grows! It is a disastrous paradox. Our scriptures say that whatever we are given we should accept as *prasad* from God. One of the most important personal characteristics toward which we should strive is the "attitude of gratitude." In our prayers that we chant each morning, there is a beautiful line that says, "Sita Ram, Sita Ram, Sita Ram kahiye, jahi vidhi rakhe Rama, tahi vidhi rahiye." It means that we should be thankful to God and keep chanting His holy name regardless of the condition in which He keeps us. We should accept more and expect less. Expectation is the mother of frustration and acceptance is the mother of peace and joy.

3. *TAPAS*—AUSTERITIES OR *SADHANA*

Through the performance of regular *tapas* (*tapasya*), we learn to be the master of our body and mind. Due to our lifelong and misguided identification with maya, we spend our lives entrapped by the belief that we are at the beck and call of our mind, emotions, and senses. We unconsciously yet readily hand over the reins of our lives to our volatile mind and insatiable senses! *Tapas* puts the control back into our hands, into the hands of our higher Self. *Tapas* does not mean only doing *japa* or fasting or doing a certain number of offerings into the *yagna* fire ceremony. *Tapas* can extend to every area of our lives. *Tapas* is being nice to our mother-in-law. *Tapas* is not shouting back when our husband or wife gets angry. *Tapas* is the practice of tolerance.

In our lives, we tend to act based only on instinct—like animals. When the feeling of anger washes over us like a wave, we yell and lash out at others. When the feeling of hunger creeps into our stomachs, we eat. When we are overcome by feelings of lust, we engage in sexual behavior. Through practicing *tapas*, we learn to have control over ourselves so that we can choose whether to act or not. *Tapas* teaches us that we are not merely lightbulbs that can be switched on and off by the incessantly vacillating mind and senses.

4. Swadhayay—Sacred Study

Swadhayay typically means "study of the scriptures." It is very important to read something spiritual, something inspiring every day. This helps keep us on track and keep our mind pure. Otherwise we tend to get lost in our own mind's sea of confusion. However, it is important to remember that scriptural study—although it is crucial—is not, by itself, a complete spiritual path. It is only one of the ten *yamas* and *niyamas*. Simple reading of the scriptures does not take you to *samadhi*. One must also put these readings into practice. One must live the scriptures, not just read a few chapters every morning or every evening.

Further, *swadhaya* also means "self-study." Introspection is one of the greatest tools of a spiritual path. Our egos, our fears, our desires, our misconceptions, and even just the hecticness of our lives keep us from truly examining our own lives. Each night we must ask ourselves,

"Where do I stand?" Am I progressing further and further on the spiritual path? A good businessman always examines his balance sheets in order to see whether he is in the red or in the black. Similarly we must examine the balance sheet of our lives.

5. Ishwara pranidhana— Devotion or Surrender to God

This is the final, ultimate commandment of leading a dharmic life. It doesn't matter what name or what form of the Divine you worship. What matters is that you are surrendered fully to God. It means our goal becomes aligning our will with the Divine Will so that we can welcome whatever comes, rather than trying to bend the Universal Plan to match our own. True *Ishwara pranidhana* is the prayer "May thy will be done." Only through dedicating all our actions to Him and His creation can we find peace, joy and meaning in life.

If we practice these ten commandments, regardless of our religion, and live them every day of our lives, we will find that our lives become full of joy, peace, and fulfillment. These may be the ten commandments of Hinduism, but they are universal in their truth, and they are just as applicable to people of all religions and all ways of life. They are the commandments of a peaceful, fruitful, and fulfilling life.

CHAPTER TEN

Drops of Nectar Across the Globe

PEACE AMIDST THE CHAOS

I T WAS A BALMY JULY SUNDAY AFTERNOON. THE NEWARK, NEW JERSEY, AIRPORT COULD HAVE PASSED FOR ANY OVERCROWDED TRAIN STATION IN ANY THIRD WORLD COUNTRY IF ONE REMOVED THE INCESSANTLY REPETITIVE AUDIO TRACKS OF

"Flight ___ scheduled to depart at ___ to ___ has been delayed due to weather. New departure timings will be posted when available." It was the end of the July 4th holiday, and as July 4 had fallen on a Thursday, most Americans took the liberty of at least a four-day weekend. Not a suit or tie was to be seen among the hordes of travelers. Shorts, T-shirts, and baseball caps decorated with any number of team logos, slogans, and stuffed creatures were the apparel of the day. Plump hands gripped thirty-two- and sixty-four-ounce cups of soda as weary vacationers sucked away their thirst through narrow straws. All available chairs had long since been occupied; travelers now sprawled on the carpets, vying for space to rest their backs against a wall.

As announcement after announcement of delayed and canceled flights filled the air, the tension in the departure hall became tangible. Parents admonished their fidgety children to stay seated while they went to berate a hapless gate agent once again. "What do you mean our flight is further delayed? How are we supposed to get home? If this flight does not take off in the next twenty minutes, I will miss the last possible connection from Chicago and won't be able to get home tonight! What are you planning to do about it, ma'am?" The gate agents and ticket agents wiped sweat out of their eyes and off their chins as they explained, over and over again, that they were very sorry for any inconvenience caused by the weather front

OPPOSITE *Pujya Swamiji at the Mahakumbhaabhishekam ceremony at the Hindu Temple of Kentucky.*

that had just moved in, and they would certainly try their best to reschedule everyone as soon as possible. If the black clouds that turned day into night weren't enough to convince travelers that there truly was a weather "condition," frequent flashes of lightening would illuminate hail-streaked runways outside the windows. But the rain did not wash away the stress of those trapped in departure halls at Newark. One after the other, as their turn arrived to approach the gate agent,

"It is no problem if your children want to wear jeans, but make sure they don't forget their genes."

would unleash storms of fury matching the hail storm outside. "I don't care what you have to do, but my flight must take off. I must reach Denver within the next three hours. Do you not understand my son has to be in class tomorrow morning? Do you not get it? He has a math test at 8:00 a.m. tomorrow morning. It is your responsibility to get us home."

After the gate agent patiently took lash after lash and requested travelers to return to their seats, the travelers would heave the rest of their anxiety onto their families. "Didn't I tell you that you've had enough soda for one day? Didn't I? And stop playing that stupid video game. The noise it makes is giving me a headache. Either put on your headphones or shut it off. We never should have come on this stupid trip. It was all because you kept pushing and pushing me."

Amid it all, Pujya Swamiji sat watchfully. His flight was delayed, of course, and he, too, would miss his connection. As always, he was the silence amid the noise, the stillness within the frenetic energy, the peace at the heart of chaos. As he watched traveler after traveler abuse the gate agent, shout at their families, pull their hair out in anguish, and eat candy bar after candy bar to numb their anxiety, he finally turned to the American *sevak* who was

traveling with him and said, "Let me understand this properly. These people, you say, have spent the last week on vacation?"

THE TEACHINGS AND THE TOUCH

Pujya Swamiji has entered the United States, as of 2011, more than ninety times. He has filled more passports with visas and entry/exit stamps than most international diplomats. He has spent more time thirty thousand feet above the ground than he has in any single location other than Rishikesh. Where most people abide by the concept "When in Rome, do as the Romans do," he follows the motto "Wherever a true Roman goes, that place becomes Rome." Wherever he goes, he carries with him not only the message and teaching of India, but also the very palpable experience of the Himalayas and the coolness of the waters of Mother Ganga. Flight attendants spend their breaks sitting at his feet, asking for his guidance. Strangers on the streets of London and Los Angeles stop and offer him the possessions in their hands. Hardened criminals in San Francisco jails cry as they hold out pictures of their children for him to touch and bless. People with no connection to India, to Hinduism, or even to Eastern spirituality find themselves inexplicably and serendipitously drawn to his talks only to find their lives transformed in an evening. Years of drought end in thunderstorms as his plane touches down in Australia. Weeks of rain and clouds break into sun as he lands in London. Patients who come to him in wheelchairs have found not only their faith but also their actual bodies restored.

"It's a miracle," people exclaim when they experience, witness, or hear about such events. Yet miracles are defined in the *Oxford English Dictionary* as "extraordinary events not explicable by natural or scientific laws, attributed to a divine agency." However, the ways of the divine hand are *through* natural and scientific laws, not above or around them. The "miracles" are therefore simply extraordinary finesse within the laws of nature and science, the result of an unimpeded connection to the source. To rub one's hands together and create heat is child's play. To consciously affect the involuntary autonomous nervous system and lower one's blood pressure or slow one's pulse through deep breathing is a basic tenet of stress management classes in schools, offices, and hospitals around the world. To add an atom of hydrogen (H) to hydrogen peroxide (HO) and turn it into water (H_2O) is part of every chemistry class. Innumerable studies at international universities and laboratories have shown the impact of even untrained energy healing on rates of recovery. If high school science students can turn hydrogen peroxide into water, if merely changing our breathing pattern can bring otherwise involuntary bodily systems into our control, if novice healers can significantly increase the speed of wound repair, it follows that one who is deeply connected to all energy and to all elements will affect and transform the world as he moves through it.

Pujya Swamiji spends several months each year out of India, bringing the touch of grace to people of nearly every religion, every walk of life, every culture, and every language. His teachings are universal. They neither require nor request the listener to become Hindu. He simply gives one the experience, the felt-sense, of being in the presence of pure, unconditional, divine love and awareness. Most of us go through life playing the role of devotee, intellectual, doctor, nurse, teacher, or engineer. Yet, most of us, beneath the roles we play and the personalities we've adopted, have a deep sense of being unworthy, impure, and filled with ignorance and darkness. That the world doesn't see this unworthiness is due to God's grace and the wonderful veil with which we cover our inner self from the eyes of the world. In Pujya Swamiji's presence, one becomes instantly and

"Let your life be a bridge," Pujya Swamiji teaches. "Don't be a barrier. Be a bridge."

distinctly aware that the veil is transparent to him, that he can see the mistakes, the ignorance, the impurity, and the unworthiness. And yet, simultaneously, from his eyes pours a continuous ocean of love. This seeming impossibility of knowing the deepest, darkest corners of one's true self and loving one unconditionally is enough to shatter the despair within which most of us live our lives. When full knowing and full loving come together as completely as they do in Pujya Swamiji's presence, pain and fear crumble. Innumerable people all over the world describe nearly identical experiences of something "bursting" and "shattering" in his presence.

The teachings that he gives sometimes take the form of wordless transmissions. At other times they are direct, verbal teachings given

OPPOSITE (top) *Pujya Swamiji at Pujya Sri Sri Ravi Shankarji's ashram in Bangalore, feeding the elephants.* ❋ *(bottom) Pujya Swamiji meditating on the coast of the Pacific Ocean in California.*
THIS PAGE *(clockwise from top) At the Yoga for Peace event in Brazil, speaking to more than 15,000 Brazilians.* ❋ *Meditating in the Swiss Jung Frau ice caves, at the highest point in Europe.* ❋ *At the Eiffel Tower in Paris.* ❋ *Giving the keynote address at the Omega conference.* ❋ *At Ground Zero, four months after 9-11.* ❋ *In San Marco's Square in Venice, feeding the pigeons.* ❋ *Leading Ganga Aarti on the coast of the Atlantic Ocean in Tenerife, Spain, with the local mayor.* ❋ *Meditating in Haifa, Israel.* ❋ *At gardens in Kyoto, Japan.*

in lectures, *satsangs*, question-and-answer sessions, or cozy *darshans* at the home of a devotee. Sometimes the teachings are given neither as specific verbal lessons nor as nonverbal transmissions. They are given simply by example. One can recognize a home in which he is staying by the fact that lights are on only in one room. "If everyone is sitting here together,

"Facebook is great, but you must also make time to face your book. Facing your own book is what is needed most."

why waste the lights in other rooms?" He regularly switches off lights in other people's homes, even if he is the first to leave a room.

"One thing, just one thing," he implores people around the world who are cooking for him. In Indian tradition, the guest is God. *Atithi devo bhava* is one of the most fundamental tenets. It literally means "Adore the guest as divine." That rule applies whether the guest is an invited friend or a suddenly appearing stranger—they are to be viewed, welcomed, and treated as divine. When that guest is their guru, many Indians are overcome with exuberance and cook lavish, extensive meals of dozens of items. "One thing," he pleads with devotees wherever he goes. Where most people would salivate at the idea of dozens of mouthwatering items—from freshly fried snacks to homemade milky desserts—Pujya Swamiji has no taste for them. "I cannot enjoy my meal with so many items," he explains.

"One thing—that's all I want. Something light, fresh, organic, and healthful." It is not merely that his dietary habits are simple, as one would expect for someone who spent his childhood fasting in the jungle, which left him without a taste for rich food. The emphasis he places on this simplicity all over the world is intended to show people—not by lectures but simply by example—that joy is not to be found in objects of the senses. A *pakora* or *samosa* or syrupy *gulab amun* does not hold the

magic key to fulfillment and contentment in life. "We must eat to live," he says, "not live to eat. When we eat to live, we eat things that are life-promoting—freshly cooked, healthful, organic, simple food. When we live to eat, we eat things that we think will give us pleasure. But then we have to keep eating, and eating and eating, because that pleasure is so fleeting. Soon we are fat and diabetic and still running after pleasure in *puris* [fried Indian bread]."

His simple ways of living—how he eats, how he travels, how minimal his needs—have changed everyone with whom he's ever stayed. He leaves behind a trail of people turning vegetarian, giving up frozen and fried food, and learning to eat salad at the age of forty or fifty, or children who are now eating fresh vegetable soup and *kichari* because "that's Swamiji food."

His lessons of simplicity extend beyond the culinary.

ONE PERSON, ONE CAR, ONE FLOWER

In the early days, crowds of people would meet him at airports around the world. Bouquets of flowers were lovingly thrust toward him as he exited customs or came through the arrivals door. He would lovingly greet everyone quickly before heading into the car that had come to take him home. Finally, in the mid-1990s as the numbers had continued to grow, he made an announcement during a lecture program in London.

It takes probably nearly an hour for each of you to get to the airport. That is two hours of driving time. Plus you naturally arrive early at the airport so you can be ready and poised at arrivals when I walk out. Thus, say, a total of nearly three hours. You park your cars in the expensive lot and pay probably five pounds to park. Then you buy bouquets of flowers costing several pounds each. And we don't even have any time to spend together. I emerge from the plane and go straight to the car. We are together later that same day or the next day at discourses and satsang programs. If fifty people

OPPOSITE *Meditating at Jung Frau, the highest point in Europe, in the Swiss Alps. "High altitude should lead to high attitude and high gratitude," Pujya Swamiji told the yatris on the alpine train ride up the mountain.*

come, that is a total of approximately 150 human-hours and hundreds of pounds sterling on parking, gasoline, and flowers, not to mention the harm to the environment from all the unnecessary driving. Save those hours. Save those pounds. Put them to good use for humanity. From now on, there shall be only one person in one car to receive me at the airport, and that one car shall not park in the lot. Rather it shall wait on the curb outside arrivals and I will walk out. Further, that one person shall bring only a simple flower.

He proceeded to impose the same rule in cities across the globe. The only slight amendment came with 9/11, when new rules forbade cars from waiting for extended periods on the curb outside arrivals at the bigger airports. Thus, he permitted one car and two people—one person waits inside at arrivals while the other parks the car at some free lot (or on the side of the road) outside the airport until the driver receives a phone call that

Pujya Swamiji has arrived, at which point the car is driven to the curb to receive him.

It is not only devotees who have had their lives touched as he travels throughout the world. Innumerable people have received seats on flights that were oversold due to his ever readiness to give up his seat when airlines ask for volunteers. Frequently, before they had even announced it, if the boarding area seems particularly crowded, he will inform the gate agents, "If you need a volunteer, I'm ready." He has fed fresh chapatis and *theplas* to countless passengers seated near him on airplanes as well as to harried flight attendants. As Pujya Swamiji doesn't eat any food that isn't home-cooked, families everywhere know to send him on flights with packed food. They also know to pack extra, as he can never eat without first feeding those around him. In fact, the first introduction to Indian food for many Western travelers may very well have come via the food they received from his hands on an airplane. Ticket agents, gate agents, and customs officials inevitably are smiling after he leaves their counter. On an early trip to Australia, the customs officer asked him (inexplicably, as he had just walked off the plane so it was obvious that he had just arrived), "Have you come here *to-day*?" Due to the officer's heavy Australian accent, with which Pujya Swamiji was unfamiliar, the young sadhu thought he had been asked "Have you come here *to-die*?" "Oh no, sir!" Pujya Swamiji exclaimed. "I've come here to *live*."

OM CHRIST

As Pujya Swamiji's impact and the demographics of his devotees have extended far beyond the Indian Hindu and even beyond the Westerner turned Hindu, a question that arises is the applicability of Hindu teachings to the non-Hindu. Pujya Swamiji is emphatic that the wisdom is universal, that it applies as much to those who worship God in the form of Jesus Christ or

Top *A youth camp in Toronto, Canada.*
Above *Feeding the poor in Durban, South Africa.*

Adonai as to those who worship Him in the form of Krishna or Shiva. The temptation for non-Hindus is to believe that in order to truly benefit from the ultimate truth of Pujya Swamiji's teachings, they need to change their religion. So, occasionally Christians and Jews request a "conversion" ceremony or offer to renounce the faith of their childhood in order to seek absolution from the despair of adulthood. "I'll believe whatever you say I need to believe. I'll worship whomever you say I need to worship, just please help me find peace," they plead. Pujya Swamiji encourages them gently to continue worshipping God in the way they always have, to renew their faith in their own religion, and to attend church or synagogue more regularly. He assures them that peace and bliss are equally available in every religion; all that is required is faith and commitment.

Typically the non-Hindu devotees are thankful for his assurances and implement his teachings along with a renewed commitment to their own religion. However, now and then a devotee is adamant, or his or her suffering seems too extensive and excruciating for a solution as simple as "go to church."

Several years ago a woman came to meet with Pujya Swamiji in Chicago. She was an American Christian, a good friend of the family hosting him. Her life was unbearable, and she was desperate for an answer. "Do you think your guru can help me?" she asked. "Of course," the family had assured her. "He can do anything." As she garnered strength to come and meet with him, she did some research on Hinduism, mantras, and miracles. When she finally came to Pujya Swamiji, she had it figured out. "I need a Hindu mantra. It will solve all my problems," she announced. Pujya Swamiji tried to convince her that there was no need for a Hindu mantra. Any sincere, earnest, and pure prayer would surely be heard and answered by God. He urged her to pray to Jesus Christ and take positive steps to turn her life around. She was firm. "No, it

must be a Hindu mantra. I have heard that they have great power and I must have one. I will renounce Christianity. I will become an official Hindu. I will do anything. But I must have a Hindu mantra."

Pujya Swamiji realized that she was obstinate and open to neither negotiation nor entreaty. Therefore, he told her to rise the following morning at 4:00 a.m., and he gave an elaborate list of rituals to be followed with regard to waking, bathing, abstaining from food, having *darshan* of the rising sun, etc. Finally he told her to bring special flowers and special herbs. The usual ritual for receiving *mantra diksha* is not nearly so abstruse. It requires little more than a bathed body, a pure heart, and earnest devotion to the guru. However, Pujya Swamiji knew that this woman had envisioned a great ceremony that would culminate in her magic mantra. In order for it to be effective, he had to play with the drama of making it as enigmatic and complex as possible.

She listened sincerely and took copious notes as Pujya Swamiji elucidated the steps she must take the following morning before coming for her initiation. She silently bowed as she left, tears filling her eyes. "Thank you," she said. "For the first time in years, I have faith that help is around the corner. I know this mantra will fix my life."

The following morning, a full half hour before Pujya Swamiji's morning silence ended and before the appointed time, she arrived. She had followed all the instructions explicitly and carried carefully wrapped bundles of the specific flowers and herbs he had requested. Pujya Swamiji led her into the temple and made her sit down in front of him. He unwrapped the flowers and herbs she had brought, offering them, along with water, to the various deities in the temple, accompanied by lengthy and elaborate mantras. He chanted far more mantras than were required and conducted a significantly more extravagant *puja* than normal. He needed her to believe that no stone was left unturned, no

"MOKSHA (LIBERATION) is
right here, every minute and every moment.
When we are free from our desires, our ego,
our jealousy, our anger, and our attachments,
then we are living in *moksha.*"

With yogacharya Sri B.K.S. Iyengar at the International Conference on Yoga at Swami Ramdev's Patanjali Yog Peeth.

ritual incomplete, and that the bestowing of a mantra was not simply an elementary act.

Finally when the *pujas* had been performed, it was time for the actual mantra transmission. Pujya Swamiji touched the feet of the deity in the temple and then lay his hand upon the top of her head, palm on her forehead and fingers extending to the crown. He closed his eyes and instructed her to do the same. "Are you ready?" he asked.

"Yes. Yes, I am," she replied in a whisper.

"Okay, repeat after me," he instructed. "Om."

"Om," she repeated.

"Christ."

Her eyes flew open, and she jumped up, startled. "What? What? Om Christ? That's not a Hindu mantra. You promised me a Hindu mantra." The trembling in her voice did not bring down its volume. Her face was red, and tears began to fall from her eyes.

Pujya Swamiji sat quietly, eyes half open and half closed. "Sit back down," he instructed her. "You must receive your mantra properly." Realizing that Pujya Swamiji was deeply serious, not playing a joke on her, and was in the midst of a sacred transmission that she had inadvertently interrupted, she returned to her seat and received the mantra of "Om Christ" with all the rite and ritual of sacred mantra initiation. Pujya Swamiji handed her a string of *rudraksh* beads, 108 holy seeds strung together into a *mala* with which she would chant her mantra each day.

To Pujya Swamiji, all names and all forms of God are equally divine. He says, "If God can only be worshipped in one way, He is not God." Whether God is called Krishna or Christ or Adonai or Allah, they are all names of the same divine, infinite, omnipotent Source. There is no inherent, objectively greater power in chanting Om Krishna than in chanting Om Christ. He explains, "If you have five children and one calls you Mom, another calls you Mama, a third says Ma, the fourth cries for Mommy, and the fifth is too young to say anything, would you love one more than the other? Would you be preferential to Ma over Mommy or to Mom over the gurgles of a toothless infant? Of course not. So, if a simple mother can appreciate and love all names, can't God?" Pujya Swamiji wanted to show her, and everyone with whom he has shared this

"Go to God. Whatever name, whatever form you worship, is no problem. Just go to Him. He accepts all names and all forms. If God can be worshipped only in one way, then He is not God!"

story since then, that attaining divine peace and bliss is not about changing one's religion. It is not about an esoteric mantra or practice belonging to a religion other than one's own. Rather, it is about surrender—full, complete, devoted surrender—to God in the name and form that one knows best. Sincerity, of the devotion and of the practice, is the wind that carries one to the Divine. The specific make and model of the sailboat is irrelevant; what matters is the strength and direction of the wind. For that reason, he did not want to initiate her into a mantra foreign to her religion. Rather, he gave the simple mantra of Christ following the requisite Om, with full knowledge that if she practiced it with earnestness, she would attain her goal.

Pujya Swamiji describes the aftermath. "I returned to Chicago a few months later and she came to see me, ecstatic. She said, 'Your mantra is really magic. It fixed my whole life.' So we see, it's not about the name or the form of the Divine. All names and forms are equal. It's about the devotion and sincerity of the seeker."

A Multivitamin for Spiritual Health

THESE DAYS WE TAKE SO MANY VITAMINS FOR OUR BODIES, TO KEEP THEM STRONG AND HEALTHY. There is also a multivitamin for our mind and heart. If you take all three of these every day and let them saturate your being, you will find true peace of the body and mind, and a deepening connection to the true Self.

1. MEDITATION

I always say that meditation is the best medication for all agitations. People have so many troubles today, mainly related to the stress in their lives. To address this anxiety, sleeplessness, and discontent, they may take pills or fill their lives with excessive material pleasures. For example, when people feel stressed, they frequently attempt to forget about it by going to the movies, shopping, drinking alcohol, or indulging in sensual pleasures. However, these are not solutions. They neither address nor alleviate the underlying issues. They are simply bandages to a wound that runs deep beneath the surface.

Yet, meditation truly calms the mind, fills the heart with joy, and brings peace to the soul. Further, the serenity and joy last throughout the day and throughout your life. Meditation is not a simple diversion that works only as long as you are actively engaged in it. Meditation is not a pill that quickly wears off and carries unpleasant side effects. Rather, meditation brings you into contact with God; it changes the very nature of your being. It brings you back to the world from which you truly come: the realm of the Divine.

As you sit in meditation, you will realize the insignificance of that which causes anxiety; you will realize the transient nature of all your troubles. You will realize the infinite joy and boundless peace that come from God and through union with your own divine nature.

Then with practice, slowly you will see that your life becomes meditation. It will not be restricted to one time and place. Yes, of course, one should have a time set aside for meditation, and there should be a quiet, serene place in which to meditate. However, even when it is not "meditation time" or even if you are away from home, away from your "meditation place," do not think that you cannot meditate. Take five minutes at work to simply close your eyes, watch your breath, focus on the oneness of us all, and connect with the Divine. Eventually, your life will become meditation.

Then, you will become a torchbearer of peace, spreading the flames of serenity, love, and brotherhood wherever you go.

2. NO REACTION

After the vitamin of meditation comes the vitamin of "no reaction," which we should practice all day. We need to learn to be calmer in our lives. We must learn to remain still and unaffected by all that happens around us. We must learn to be like the ocean. The waves come and go, but the ocean stays. Even a large rock, thrown from a great distance, with great force, will only cause temporary ripples in a small area on the surface. Most of the ocean, and particularly the depths of the ocean, will remain unaffected.

Typically in our lives we act like the water on the surface, allowing ourselves to get tossed around by every passing wave or gust of air. We must learn, instead, to be like the calm, undisturbed water in the depths of the ocean itself, unaffected by small, transient fluctuations.

I am using the analogy of the waves of the ocean, but the waves I am really talking about are the waves of

anger, anxiety, jealousy, greed, and lust, which are just as vast, just as strong, and just as restless as the waves of the sea. We must let these waves come and go, while remaining calm and undisturbed.

Frequently, we act as though we are lightbulbs and anyone who wants can simply switch us on or off. The smallest comment, look, or action of another changes our mood by 180 degrees. So frequently, we may be in a wonderful mood, and someone at the grocery store is rude to us, or someone on the freeway passes in front of our car, or a friend is cold and distant. Any of these things immediately switches our mood off as though it were a lightbulb.

Instead, let us take whatever comes as *prasad* (a blessing) and as a gift from God. Let us remain calm and steady in the face of both prosperity and misfortune. We must not lose our vital energy in this constant action and reaction to everyone around us.

THE CRUCIAL SPACE— ### BETWEEN A THOUGHT AND AN ACTION

Whenever I talk about "no reaction," people frequently say that it is impossible. "How is it possible not to react when someone makes you angry or makes you sad?" they ask. Here it is very important to distinguish between feelings and actions. We are human, and part and parcel of being human is the softness of our hearts, the sensitiv-

ity of our emotions, our susceptibility to joy, pain, anger, and pleasure.

"No reaction" does not mean that we become indifferent and stoic or that our hearts turn to stone. It does not mean that we should not feel emotions in response to daily happenings. What it does mean is twofold. First, it means that we do not let these emotions overpower us, that we learn to become like the calm, stable depths of the ocean rather than like the turbulent waves. Second, it means that, although we may feel the emotion, although we may have an immediate, instinctive reaction in our heart and mind, we do not have to act out this reaction.

Thoughts come. That is natural and human. Only after great *sadhana* does one learn to master one's thoughts. So, we must accept the thoughts and the emotions as human and mostly inevitable. However, what we do based on the thoughts and emotions is our decision. That is where we must focus our attention. To try to become thoughtless is a great *sadhana* and one that will take us to the peaks of divine realization. However, that is not what I'm discussing here, because that is a practice only for those whose lives are committed and dedicated to *sadhana*.

Rather, for all those living in the world, living with careers, families, and all aspects of a householder life, it is unrealistic to expect to attain a state of thoughtlessness in a short time. Yet that does not doom you to a life of underscoring Newton's law that for every action there is an equal and opposite reaction. It does not doom you to a life of negative reactions to life's pains and difficulties.

If you become quiet and still, you will notice that between every thought and action there is a space, a brief moment of time, a gap. First there is the thought that we want to act (for example, "I'm so angry I am going to slap her"). Then there is a space. Then there is the action (actually picking up our hand and slapping her). The action may seem instantaneous if you are not aware. It may seem to you that you had no choice, that the reaction just came immediately. However, if you practice being aware, you will find that there is always a space after the thought or emotion and before the action. It may only be a split second. But it is there.

Grab that space. In that space you must find the restraint not to act. Have the feeling or thought, if you must. No problem. Acknowledge it. Try to remove it from your mind through prayer, good work, and *japa* (chanting of God's name). But, even if the thoughts seem intractable, still you must realize you have the power not to act on them. Tell yourself, "Okay. I have these thoughts of anger or jealousy or pain. I realize it. Temporarily I accept them, because it seems that right now there is nothing I can do about them, but I'm not going to act on them."

The more you practice focusing on the space, the more you will be able to grab it. At first it will seem elusive, but with time you will find that the space becomes longer and more conscious. You will find that you really do have a choice about whether to spread pieces or to spread peace.

Responding negatively is easy. Fueling the fire of anger with more anger is easy. Meeting criticism with criticism is easy. Spreading pieces is easy.

The challenge comes when we want to spread peace. That is what we learn by grabbing the space. In that moment we have the divine opportunity to meet pieces with peace, to douse the fire of anger with the water of compassion.

The Buddha said that he was like a river. Even the strongest, raging fire cannot last a moment if it is placed into the deep waters of a river. Similarly, if someone came to him full of burning flames of anger, the flames were immediately extinguished by the flowing river of his love.

If we want to be torchbearers of peace, we must first become rivers of love, dousing all flames of discord in the waters of our own compassion and serenity.

3. INTROSPECTION AND THE "SURRENDER" MANTRA

Each night, we must examine the balance sheet of our day: What were our successes? What were our failures? What are our plus points? What are our minus points? Then, thank God for the successes and pray for strength that tomorrow there may be fewer failures. Lastly, turn it all over to God and go to sleep with a clean slate.

There is a beautiful mantra that we all should chant every night to bring deep peace to our beings.

kaayena vaachaa manasendriyairvaa
buddhyaatmanaa vaa prakriteh svabhaavaat
karomi yadyat sakalam parasmai
naaraayanaayeti samarpayaami

It means, "Oh Lord, whatever I have done, whatever actions I have performed—whether through speech, through thought, through my senses, through my mind, through my hands, or through just the nature of my existence—I lay it all at Your Holy Feet. Every aspect of my life and existence are completely surrendered to You." By chanting this mantra, sincerely, deeply, and devotionally every night, we remove any vestiges of ego that may still be lingering, clinging, and preventing us from being in peace.

CHAPTER ELEVEN

Sacred Journeys—Outer and Inner

YATRA TO THE ABODE OF SHIVA

CLOUDS OF DUST RISING FROM EVERY DIRECTION FULLY OBSCURED THE VIEW OF THE BARREN LANDSCAPE. FIFTY JEEPS SPREAD OUT ACROSS THE PLAINS, SWERVING IN AND OUT OF INVISIBLE PATHS, PASSING EACH OTHER WITH BLINDING, BILLOWING clouds of dust. Who was following whom? There seemed to be no leader, as the speed and position of each vehicle changed as the day wore on. Cars stopped periodically for their passengers to go to the bathroom behind a meager patch of tumbleweed or in a slight ditch, or for any avid photographers to try futilely to capture the 360-degree landscape in the two dimensions of a camera's viewfinder. How did the drivers know the way? No signs, no paved roads, no mountain any more descript than the one preceding it. A journey to the center of nothing and the center of everything. Occasionally the caravan would pass a makeshift village of nomads—rugged cloth tents that couldn't possibly stand a chance against the whip-ping winds blowing across the plains or the biting cold that blanketed the landscape at sundown. Children with faces that had never been washed by anything other than their own tears stood by the edge of the nonexistent road, waving their arms excitedly, yelling "hi, bye" to each passing car.

The mountains followed each other religiously, without beginning or end, as the cars continued their pathless journey over a barren landscape that threw up clouds of dust behind each set of wheels.

Pujya Swamiji had given the injunction, "Less chatting, more chanting," the previous evening before the *yatra* began. He urged the *yatris* to silence their tongues

OPPOSITE *Leading chant of Om Mani Padme Hum at a large monastery in Lhasa on the way to Mount Kailash and Lake Mansarovar in Tibet.*

that they might find silence in their minds. The injunction was unnecessary. The experience of traveling to Mansarovar and Mount Kailash defies language. There are no words. There is also no energy to speak. The altitude, the piercing cold turning to desert heat turning back to piercing cold with each movement of the sun and clouds, the inescapable dust—in mouths, in noses—are enough to render them silent. There is no option but to travel inward.

Suddenly the silence in the car was broken as the driver exclaimed, perhaps the only words he knows in English, "Yes, yes," and

"Travel light on your journey in life. Your desires and expectations are heavy baggage, which slow you down and thwart your progress. Let them go."

gesticulated to a group of cars passing in the other direction. The approaching car had honked its horn and motioned for the driver to stop. As he lowered his window, so did the driver of the oncoming car, and the two drivers exchanged greetings in Tibetan. The windows were caked with dirt, and hence it was impossible to discern the faces of passengers in the back. The back doors opened and three Indian pilgrims bundled up in ski jackets and wool hats staggered out into the windy day and approached Pujya Swamiji's car.

He opened his window and then his door so they could approach and speak to him easily. Falling at his feet and grasping his ankles, one of the women began to sob. A gentleman with her explained that they had come from London and they knew Pujya Swamiji well, although he may not know them. They had been to several of his lectures in London but never imagined they would be so close to him, particularly in such a sacred, holy place. As the woman raised her tear-streaked face, the man continued. They had come for *yatra* with a large group from the United Kingdom. Every-

thing was arranged well, and the travel agents were courteous and professional. However, two members of the group became sick due to the altitude and had to be evacuated. The group just received the news that one of them had died on the way back to Katmandu.

Pujya Swamiji consoled them lovingly and invited them all to come to Rishikesh for the sacred final rites ceremony. They bowed at his feet and continued on their journey, awed by the grace of God that had sent the guru exactly when and where they had needed him.

Although their hearts were lightened, a weight grew upon Pujya Swamiji's. A death that could have easily been prevented had even basic care been available. Needless suffering. A young widow and fatherless children. Could nothing be done to prevent this sort of tragedy?

Three days later, when the jeeps arrived at the banks of Lake Mansarovar, after all the *yatris* rose from the ground on which they had instinctively lay in reverence and awe, after the silence had lifted, Pujya Swamiji looked around and realized there truly was nothing. Along the way, of course, there had also been nothing, not even bridges over the flooding rivers through which the jeeps had to be pulled by rope. However, the *yatris* had all believed that, upon arrival at this most sacred pilgrimage site, at this place to which Hindus, Jains, and Buddhists yearned to go, that there would be *something*. Yet, save for the sturdy cloth tents erected in advance by the travel agency, including separate large tents for dining and *puja*, there really was nothing at all.

There was not even a makeshift shelter to which someone could go to get warm. The tents were eight- and ten-person tents, held to the ground by flimsy metal spikes with at least half a foot of space between the bottom of the tent and the hard, cold earth. Those six inches served as funnels for the whipping wind as soon as the sun dipped behind the mountains. Inside the tents was no warmer than outside.

Lake Mansarovar — the view from the Parmarth Ashram, constructed on the banks.

"Something must be done," Pujya Swamiji said. "We must build an ashram here so people have a safe, warm place in which to stay and where we can provide medicine and medical services."

"Maharajji, it's impossible," the devotees said. "This is China, not India. How are you possibly going to build an ashram in China?"

Pujya Swamiji replied, "It must be done. It is a necessity for the *yatris* who come full of devotion and piety. It also would be a great benefit for the local people. It will be done."

As the *yatris* bathed in Lake Mansarovar, performed *puja*, and gathered together for devotional singing, Pujya Swamiji befriended the drivers and local guides. They spoke nei-

ther English nor Hindi. He spoke no Tibetan. However, slowly as their trust in the long-haired, orange-robed "Lama" grew, they became willing to converse in his language of love. Pujya Swamiji learned that the area was controlled by local government and military authorities based in Taklakote, approximately five hours away. The distance was not that far, but due to the ubiquitous absence of paved roads, the journey took half a day. He told the drivers and guide to get a message to the authorities that he would like to meet, that he would like to offer his service in building a permanent lodging facility for the *yatris* that could be used as a source of income for the community.

THIS PAGE (top row) *Mansarovar yatra in 1998 with Pujya Swami Gurusharananandji and Pujya Bhaishri.* ❋ (middle row) *Leading the children of Paryang in a song.* ❋
(bottom row) *At the Saga Dawa Festival in Kailash in 2006 with a local rimpoche.* ❋ *An old medicine woman.*
OPPOSITE (clockwise from top left) *The local villagers prepared a sign welcoming Pujya Swamiji for the inauguration of the Mansarovar ashram in 2003.* ❋ *Contract signing ceremony in Katmandu, December 2000.* ❋ *Governor of the Ngari Prefecture (in which Mount Kailash lies) congratulates Pujya Swamiji during the contract-signing ceremony.* ❋ *Official inauguration of Mansarovar ashram in 2003.* ❋ *With Pujya Shri Shankaracharyaji Swami Divyanand Teerthji and Pujya Rasayani Babaji on yatra in 2006.* ❋ *Performing aarti with the village chief and local villagers of Mansarovar.* ❋ *Giving bindis to the children of Paryang.*

CHIEF H.H. SWAMI CHIDANANDA SARASWATI(MUNIJI)AND HIS
INDIA HERITAGE RESEACH FUNDATION MEMBER ARE HEATLY
WELCOME TO KAILASH AND MANASAROVAR VIST

"We Are on Yatra"— A Yatri's Remembrances

Here on *yatra*, looking out over the incredible mountains, stretching out as far as you can either see or imagine—reducing you, your jeep, your entire life into nothing more than a grain of sand, blowing by the side of the road—the mind, eyes, ears, and senses just dissolve into the thin air, burning one minute and freezing the next.

"We're on *yatra*" is the motto, making anything else seem like absurdly superfluous gibberish. Even my fears and tears just dissipate into the clouds as they embrace the mountaintops, obscuring from our view the true height of their majesty.

The quiet—of my tongue, of my mind. The voices around me just swirling above me, to my sides, but unable to penetrate inside to disturb the incredible stillness.

"We're on *yatra*." *Yatra* to what? From what? *Yatra* from a life of petty concerns, of overestimated needs, of empty words, of excessive reliance on others, on external focus. *Yatra* to a mountain that will make us realize the simultaneous nothingness and everythingness of our beings. Nothingness: the futility of our attempts to exercise control and power, for who could so much as leave a lasting footprint on the sands of Shiva's mountain? The superfluity of our endless obtainment of material possessions—who could carry a mansion to Lord Shiva's feet? We can barely carry our bodies. The irrelevance of the concerns that saturate our daily life—now it is simply a matter of food, water, sufficient oxygen, and a prayer against rain.

Yet, with this ego-annihilating nothingness, there is a simultaneous ecstatic realization of our oneness with the sands of which the mountain is made; of our inextricable link to the glorious height of the mountain; of our brotherhood with the never-

Pujya Swamiji on Mount Kailash, praying at the stream that runs through the mountainous valley.

washed faces and empty bellies of the people whose lives begin and end in this vast sea of simultaneous emptiness and overflowing abundance.

In a military camp. Can't go here. Can't go there. Don't cross this line. No pictures. An irony from a storybook: a land barren as far as the eye stretches, days without so much as sight of a store, a telephone, a building other than sheet metal and cow dung shacks. Thousands and thousands of miles of sand mountains, of rivers running into nameless lakes, of children standing by the side of the dirt that passes for a road, yelling "Hi . . . Bye" to every passing car. And so many military camps. Protection of what? From whom? Do these army men even know the land they are barricading? Have they walked the path of Brahma's mind? Have they fallen in *pranam* at Shiva's feet? Do they bathe reverently in the crystal clear lakes that act as perfect mirrors for the peakless mountains? I do not think so. So why the fervent protection? Why the absurd rules? How to draw a border line in miles and miles of changeless sand? How to say, "This is our land, this is your land?" And why protect it if they don't worship it? Why hold so tenaciously to it?

"We are on *yatra*." A true journey from one frame of reference to another, from one world with one set of assumptions to another. In this new world of saints sleeping on wooden boards, crammed into rooms that haven't been cleaned this century, forced to use makeshift toilets . . . in this world of tears on mountainsides covered with snow, in this world of great saints building snow babies out of the meager ice covering, in this world of mountains that steal your thoughts before you think them . . . perhaps in this new world, perhaps it makes sense.

The sand and tumbleweed landscape suddenly gives way to a lake of majestic proportion—crystal clear, tinged with purple and blue hues as the evening sun casts its last rays of light on the waters. The lake seems to be a mirage—a vast pool of lush beauty in this arid land, a gift sent from Heaven as we get closer to the abode of God.

The vans all stop; no one needed to coordinate it. We silently emerge from the cars, pulled by a strength and power to which we are helpless. Some immediately fall to the ground in *pranam*; others simply gaze into the divine sight. I burst into tears, which quickly become sobs, as though wresting from me parts of my heart I didn't even know were there.

I was not expecting to be affected in that way. A beautiful lake, beautiful mountains, invigorating hiking, the joy of being on Mother Earth's territory. That was my expectation. Yet, here I am, brought to my knees as I shake with emotion in front of a God I am not supposed to worship.

I fall to *pranam* at Swamiji's feet, the tears unstoppable. If I could just stay there, forever, at the feet of the man who has done this to my soul . . .

I look back and forth: his face, glowing in the light of the setting sun; the holy waters of this lake formed of Brahma's mind; the distant towering peak of Mount Kailash, the most sacred of mountains, upon whose peak Lord Shiva resides. Back and forth: him, the lake, the mountain. It is as though they simply merge together into one undeniable, completely consuming presence of God. I cannot meet his eyes. It is too much for me. What will happen if you look into the eye of God? I am already too overwhelmed to find out.

Slowly, all the jeeps arrive and we gather into a semicircle of prayer—Maharajji, Swamiji, and Bhaishri in the center, facing the lake, but clearly seeing beyond it. As each car arrives, people instinctively fall to *pranam* at the lake, the mountain, and our leaders who have brought both our bodies and our souls to God.

Parmarth Kailash-Mansarovar Ashram in Paryang, outside and inside one of the halls.

The following day, as more than two hundred *yatris* gathered at the feet of Pujya Swami Gurusharananandji and Pujya Sant Shri Rameshbhai Oza for the sacred and auspicious Shiv Abhishek ceremony, Pujya Swamiji was nowhere to be found. Finally, a concerted search discovered him in a tent at the far end of the compound sitting on a wooden bed next to a Chinese official bedecked in full military camouflage. His left hand rested gently on the official's shoulder as his right hand held a palmful of cashew nuts from which the official was eating, slowly and with hesitation. "It's okay," Pujya Swamiji was urging him. "They're good to give strength to the body. Have another." As the small search party entered the tent, he quickly instructed, "Bring this man a cup of hot tea," before they could even ask what he was doing.

"But Maharajji," one of them said. "The *abhishek* is beginning. They are waiting for you to start."

Pujya Swamiji looked at the round face of the Chinese official next to him on the bed and then at the three *yatris* standing eagerly in the doorway of the tent. "Go ahead with the *abhishek*," he said. "Please request Pujya Maharajji and Pujya Bhaishri to begin the ceremony. I will come later. In the meantime, bring this man a cup of tea. My *puja* is here."

This military head of the local Ngari Prefecture provided Pujya Swamiji with the details of who could grant permission for construction, who were the people to contact, and what would be the proper way.

That *yatra* to Lake Mansarovar and Mount Kailash in 1998 was a great success. Beautiful weather, the ability to complete the full Kailash circumambulation, and the company of Pujya Swami Gurusharananandji and Pujya Bhaishri made Pujya Swamiji's first journey to the sacred land a joyous and blissful experience. However, as he explains, "My true *yatra* was only beginning. The *yatra* to the abode of Lord Shiva had ended, but my *yatra* to build the much-needed facilities in the area had just begun."

Over the next two years he wrote letter after letter to various government officials, requesting nothing more than their permission to construct lodging and medical facilities for the benefit of *yatris* on the banks of Lake Mansarovar. All expenses would be

THIS PAGE *Pujya Swamiji is sure to always include a visit to the Paryang school in the Mansarovar Kailash yatra itinerary.* ❋ (top row) *He brings gifts ranging from blankets to pens, notebooks, and sunglasses. Even more important, he brings the gift of love.* ❋ (middle row) *Children in the classroom of the school in Paryang.* ❋ (bottom row) *Pujya Swamiji leads the children in singing "I love you, you love me, we are one, one family."*

covered by his foundation. All income would go directly to the local people. He simply needed the permission to build. Finally, as winter snow flurries moved into the region of Ngari, as any and all traces of *yatris* were covered by the annual frost, he received an invitation to come to Katmandu for an official contract-signing ceremony. The Chinese government officials would travel from Lhasa and he would travel from India.

Finally, just a few weeks before the dawn broke on 2001, the contract was signed between India Heritage Research Foundation and the government of the Ngari Prefecture, Tibet Autonomous Region, People's Republic of China, for the construction of a rest house on the banks of Lake Mansarovar. A beautiful certificate was presented to Pujya Swamiji in which his gift was gratefully accepted by the people.

In July 2003, Pujya Swamiji inaugurated the Parmarth Mansarovar Ashram with nearly two hundred *yatris* from around the world.

Later additions included medical rooms as well as a *satsang* hall where innumerable spiritual leaders have led hundreds of *yatris* in prayer, *kirtan*, and meditation and even have delivered *katha* (the verbal, melodic recitation of scriptures, frequently with song and dance). "A *katha* on the banks of Lake Mansarovar?" It is a Hindu's unimaginable dream. To Pujya Swamiji, it and everything is simply "by God's grace."

In September 2009, Pujya Swamiji inaugurated his third ashram in the sacred region. After the ashram was built on the banks of Lake Mansarovar, he had one built in Paryang, the village in which all *yatris* stay the day before arriving at Mansarovar. On the *yatra* of 1998, when he had stayed in the makeshift "guest house" with neither floors nor doors, there had been not even running water. The Parmarth Kailash-Mansarovar Ashram in Paryang, inaugurated in 2006, had not only twenty-five rooms—doubles, triples, and quads—but also full bathrooms with showers and water

A young Tibetan child from a village near Darchen.

warmed by a generator. Boring wells in a land where they could not even conceive of water flowing from a pipe, down comforters and curtains for the windows in an ashram built where only pack dogs had roamed before, a regular source of employment for local people—these are the gifts of the Paryang Ashram.

"I love you. You love me. We are one, one family." Pujya Swamiji sang over and over into a small microphone attached to the bullhorn, enunciating each syllable with the utmost care. The children looked on, mesmerized, their sun-baked and wind-cracked faces crinkling into smiles. They pushed forward, leaning on tiptoes to see this saint who sat on a tiny metal school chair in the yard, the one who had placed new sunglasses on their faces a few minutes earlier. "I love you," he sang and then held the microphone out into the crowd of children motioning with his other hand for them to repeat. It took a few tries. Finally, in a joyful burst of exuberance they understood. "I love you," they sang back to Pujya Swamiji, some loudly, some softly, all giggling. "You love me," he sang. Holding the microphone out to them again, he encouraged, "You love me." They understood. "You love me," they shouted. "We are one, one family," he led. Quickly after only a few tries, they could sing along. The chorus began in full earnest. "I love you," Pujya Swamiji sang melodically.

OPPOSITE *Parmarth Kailash Mansarovar ashram at Dirapuk, from where the view of Mount Kailash is the clearest, closest, and fullest. It is reachable only by foot; hence, all luggage is carried on yak back.*

"You love me," they shouted back, falling over each other in laughter. "We are one, one family," Pujya Swamiji, the children, and all the *yatris* sang together. The cement school yard of the Paryang school became a site of inter-faith, inter-culture, inter-language love. A program that had begun with the children lining up trepidatiously to accept gifts of pens, pencils, blankets, notebooks, snacks, and sunglasses concluded with the same children dancing arm in arm with the *yatris*, as *rishikumars* played percussions on the bottom of empty water drums.

The third ashram was built in Dirapuk at the unprecedented height of seventeen thousand feet, on the rugged mountainside of Kailash. When pilgrims undertake the three-day circumambulation of Mount Kailash, they spend the first night, approximately twelve miles into the journey, in a place called Dirapuk. It is the most difficult and treacherous night, for one has gained significant altitude and must be prepared to cross the pass on the following day. Yaks that go to sleep on the dirt awake with icicles hanging from their tails.

Prior to the construction of the ashram, pilgrims slept in tents carefully weighted down with heavy rocks to prevent a storm from carrying them down the mountainside. A late-night bathroom call meant braving the whipping, icy, high-altitude winds and even rain or snow.

In a land inaccessible by four-wheel vehicle, a two-storied ashram has now been built, the Parmarth Kailash-Mansarovar Ashram - Dirapuk. Attached bathrooms, running water, heavy down quilts, and insulated windows are provided for the weary pilgrims. A large dining hall with an adjacent kitchen permits everyone to gather indoors, around enormous pots of water boiling for tea or soup, and to stay warm and safe.

"Kaam karo aur aage badho," is Pujya Swamiji's motto. "Do your work and then move on." Thus, years pass in between his personal trips to the sacred land, with the ashrams now in the able hands of local people.

In the decade since inaugurating the Parmarth ashram on the banks of Lake Mansarovar, Pujya Swamiji has undertaken beatification and renovation programs in other holy areas, including most significantly the land of Gangotri, the source of Mother Ganga. The Gangotri beautification program includes not the construction of ashrams, for there are already ashrams. Rather, it involves essential infrastructure to restore a polluted town, its natural beauty obscured by unchecked encroachment, into a place as clean, pure, and unobstructed as the waters of Ganga Herself.

Typically, when people pack for a *yatra*, their luggage includes warm clothes, perhaps sunscreen or mosquito repellant, a camera, and other basic essentials. When people pack for a *yatra* with Pujya Swamiji, their belongings must also include sturdy trash bags and rubber gloves, for they will most certainly find themselves picking up litter along the way. Their belongings should also include pens, pencils, and packs of healthy biscuits or nuts to distribute to needy people in the villages through which they travel. However, should they forget these items, it is not a problem, because Pujya Swamiji himself is always prepared. His typical luggage comprises a tiny handbag for his clothes and several large suitcases full of items for distribution to the impoverished villagers he inevitably will meet on the way.

Despite the various final destinations of the *yatras* he has led, to Pujya Swamiji the goal of all *yatras* is the same: connecting with the Divine within. "It is not," he exhorts, "about Bhagawan Shiva in Kailash or Kedarnath or Lord Narayanaya in Badrinath. Yes, these are sacred and holy places with divine energy. But the goal of traveling on *yatra* is to find Shiva within, to find Narayanaya within. That same divinity that resides in the holy places also resides in your heart. *Yatras* are not only outer journeys. They are inner journeys."

OPPOSITE *(clockwise from top left) On* yatra *in Govardhan Vrindavan, cleaning and offering respect to the rock, which represents Govardhan Hill.* ✷ *On the way walking from Gangotri to Gaumukh (the glacial source of Mother Ganga).* ✷ *On* yatra *trekking to the Valley of the Flowers near Badrinath in the Himalayas.* ✷ *Some of the* yatris *take rest with Pujya Swamiji along the way of the trek to Gaumukh.* ✷ *At Hemkund Sahib, a lake holy to the Sikhs, near Badrinath in the Himalayas.* ✷ *Picking apples in an orchard on the descent from Badrinath* yatra.

Glossary

AARTI A ceremony performed to any manifestation of the Divine—including deities in Hindu temples, ancestors, the guru, or a sacred aspect of nature—during which the worshipper offers articles representing the five elements (such as flowers, burning candles, water, incense) to the divine image.

BHAGAVAD GITA A seven-hundred-verse section of the ancient Sanskrit epic *Mahabharata*, regarded by most Hindus as the words and message of God and recognized by scholars and philosophers of various traditions as one of the most important texts in the history of religious literature and philosophy.

BRAHMACHARI Celibate student within any of India's traditions of spiritual training.

DARSHAN Literally "vision" of the Divine, often used to indicate the experience of beholding the deities in a temple or looking into the eyes of a holy person.

DHOTI Traditional dress for men in Indian culture, made of a single length of three to four yards of cotton or silk cloth wrapped around the waist, with ends tucked into the waistband.

JAPA Recitation of God's names, a mantra, or other sacred sound, often done while turning sacred beads resembling a rosary.

MALA Strand of 108 beads used to count recitation of divine names, mantras, or prayers.

MANDIR Temple, place of worship. A characteristic of most mandirs is the presence of a *murti* (carved or naturally existing deity) to whom the temple is dedicated.

MAYA "That which is not," illusion, the energy that veils a living entity's awareness of his divine Self and due to which one identifies with the temporal body and fluctuations of the mind rather than with the eternal, changeless, infinite soul.

PUJA A religious ritual or sacred ceremony, frequently involving the offering of various natural articles such as flowers, rice, and incense.

RISHI A "seer," a spiritually elevated man or woman who knows the inner meaning of scripture.

SADHU An ascetic, a wandering monk, dedicated to achieving full spiritual awakening through meditation and contemplation.

SEVA Selfless service, work done as an offering to God or the guru.

SWAMI An ascetic or yogi who has been initiated into a religious monastic order. The term usually refers to men but can also apply to women who have taken the oath of renunciation and abandoned their social and or worldly status to follow this path.

TAPASYA A self-discipline or austerity undertaken as part of a sincere spiritual path, willingly expended both in restraining physical urges and in actively pursuing a higher purpose in life.

YAGNA A ritual of sacrifice derived from the practices of Vedic times, performed to purify the ground, the environment, and those who are performing it, as well as to please the gods or to attain certain wishes. An essential element is the sacrificial fire into which oblations of natural items such as grains, seeds, ghee (clarified butter), and coconuts are offered, as everything that is offered into the fire is believed to reach the gods and to purify the performers.

Acknowledgments

A book of this kind is not accomplished by one person. It is the experience of God's grace, which flows forth through different people in different ways. A freshly baked, nourishing loaf of bread may be assembled by one cook in the kitchen, but it requires someone to plant the wheat, and someone else to water it and remove any pernicious weeds. It requires someone to harvest the wheat and grind it into flour. Someone needs to churn fresh milk into soft butter. Someone else collects salt crystals from evaporated ocean water. Yet, even with all of the ingredients in place, without a warm, temperate place in which the dough can rise, and without the strong heat of an oven or hot sun, the wheat, butter, yeast, and salt still could not become bread. The number of people who gave their time, energy, experience, and expertise to this project is phenomenal. From the moment I mentioned that I was writing Pujya Swamiji's biography, the outpouring of support has felt like the current of Mother Ganga—boundless and ceaseless. There are a few people, though, without whom this project truly could not have come to fruition.

I would like to thank Dr. Kim Chernin, for doing a wonderful job of editing the manuscript and also for her constant encouragement regarding its quality—in both style and content. Also, special thanks to Arielle Ford, for reading the manuscript and assuring me that this book would be both inspiring and meaningful to devotees and also of great value to the general public. Dawn Baillie has played an essential role in helping with the design and layout. Michael O'Neill lovingly gave us permission to use his gorgeous images of Pujya Swamiji and the *rishikumars*

(including the cover image). Ian Shive traveled to Rishikesh with Raoul Goff specifically to shoot pictures of Pujya Swamiji, Ganga, and the Himalayas for this project. His outstanding images grace many of the full pages and double-page spreads throughout the book. Dr. Naval Kant generously provided the majority of photos of Pujya Swamiji in America between the years 1980 and 1995.

This book would not have been possible without our financial sponsors. Lily Bafandi, Satya & Kishan Kalra and Hersha & Hasu Shah provided the generous donations, which made this book possible. Each of them came forward immediately and selflessly to offer their *ahuti* into this divine *yagna*.

The wonderful team at Mandala publications, under the leadership of Raoul Goff, has put this book together. They have created an exquisite book that gives form to Pujya Swamiji's grace. Raoul's entire team, from Jan Hughes, who expertly oversaw production, to Dasha Trojanek, who lovingly designed the pages, has been a pleasure and joy to work with. Of course, they are guided at every step by Raoul's vision and devotion, which give the final product such a special touch. Joshua M. Greene has served not only as my liaison at Mandala but as a personal friend and mentor at every step along the way. His devotion to Pujya Swamiji, his love for this project, and his effusively positive encouragement have been invaluable pillars of support.

Most of all, I lay my gratitude at Pujya Swamiji's feet. He is the sun that has shined upon this project and that shines upon my life and the lives of countless others around the world.

"PRAYER IS calling back
home. It brings us into
divine connection."